Critical Issues for Clinton's Domestic Agenda

Edited by
DEMETRIOS CARALEY

Special Introduction by Bill Green

THE ACADEMY OF POLITICAL SCIENCE
NEW YORK

Editor's Preface

The purpose of this volume was to publish between a single set of covers recent analyses of major items of unfinished business on the nation's domestic agenda.

The Clinton administration has found it impossible not to give more attention than planned to issues of foreign policy and national security despite the ending of the cold war and the breaking up of the Soviet Union. Still the day-to-day quality of life experienced by Americans is directly affected by domestic problems such as poverty, crime, homelessness, inadequate health care, discrimination against women and racial minorities, and the many facets of deterioration in American cities. These problems are still pressing.

All the articles in this collection have been reprinted from recent issues of *Political Science Quarterly* as they were originally written. We hope that this publication will enlighten the ongoing debate on public policy problems and their solutions. The high level of analysis is typical of the articles appearing in the *Quarterly* since 1886, both on a wide range of domestic political processes and policy problems and on subjects of foreign and military policy.

This volume, like the *Quarterly*, is published by the Academy of Political Science. Since it was founded in 1880, the Academy has endeavored to make the knowledge of experts available to policy makers and to the wide audience among the general public who are interested in serious discussion of the most significant issues facing our nation. As an organization, the Academy makes no recommendations on political or policy questions. Moreover, the views of the authors are their own and not necessarily those of the organization with which they are affiliated.

I wish to thank the authors of the articles in this collection for having originally published with *Political Science Quarterly* and for now giving permission to reprint them in this volume. I am especially grateful to Bill Green, member of Congress from 1978 to 1993 and a director of the Academy of Political Science, for writing the special introduction to the volume. Finally, I wish to express my sincere thanks to Cerentha Harris, the *Quarterly*'s managing editor, for taking on the task of transforming a set of selected articles into a published book.

DEMETRIOS CARALEY
Editor, *Political Science Quarterly*

Critical Issues for Clinton's Domestic Agenda

Contents

The articles in this volume are reprinted from the following issues of
Political Science Quarterly:

Demetrios Caraley, "Washington Abandons the Cities," 107 (Spring 1992): 1–30.

Paul E. Peterson, "The Urban Underclass and the Poverty Paradox," 106 (Winter 1991–92): 617–637.

William Julius Wilson, "Another Look at *The Truly Disadvantaged*," 106 (Winter 1991–92): 639–656.

Thomas R. Oliver, "Health Care Market Reform in Congress: The Uncertain Path from Proposal to Policy," 106 (Fall 1991): 453–477.

Margaret Weir, "Innovation and Boundaries in American Employment Policy," 107 (Summer 1992): 249–267.

Donna Wilson Kirchheimer, "Sheltering the Homeless in New York City: Expansion in an Era of Government Contraction," 104 (Winter 1989–1990): 607–623.

Dona Cooper Hamilton and Charles V. Hamilton, "The Dual Agenda of African American Organizations Since the New Deal: Social Welfare Policies and Civil Rights," 107 (Fall 1992): 435–452.

Georgia Duerst-Lahti, "The Government's Role in Building the Women's Movement," 104 (Summer 1989): 249–267.

Loree Bykerk and Ardith Maney, "Where Have All the Consumers Gone?" 106 (Winter 1991–1992): 677–693.

Robert Y. Shapiro and John T. Young, "Public Opinion and the Welfare State: The United States in Comparative Perspective," 104 (Spring 1989): 59–89.

Robert B. Reich, "What is a Nation?" 106 (Summer 1991): 193–209.

Looking at the Domestic Agenda:
A Special Introduction

BILL GREEN

The articles in this collection set forth leading issues that must be addressed in any domestic agenda for President Clinton. They also raise important questions as to the setting of priorities in dealing with the agenda.

Two of the articles, Paul E. Peterson's "The Urban Underclass and the Poverty Paradox" and William Julius Wilson's "Another Look at *The Truly Disadvantaged*," focus on the "underclass" problem. Though they take somewhat different views of the problem, together the two articles have more agreements than disagreements: In the 1970s the trend of steadily declining poverty rates ended and the percentage of households in poverty increased. That phenomenon was accompanied by a rapid growth in female headed families, and also by a flight of manufacturing jobs to the suburbs. The problem has reached a critical mass primarily in the big cities of the Northeast and Midwest. There is no consensus as to whether the problem is primarily caused by social breakdown or the lack of economic opportunity, with Peterson emphasizing the former and Wilson the latter. Still there is not as much disagreement between them as some may think; Peterson acknowl-

BILL GREEN was a member of the House of Representatives from 1979 to 1993. He served on the Appropriations Committee, and was ranking minority member on the Subcommittee on Veterans, Housing, Urban Development, and Independent Agencies. Before serving in Congress he was Regional Administrator of Housing and Urban Development in the New York area. He is also a director of the Academy of Political Science.

edges, for example, that the tight labor market around Boston in the mid-1980s did reduce inner city unemployment in Boston, but unfortunately the "Massachusetts miracle" came to an end before one could see the impact on social indicators.

Nonetheless the difference between the two perspectives is important. If the underclass problem is primarily an employment problem, then such measures as enterprise zones and improving reverse commuting from inner cities to suburban factories may be the answer. On the other hand, if a breakdown in family structure is the root cause, the problem becomes more complicated. Some, like Charles Murray in *Losing Ground* and on the pages of *Political Science Quarterly*, have argued that a complete revamping of the welfare system is a solution. Others point out that the growth in out of wedlock births and female headed families is not unique to the underclass but permeates our society, though showing up in its most aggravated numbers and with its most pernicious results in the inner cities. If it is going to take a societal revolution to deal with the problem, government alone — at least in our democratic, pluralistic society — may not be able to solve it.

Two of the other articles show that others have faced similar policy decisions in the past. Margaret Weir's "Innovation and Boundaries in American Employment Policy" explains how the War on Poverty became separated from larger economic policy making and questions whether it was wise. Similarly, Dona Cooper Hamilton and Charles Hamilton, in "The Dual Agenda of African American Organizations Since the New Deal," trace the choices made by African American groups between focusing their efforts on "civil rights, race specific" issues and focusing on broader social welfare initiatives that would benefit African Americans only as part of a larger polity.

Donna Wilson Kirchheimer's "Sheltering the Homeless: Expansion in an Era of Government Contraction" deals with one particular segment of the underclass, the homeless. She focuses primarily on the processes both formal and informal which led New York City to assume responsibility for running a major homeless shelter program. I quarrel with her in her assumption that the problem could have been solved if only "permanent housing" had been provided instead of shelters. At least as to the single adult homeless I believe the pervasiveness of substance abuse, and to a lesser extent serious mental illness, is now generally acknowledged. It will be interesting to see if the Clinton administration's health care reform program ultimately provides resources to deal with those problems. I fear that the politically sexy emphasis by the administration on gaps in insurance coverage rather than gaps in service delivery may leave the health problems of the urban poor no better tended to than they are today.

Demetrios Caraley, in "Washington Abandons the Cities," notes the considerable drop since 1978 in federal discretionary funding (in real dollars) that flows to city governments from Washington. Plainly that has left mayors with fewer resources to deal with inner city and homeless problems. However, what I find fascinating in Caraley's article is Table 1, which shows that the decline in largely discretionary dollars flowing to city governments is almost exactly matched by the increase in entitlement dollars flowing directly to the urban poor. In this respect what has happened to the cities' portion of the federal budget reflects what has happened to the federal budget as a whole: the entitlements are crowding out discretionary federal spending.

After one reads Shapiro and Young's "Public Opinion and the Welfare State: The United States in Comparative Perspective," one understands why. Despite variations over time and among age groups, there is strong support for social welfare entitlements. In contrast, Shapiro and Young point out there has been a drop in public support of federal funding for state and local governments.

The federal budget problem is reflected in two of the other articles. "Health Care Reform: The Uncertain Path from Proposal to Policy" by Thomas Oliver tells the story of the policy debate in the late 1970s and early 1980s between what were then perceived as the two major health care choices, increasing competition among health care providers versus national health insurance. In the end, Oliver relates, the budget pressures being generated by the Medicare program, which was predicted to run out of money by the late 1980s, overwhelmed the policy debate between the two alternatives, and Congress in 1983 adopted a Reagan administration initiative to hold down hospital charges to the Medicare system through the diagnosis-related groups approach. This is surely a cautionary tale for the Clinton administration as the health care debate wears on.

The major thrust of Robert B. Reich's "What Is a Nation," which he wrote as a Harvard professor, is the need to spend more on elementary and secondary education, job training, and physical infrastructure. What is more controversial is his proposal to provide the funds through increases in tax rates on the top fifth in income of the population, a proposal that the administration he has now joined as Secretary of Labor has obviously embraced. Not everyone agrees that this will work. As a former Harvard colleague of Secretary Reich, Professor of Economics Robert J. Barro, has written in the *Wall Street Journal*:

> A key issue, however, is whether increases in marginal tax rates at the top will raise any revenue at all. The history of responses to tax-rate changes from 1981 to 1991 suggests that the receipts generated by this part of the fiscal package probably will be close to zero and may actually be negative. Upper-income people are very 'responsive' to changes in the tax code: that is, they readily move their money around or change their behavior in response to new tax law. (Higher Taxes, Lower Revenues, Wall Street Journal, July 9, 1993.)

The two remaining articles in this collection deal with particular interest groups. Loree Bykerk and Ardith Maney, in "Where Have All the Consumers Gone?" spell out how an interest group—the consumer movement—has used the Congressional hearing process to make its case. Georgia Duerst-Lahti, in "The Government's Role in Building the Women's Movement," shows how an executive branch entity—in this case the Women's Bureau—can provide leadership and direction for an interest group.

Taken together, the articles in this collection illuminate not only major policy issues that the administration faces in pursuing a domestic agenda but also some important process issues that will confront the administration and its allies as it seeks to turn that agenda into reality. This collection is must reading, both for policy makers in the Clinton administration and in Congress who need to confront and remedy these problems, and for the general public whose support and understanding is necessary in a democratic political system like our own.

Washington Abandons the Cities

DEMETRIOS CARALEY

The New Federalism of the Reagan and Bush administrations has succeeded in reversing fifty years of American domestic policy by cutting back the constellation of federal grants to local and state governments that the federal government used to help poor people and needy city jurisdictions. These cutbacks accelerated the drift of large cities, especially the older ones of the East and Middle West, into underserviced, violence-ridden, crack-infested, homeless-burdened, bankruptcy-skirting slum ghettos. On top of this, the Bush administration's inability to maintain economic prosperity combined with its unwillingness to engage in traditional countercyclical spending through grants to city and state governments has brought many cities their worst fiscal and service crises since the Great Depression of the 1930s.

Even at the beginning of the Reagan administration in 1981, the social and economic conditions in the nation's large cities had not been robust. Poverty rates, the percentage of city populations living in poverty areas,[1] and violent crime rates had been high both in historical terms and in comparison to suburban rings where better-off families and thriving businesses were moving. (See Figures 1 and 2.) Among some subgroups of the central city population, the poverty rate was so high as to be almost unbelievable: for black children under age six in female headed families: 75 percent; for similar white children: 62 percent. The economic bases of central cites had been weak and unable at existing tax rates to generate the revenues needed to maintain—let alone improve—their low

---

[1] The census bureau defines poverty areas as census tracts where over 20 percent of the population is below the poverty threshold. The rest of the population in those tracts, while not poor itself, is exposed to the many destructive behaviors and attitudes of the poor.

DEMETRIOS CARALEY is Janet Robb Professor of the Social Sciences at Barnard College and the Graduate Faculties of Columbia University. He has published books and articles on both national and urban politics and policies.

FIGURE 1

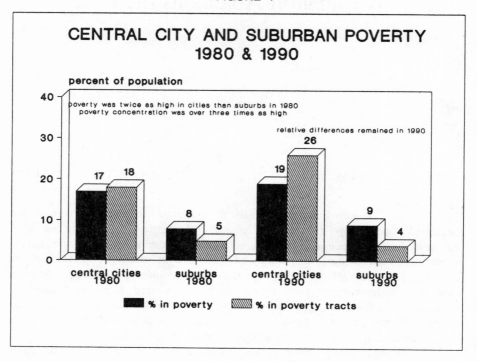

CENTRAL CITY AND SUBURBAN POVERTY
1980 & 1990

percent of population

poverty was twice as high in cities than suburbs in 1980
poverty concentration was over three times as high

relative differences remained in 1990

% in poverty   % in poverty tracts

quality of housekeeping services or to maintain and rehabilitate their aging infra-structures. These central cities had not been able to eliminate or even stop the expansion of slum neighborhoods with their deteriorating housing and ineffective schools in which large numbers of minority poor lacking jobs and job skills were concentrated. Nor had central cities been able to stop white flight or black, middle-class flight to the suburbs.

Moreover, during the Reagan administration, three sets of additional un-healthy conditions developed that were concentrated in large cities and imposed still greater burdens on their governments. First was the twin epidemics of crack-cocaine addiction and the routine murders and other violent crimes associated with its selling and use. Second was the AIDS epidemic with the horrors it imposed on its victims and its expensive public health costs. The third morbific develop-ment was the major expansion of homelessness—not only down-and-out indi-vidual males but entire families—and of large-scale begging on the streets and other public places.

Finally, in the Bush administration, the economic recession beginning in 1989 in the Northeast and then spreading to the nation as a whole caused drastic

FIGURE 2

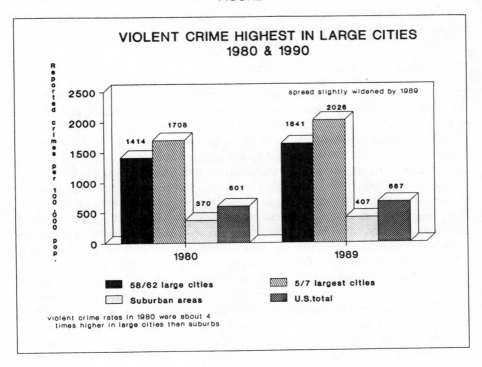

shortfalls in city-generated revenues leading to crushing deficits in city budgets and savage cutbacks in services and programs.

The remainder of this article will examine the two myths on which the Reagan/ Bush New Federalism ideology was based, the extent and impact of cuts in grant programs to city governments and poor people, and the prospects for the federal government turning around from simply abandoning large cities to resume the role of what I call the bailer-out-of-last-resort.

POLITICAL MYTHS AND POLITICAL REALITIES

The language of the Reagan/Bush administration's New Federalism cutback policy has contained many allusions about returning to local and state governments the power to make choices about what mix of taxes, essential housekeeping services, amenities, and benefits and services for the poor their citizens should have. Local and state governments, it was argued, are closer to the people than is the federal government. This position rests on two myths: every city and state jurisdiction has enough taxable resources to be afforded a real choice, and the federal government's intervention to fund grants to localities and states and individual benefits for the poor has been a usurpation that took place against the wishes of city and state officials and electorates.

The Superiority of Local Choice Myth

The myth that every city government with its limited geographic tax reach had the same real choice of what services, amenities, poverty benefits, and taxes it wanted to provide and impose was simply false. Every study of the capacities of city and state governments by the Census Bureau, Congress, the Advisory Commission on Intergovernmental Relations, and scholars in universities and think tanks provides evidence to demonstrate that falsity.[2] (See Figure 3.)

One set of statistics easily available from the 1980 census and reflecting conditions at the beginning of the Reagan administration shows that the richest city, San Jose, had a median family income of $25,598 — over twice the income of Newark's $11,989.[3] When suburban rings are also included in the comparison with large cities, eleven suburban rings — those of Washington, DC, San Jose, Chicago, New York City, Detroit, Houston, Newark, Milwaukee, San Francisco-Oakland, Minneapolis-St. Paul, and Seattle — had median incomes higher than the city of San Jose.[4] At the other end of the scale, of the twenty-five places with the lowest median income, twenty-two were central cities and only three were suburban rings — those of El Paso, Tampa, and Albuquerque. When the poverty rate is examined as one measure of the need for expensive services and programs, the range again is extremely wide — from 32.8 percent for Newark to 3.4 percent for Milwaukee, a difference of 9.6 to 1. Finally, when we calculate the amount of median family income available to be taxed for each percent of poverty, as an indicator of fiscal capacity and hence of the ability to make real choices, the range becomes tremendous. The Washington, DC suburban ring has

[2] One of the first such analyses appeared in this journal. See Richard P. Nathan and Charles Adams, "Understanding Central City Hardship," *Political Science Quarterly* 91 (Spring 1976): 47–62; see also Katherine L. Bradbury, Anthony Downs, and Kenneth A. Small, *Urban Decline and the Future of American Cities* (Washington, DC: Brookings Institution, 1982); Peggy Cuciti, "City Need and the Responsiveness of Federal Grant Programs," Report of the U.S. House of Representatives, Committee on Banking, Finance and Urban Affairs, Subcommittee on the City, 95th Congress, 2d sess., 1978; and Richard P. Nathan and Charles F. Adams, Jr., "Four Perspectives on Urban Hardship," *Political Science Quarterly* 104 (Fall 1989): 483–508.

[3] These statistics are calculated from U.S. Department of Commerce, Bureau of the Census, *1980 Census of Population, Vol. 2, Subject reports, PC80-2-2, Poverty Areas in Large Cities* (Washington, DC: 1984), Tables S-2 and S-3.

[4] The numbers given by the Census Bureau for the "Remainder of Metropolitan Area" or suburban rings are, of course, only statistical artifacts and represent no real governmental jurisdiction. Each ring may have from twenty to a hundred suburban municipalities, which themselves vary in capacity. But the differences between central cities and the aggregate of local governments in suburban jurisdictions is so wide that it is not misleading for the Census Bureau to make comparisons between central cities and their suburban rings as wholes.

FIGURE 3

DISPARITIES IN RESOURCES AND NEEDS
42 Largest Cities and Their Suburban Rings

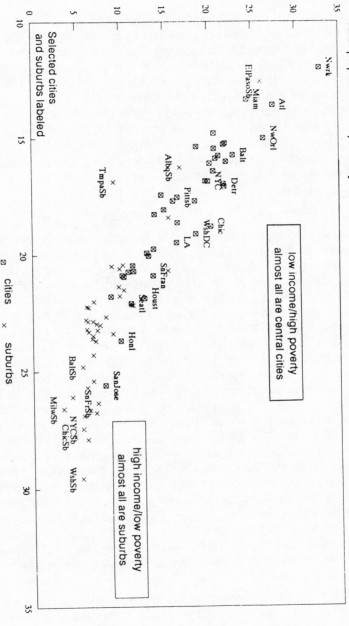

% of population in poverty

Median family income (in thousands)

⊠ cities   × suburbs

Selected cities and suburbs labeled

low income/high poverty almost all are central cities

high income/low poverty almost all are suburbs

Nwrk, ElPasoSb, Miam, Atl, NwOrl, Balt, AlbqSb, Detr, NYC, Pittsb, Chic, WshDC, LA, TmpaSb, SnFran, Houst, Seatl, Honl, BaltSb, SanJose, SnFrSb, MilwSb, NYCSb, ChicSb, WshSb

$5,375; the city of Newark has only $366 for each percentage of poor in their populations, a difference of 14.7 to 1. Figure 3 and the appendix show the great disparities even among central cities in resources relative to their poverty needs and the great disparities between central cities and suburban rings, with broad concentration of cities in the high need/low resources quadrant and suburban rings in the high resources/low poverty need quadrant.

Clearly, real choices are open only to wealthy jurisdictions with modest poverty needs, while poor jurisdictions have choices only in theory. In actuality, poor jurisdictions do not choose but are simply forced into the provide-less, cut-more, and tax-more, vicious circle that, as will be explained, makes cities less and less attractive to families and businesses wealthy enough to move away.

The Federal Usurpation Myth

In reality, almost all federal programs were taken on because city or state officials indicated either an unwillingness or an incapacity based on a mismatch between resources and needs to deal with the problem to which the federal program was responding. State and local government participation has been voluntary in virtually all grant programs; indeed, local and state governments did not get supplanted by a federal bureaucracy but were the governments that actually administered, albeit subject to federal regulations, the programs receiving federal aid. Also, federal grant and individual aid programs were not developed in a vacuum by some federal establishment insulated in Washington, DC, with little contact or awareness of local and state conditions and needs. Generally, federal programs were developed in full consultation with local and state officials who both testified and lobbied on different aspects. They also were approved by a Senate whose membership is elected from the fifty states and a House of Representatives elected by 435 local subdivisions of states. In this kind of governmental system, no federal program that has strong opposition in many states or localities can pass. Thus the federal involvement with social welfare and other grants to local and state governments reflected not a usurpation, but the traditional pattern in American government that if a serious domestic problem is to be solved, all levels of government including the federal must join in a cooperative effort to cope with it.

Moreover, the Founding Fathers foresaw this potential expansion of the federal role. James Madison, no friend of federal usurpation, asked rhetorically in *The Federalist* Nos. 45 and 46:

> . . . if . . . the Union be essential to the happiness of the people of America, is it not preposterous to urge as an objection to a government, . . . that such government may derogate from the importance of the governments of the individual States? Was, then, the American Revolution effected, was the American Confederacy formed, was the precious blood of thousands spilt, and the hard-earned substance of millions lavished, not that the people of America should enjoy peace, liberty, and safety, but that the governments of the individual States, that particular municipal establishments, might

enjoy a certain extent of power and be arrayed with certain dignities and attributes of sovereignty? . . . [A]s far as the sovereignty of the States cannot be reconciled to the happiness of the people, the voice of every good citizen must be, Let the former be sacrificed to the latter . . . .

If . . . the people should in future become more partial to the federal than to the State governments, the change can only result from such manifest and irresistible proofs of a better administration as will overcome all their antecedent propensities. And in that case, the people ought not surely to be precluded from giving most of their confidence where they may discover it to be most due. . . . .[5]

THE IMPACT OF THE REAGAN/BUSH CUTS IN FEDERAL AID

During the depths of the Great Depression of the 1930s, the federal government began to take on major responsibilities toward the poor and toward local and state governments.[6] Over the decades, especially in the 1960s, it added various, mostly categorical, social welfare programs to cover more categories of activities and individuals defined by the federal government as being most in need. It raised funding levels. It established grant programs that delivered aid directly to local governments, bypassing the state governments of which local governments were legal creatures. It established block grants and skewed allocation formulas for grant programs in order to target funds more to the so-called hardship cities and areas (those older and larger urban areas with large poverty populations primarily in the East and Midwest snowbelt) rather than spread those funds evenly among all cities and states. It amended eligibility standards from time to time to make it easier to qualify for individual benefits such as welfare, food stamps, and housing assistance. It increased benefit levels both to raise the minimum assistance being provided to the poor and needy and to compensate for inflation.

When the Reagan administration took office in 1981, the main problem areas for which there were major federal grant and social welfare spending programs were:

• poverty and unemployment among families and individuals: grants for cash welfare payments (Aid to Families with Dependent Children or AFDC), food stamps, housing assistance, legal services, medical services (Medicaid), and public

---

[5] Alexander Hamilton, James Madison, John Jay, *The Federalist Papers* (New York: Mentor Books, 1961), 288-289, 295.

[6] Some limited and sporadic forms of federal assistance to local and state governments date to the early 1800s. Federal financial aid programs to cities and states are based primarily on Congress's so-called spending power, which derives from Congress's constitutional authority "to lay and collect taxes . . . to pay the debts and provide for the common defense and general welfare of the United States." (Article I, Section 8.) As Congress exercised it since adoption of the Constitution and as the Supreme Court eventually ruled in 1936 in the case of *U.S. v Butler*, 297 U.S.1(1936), this clause permits the spending of federal monies not only in the substantive areas that Congress can regulate under its various enumerated powers but also for any purpose that comes within the meaning of the broad terms "general welfare" or "common defense" of the United States.

service jobs and job training (Comprehensive Employment and Training Act or CETA);

• physical decay and deteriorating economic bases of cities: community development block grants (CDBGs), urban development action grants (UDAGs), and economic development (EDA) grants and loans to local governments;

• education: grants to local school districts for compensatory services for disadvantaged students;

• transportation: grants to local and state governments for highways and for mass rail and bus transportation; and

• general purpose financial assistance: general revenue sharing payments to local governments.[7]

Fortunately for needy cities and poor persons, not all the cutbacks proposed between 1981 and 1991 by the Reagan/Bush administrations were adopted. But as Table 1 and Figure 4 show, the cuts in grant programs that benefited city governments were drastic: from 1980 to 1990 a cut of 46 percent or some $26 billion in constant 1990 dollars. As a consequence, the vast majority of large central cities of metropolitan areas were hurt; the disparities that already existed between rich and poor local and state jurisdictions got larger; and all of the previous factors in combination produced a constant ratcheting down of city services generally and an inability to raise the level of benefits and services for the poor, except in medical coverage. Finally, the economic recession beginning in 1989 in the Northeast and spreading broadly since 1990 further aggravated the situation by sharply reducing the revenues generated by city governments themselves and thus produced budget deficits that had to be eliminated with still more rounds of cutbacks in services and programs and increases in taxes.

The vast majority of large central cities were hurt.

Especially in the East and Midwest, central cities were already suffering in 1981. They had the greatest mismatch between needs for poverty-related services and benefits, for the improvement of housekeeping services, and for maintenance or replacement of aging infrastructures, on the one hand, and the availability of fiscal resources to pay for them, on the other. Consequently, they were heavily dependent on federal and state aid. In fiscal 1980 at the end of the Carter administration, six large cities—Newark, Baltimore, Buffalo, San Francisco, Milwaukee, and New York City—had from 50 to 69 percent of their general expenditures funded by federal and state aid, while another eleven cities received federal and state aid covering 40 to 50 percent of their general expenditures. By 1989 only three—Baltimore, Newark, and Buffalo—got over 50 percent of their expendi-

---

[7] Not all the funds expended through these programs went only to large cities or poor people living in them; large city governments and their poor residents got very large proportions of most of these grants.

TABLE 1

Trends in Federal Grants for Poor People and Poor City Governments Outlays in Constant 1990 Dollars (In Millions)

	1980	1990	CHG80–90 (%)	CHG80–90 ($)
Benefits Primarily to Individuals				
Medicaid	22,138	41,103	86	18,965
Housing assistance	7,257	13,561	87	6,304
Welfare payments	10,983	12,246	12	1,263
Supplemental feeding (WICS)	1,137	2,197	93	1,060
Food stamps	13,808	13,793	– 0	(15)
Child nutrition prgm	5,363	4,978	– 7	(385)
Community services prgm	868	350	– 60	(518)
Justice assistance	799	244	– 69	(555)
Totals	62,352	88,472	42	26,120
Totals excluding medicaid	40,214	47,369	18	7,155
Benefits Primarily to Governments				
General revenue sharing*	10,832	0	– 100	(10,832)
Public service jobs & job training	9,820	3,042	– 69	(6,778)
Community development block grants	6,189	2,818	– 54	(3,371)
Social services block grant	4,383	2,749	– 37	(1,634)
Urban mass transit	4,963	3,728	– 25	(1,235)
Compensatory education	5,345	4,437	– 17	(908)
Local public works	660	0	– 100	(660)
Economic development asst	717	160	– 78	(557)
Urban development action grants**	357	209	– 41	(148)
Federal aid highways	13,760	13,854	1	94
General antirecession assistance***	0	0		
Totals	57,026	30,997	– 46	(26,029)
* Large-city part of gen. rev. sharing (cities > 300,000):	1,758	0	– 100	(1,758)

** UDAGs were terminated in 1988 and outlays will drop to zero in early 1990s.
*** General antirecession assistance had been $2.664 billion in 1978

Source: Calculated from *Budget of the United States Government, fiscal year 1992*, Part Seven, Historical Tables 11.3 and 12.3.

tures from federal and state aid, with the top percentage dropping to 55 for Baltimore. The number of cities getting from 40 to 50 percent dropped from eleven to two — Milwaukee and Boston. The aid New York City received dropped from 52 percent of its general expenditures in 1980 to 36 percent in 1989. Indeed, if New York City had held on to the same percentage of its general expenditures funded by federal and state aid in 1989 as in 1980, it would have had some $4 billion more to spend and not had a budget crisis in 1990 and 1991, when it was forced to cut services and raise local taxes.

When aid from the federal government alone is looked at and in programs where aid went directly to city governments of cities over 300,000 in population,

FIGURE 4

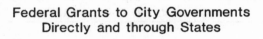

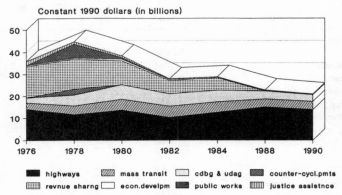

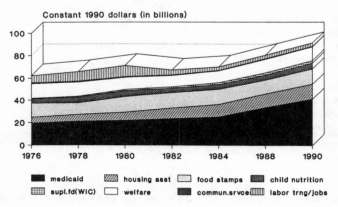

FIGURE 5

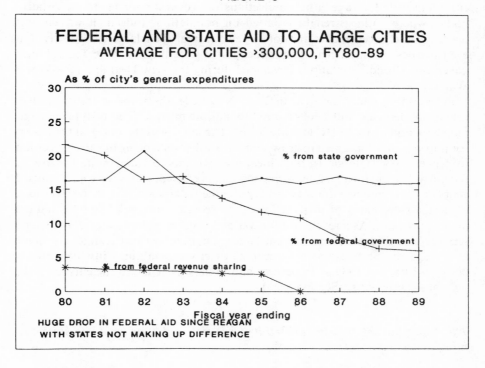

FEDERAL AND STATE AID TO LARGE CITIES
AVERAGE FOR CITIES >300,000, FY80-89

As % of city's general expenditures

% from state government

% from federal government

% from federal revenue sharing

Fiscal year ending

**HUGE DROP IN FEDERAL AID SINCE REAGAN
WITH STATES NOT MAKING UP DIFFERENCE**

from 1980 to 1989[8] the total amount of such aid dropped by some $1.8 billion from an aggregate of $5.2 billion in 1980 to $3.4 billion in 1989, a 35 percent cut. When adjusted for inflation, the cut is much sharper, a drop of over $5 billion in 1989 dollars. Still another way of looking at the impact is in terms of what the average percentage of these large cities' expenditures was covered by federal aid: in 1980 it was 22, and by 1989 it had dropped to 6. (See Figure 5).

The elimination of some targeted federal categorical programs that provided aid to city governments directly — general revenue-sharing payments and urban development action grants — and the diminution of others — like community development block grants, economic assistance grants and loans, and mass transit grants for capital and operating expenses — meant that cities had to look to their states for replacement of such aid or cut their own services further. Yet in no state was the population of large cities — for the purposes of this analysis those

[8] The figures for fiscal years ending in calendar 1989 are the most recent available from the Census Bureau. All the comparisons of federal and state aid come from the annual publication, U.S. Department of Commerce, Bureau of the Census, *City Government Finances*, Series GF, No. 4, (Washington, DC: various years).

of 300,000 or above — anywhere near a statewide majority. This meant that these cities had little leverage either in elections for governors or in state legislative bodies where voting strength is based on population. Indeed, it was in part because state governments did not in general treat their large cities fairly, but even at times exploited them in the allocation of state aid, that direct federal-local government funding relations developed during the New Deal and post-World War II eras.

Furthermore under the Reagan/Bush New Federalism, the states themselves also lost federal aid and were required to allocate more of their own revenues as matching dollars to AFDC and Medicaid. The latter was the one grant program for the poor that continued to grow sharply. Rather than being in a fiscal position to deliver more state aid to their local governments to compensate for loss of federal aid as the Reagan administration had predicted, states were hard pressed simply to generate new revenues to replace the federal aid they themselves lost, especially since many of them followed the federal example after 1981 and cut income tax rates. As a result, aid for welfare, other poverty-related benefits and services, and general operations that came to large cities from the states also came into jeopardy. State aid as a percentage of city expenditures just held steady between 1980 and 1989 at 16 percent and in no way replaced the cuts from the federal governments. (See Figure 5).

The disparities that already existed between rich and poor local and state jurisdictions got larger.

The assignment to localities and states of more funding responsibilities for social welfare programs and for general governmental operations meant that there was a tremendously wide range in the ability to replace federal aid with funds generated by local and state taxes even in a prosperous national economy. Jurisdictions with high taxable resources and low concentrations of poor people — for example, thriving high-tech areas and high-income suburbs — had the capacity to keep services high, to continue to provide (if they chose) the preexisting levels of benefits to the small concentrations of poor people within their borders, and to keep tax rates low. Jurisdictions with low taxable resources and high concentrations of poor people — for example, the larger, older declining cities primarily of the East and Midwest with high concentrations of ghetto poor and snowbelt states with high levels of structural unemployment — had little or no capacity to substitute locally- and state-generated revenues for lost federal aid.

Many of these poor local jurisdictions were already in 1981 imposing high taxes relative to the low level of services they provided. Some had tax rates approaching or actually at state legislative or state constitutional limits. All were subject to local city charter requirements and state legislative or state constitutional mandates for annual balanced budgets. And all feared that increases in local taxes, even if technically possible, would be counterproductive by providing greater incentives for mobile, high-income families and prosperous businesses that still remained to move out. By moving out, these families and businesses would be avoiding tax increases for themselves and further eroding the fiscal capacity of the jurisdictions they left. Such erosion would cause further increases in the tax rates to make up for a smaller tax base and/or cause further reduction of services and benefits. There was thus a strengthening of the vicious circle for wealthy jurisdictions to become even wealthier and fiscally stronger as they attracted still more upper-income families and prospering businesses. And as the other part of that circle, poor jurisdictions became poorer and incapable of continuing even the lower levels of services and benefits they previously provided as they lost still more of their economic base and also lost targeted federal aid such as all of general revenue sharing, all of urban development action grants, and significant amounts of community development block grants and mass transit grants.

All of the previous factors in combination produced a constant ratcheting down of city services generally and an inability to raise the level of benefits and services for the poor except in medical coverage.

As some jurisdictions were perceived as having low tax/high essential services/ low poverty services profiles, other jurisdictions in order to stay competitive or to meet balanced budget requirements found it necessary or expedient to reduce services and benefits to the poor and their neighborhoods even more in order to keep their own low tax/essential services/poverty services mix competitive. This stimulated still more jurisdictions to cut poverty services to remain competitive. In their spending on welfare, for example, states, which are allowed to set benefit levels but also mandated to match up to 50 percent of their costs, either cut those levels or did not increase them to keep up with inflation.

The so-called safety net programs — welfare payments, food stamps, Medicaid, child nutrition, and supplemental feeding for women, infants, and children (WIC) — were able as a whole to resist cuts between 1980 and 1990 even when measured in constant dollars. The special standing of these programs was officially recognized both in the Gramm-Rudmann-Hollings Act of 1985 (GRH) and in the Budget Enforcement Act of 1990 (BEA) by making them exempt from automatic cuts through sequestration.[9] But even the level of spending on pro-

---

[9] The GRH mandated a balanced budget by 1991 through cuts in spending and set deficit reduction targets for each year until 1991. To enforce the deficit reduction process, the act provided that if the targets were not met by the regular legislative and appropriations processes, automatic sequestration orders would be issued making across-the-board spending cuts sufficient to meet the deficit targets. It required that half the cuts come from military programs and half from domestic programs, but protected some domestic programs like social security, AFDC, Medicaid, food stamps, and WIC (a special food program for women, infants, and young children). The BEA was Title XIII of the Omnibus Reconciliation Act of 1990 which incorporated into law the fall 1990 White House-congressional budget summit agreements. It relaxed in two major respects the constraints of Gramm-Rudman-Hollings for fiscal years 1991–1995: There was no longer a calendar deadline for reaching

grams for poor persons in 1980 was not decreasing but allowing the rate of poverty in cities to increase. Therefore, the very major accomplishment – as compared to other domestic programs – of not taking cuts in these programs for central city poor individuals and families did not produce any improvement in their fortunes. Despite the growth in total spending, the average AFDC benefit dropped from 1980 to 1990 in terms of constant 1990 dollars from $3506 to $3218 per family and from $1205 to $1116 per recipient. For food stamps the average benefit dropped from $719 to $690. The only major exception was the extension of Medicaid coverage to pregnant, working poor women and their small children who were not on welfare. Together with the rapid rise in medical costs, this forced a major 86 percent or 19 billion, 1990 constant dollar expansion of spending for Medicaid between 1980 and 1990. (See Figure 4 and Table 1.)

Ironically, even this expansion of Medicaid coverage was a two-edged sword in its impact on city governments. On the one hand, it went against the thrust of the Reagan/Bush administration's cutback policy of not improving grant and aid programs for the poor and therefore helped cities by making some of their working poor families eligible to receive free medical care. On the other hand, this federal generosity was expensive for states and some local governments. Medicaid, like AFDC, requires matching funds from all states with the matching rate for many states with large cities being close to or at the maximum of 50 percent. In some states, the state requires part of those matching funds to come from local governments. The most costly situation for city governments is in New York where federal rules require the state to match 50 percent of Medicaid spending with its own funds and New York State itself requires its cities and other local governments to absorb one-half of the nonfederal share – again the highest matching rate – or 25 percent of the total bill.[10] This helped produce a fiscal 1989 budget expenditure for Medicaid in New York City of some $2.6 billion.

---

a balanced budget. Instead declining budget-deficit targets allowed a deficit of $83 billion by fiscal 1995. Separate spending caps were set for each year in three areas of spending – defense, international, and domestic – at a level that would reduce the overall budget deficit by a specified amount. But those caps were in a sense floating, since they could be revised to reflect changing economic and technical assumptions. Within each of those caps, changes up or down could be made in discretionary spending or in taxes as long as the net impact canceled out – referred to as the pay-as-you-go process. To enforce these caps, there was provision for very complicated sequestration procedures that would originally apply only in the broad category breaching the cap, but with Social Security, AFDC, Medicaid, food stamps, child nutrition, and WIC still exempt from sequestration. In the fourth and fifth year of the BEA the separate caps would be replaced by one overall cap so that cuts and additions could be made across the categories of defense, international, and domestic spending. There was also a provision for breaching the spending caps if the president designated that extra spending was for emergency purposes. The entire sequestration process could be suspended if Congress passed a joint resolution (requiring presidential approval or an extraordinary majority to override a veto) recognizing very low or no economic growth, since revenue loss would prevent the deficit reduction targets from being met.

[10] The matching rate in 1992 for Alaska, California, Connecticut, Illinois, Maryland, Massachusetts, Nevada, New Hampshire, New Jersey, New York, and Virginia was 50 percent; the lowest rate of matching was for Mississippi at 20 percent. Of states with large cities, only the following required

Even more important for city governments, the flip side of protecting individual safety net benefits for the elderly and poor was that in order to meet the GRH deficit targets and BEA spending caps, the unprotected domestic grant programs like community services, job training, mass transit, community development block grants, community development action grants, general revenue sharing, and economic development, took disproportionately large cuts, and those domestic discretionary programs became in the aggregate a smaller and smaller part of the remaining budget.

Sometimes the cuts in unprotected programs for city governments were made not even in order to help safety net programs for poor people. In 1988, Congress eliminated all funding for community development action grants and ended that program in order to provide a major funding increase for NASA's space station.

The economic recession beginning in 1989 in the Northeast and spreading broadly since 1990 further aggravated the situation by sharply reducing revenues generated by city governments themselves and thus produced budget deficits that had to be eliminated with still another round of cutbacks in services and programs and increases in taxes.

This recession also reduced the revenues of the state governments and by expanding welfare and Medicaid rolls, forced states to use more of their revenues as matching dollars in these programs. Thus at best the states' ability to replace funds cut by the federal government was restricted and at worst state governments were forced to make cuts in previous levels of their own aid to local governments. In the fall of 1991, for example, the Michigan legislature abolished all relief or welfare that was not AFDC and thus was not partially federally funded; this meant that single men or women or couples without children would receive no cash assistance. Other states — including traditionally progressive ones like New Jersey and New York — were considering and adopting similar reductions of welfare benefits in the winter of 1991–1992.

In addition, because of a combination of what I call the Washington "don't bother us, we're broke" mentality with respect to domestic problems and the Reagan/Bush ideology of abandoning city and state governments to sink or swim on their own, the federal government did not in 1990 or 1991 legislate antirecession, countercyclical programs like emergency public works, emergency public service jobs, or countercyclical cash payments. Congress had done this over President Gerald Ford's veto in 1976 and again with President Jimmy Car-

---

matching of the state share: California, 10.8 percent; Colorado, 42.7 percent; Indiana, 40 percent; Minnesota, 15 percent; New Jersey, 25 percent; New York, 50 percent; and Ohio, 5 percent. Committee on Ways and Means, U.S. House of Representatives, *Overview of Entitlement Programs: 1991 Green Book: Background Material and Data on Programs within the Jurisdiction of the Committee on Ways and Means* (Washington, DC: U.S. Government Printing Office, 1991), 609–611, Tables 13 and 14.

ter's support in 1977 and 1978; various kinds of countercyclical spending were traditional in earlier post-World War II recessions. The antirecession package voted by Congress in 1976 and 1977 sent about $8.5 billion to city and state governments which if emulated during the 1990-1991 recession would have amounted to $17 billion in 1990 dollars.

THE FUTURE OF BAILER-OUT FEDERALISM AND CENTRAL CITIES

For the some fifty years preceding the Reagan/Bush administrations, American federal aid policy was based on the premise that only the federal government could afford to fund benefit and services programs for poor people and grants programs for poor cities and states. It was considered right and just for the federal government to do so. Unlike that of a particular city or state, the federal government's tax reach is all encompassing; taxpayers cannot move to lower-tax jurisdictions to reduce the amount of their income taken by taxes. From World War II to the 1970s, the federal government had the most productive tax system, able to raise increasingly larger increments of revenue with each increment of economic growth or of inflation. Only the federal government is allowed to run a deficit in its annual budget and thus is capable through borrowing of spending more than it raises in revenues. And only the federal government's expenditures, tax rates, and borrowing are never subject to public referenda. Finally and most importantly, it was widely felt that the federal government was ultimately the bailer-out-of-last-resort for keeping services and benefits in all localities and states above some minimal threshold and for intervening to help with major problems that could not or were not being successfully addressed by local or state governments.

The amount of federal aid was never enough to turn cities around and solve the problems of concentrated slum poverty, drugs and crime, and aging infrastructure. Furthermore, money alone could not cure all problems, especially those requiring complicated changes of attitudes and behavior to improve learning in schools, reduce welfare dependency, and bring down crime rates.[11] But the level of federal aid made available directly to cities and indirectly through state governments at least kept conditions from deteriorating as rapidly and explosively as they have over the past ten years. It was also important to city officials and populations that the federal government cared.

Starkly put, the Reagan/Bush administrations' ideological posture was that it no longer wanted, could not afford, and did not deem it legitimate to be the ultimate subsidizer of poor people and poor local and state jurisdictions. The one exception was to actually expand Medicaid coverage to working poor, pregnant

---

[11] See Demetrios Caraley, "Is the Large City Becoming Ungovernable" in Robert H. Connery and Demetrios Caraley, eds., *Governing the City* (New York: Frederick Praeger, 1969), 206–223; Demetrios Caraley, *City Governments and Urban Problems* (Englewood Cliffs, NJ: Prentice-Hall, 1977), chaps. 17–20.

women and their small children and to increase the maximum refundable earned income tax credit for working poor families. Both of these steps were designed to give incentives to some working poor families to keep working and not become welfare recipients. One of the central premises of the Reagan/Bush administrations' cutback policies was that it was precisely the federal tax system's productivity in taking a larger and larger tax bite out of the economy that had caused the economy of the 1970s to be so sluggish. With the stagnant but still inflationary economy of the 1970s, that bite was not coming out of real economic growth but out of the living standards of the broad middle class as it was subjected to inflation-driven bracket creep. The overriding domestic objective of the Reagan administration was, therefore, to spur vigorous economic growth with tax cuts and to rely on that projected economic growth to trickle down and take care of the problems of the poor.

The prospects for cities seeing a return once again to a more benevolent, bailer-out-of-last-resort federal government essentially depends on the federal government's self-perceived and actual budgetary constraints. It also depends on political factors such as party control in the White House, distribution of party strength in Congress, and the disposition of the American population between central cities and suburbs and between the Northeast-Midwest snowbelt and the southern and western sunbelt. Finally and perhaps most fundamentally, it depends on elite beliefs and broad public opinion — essentially the dominant public philosophy — about the responsibility of the federal government for dealing with problems of individual and family poverty and distress and for alleviating extreme disparities among local and state governments in fiscal stability and services delivered for each tax dollar collected.

Budgetary Constraints

To understand how fiscal conditions affect federal funding of programs for poor cities and poor people, it may be useful to flash back to the 1960s, when the federal government's condition was not one of fiscal stringency but of plenitude. Writing in 1966, Walter W. Heller, who had been chairman of President John F. Kennedy's and President Lyndon B. Johnson's Council of Economic Advisers, postulated that with a continuously growing economy, the then existing rates of the federal tax system would produce built-in average increases in revenues of $7 to $8 billion a year in excess of those needed to meet rising federal expenditures.[12]

Unfortunately for the treasuries of city and state governments, the escalation beginning in 1965 of the war in Vietnam absorbed all the expanded revenues that became available. But even as expenses for the Vietnam war began to contract between 1969 and 1972 with the reduction of the American ground force commitment, no new fiscal or peace dividends became available to be diverted to social

---

[12] Walter W. Heller, *New Dimensions of Political Economy* (New York: Norton, 1967), chap. 3.

welfare needs. First, the general reduction in personal and corporate income taxes that had been legislated in 1964, 1969, and 1971 seriously weakened the previous capacity of the federal revenue-raising system to generate large amounts of new revenues year after year. Second, just as federal tax collections were showing a substantially smaller automatic annual growth, expenditures for domestic programs, of which social security transfer payments and social welfare-oriented Great Society grant programs were a big chunk, began in 1965 to increase much more sharply than in the past and faster than the growth in the nation's economy.

The implication of these trends for domestic social welfare programs was simply that with the existing federal tax structure and even a nonrecessionary economy the projected automatic growth in domestic expenditures alone had begun to exceed the projected annual gain in revenues yielded by economic growth. Any new or expanded social welfare grant programs could not, therefore, be funded by the federal government painlessly out of fiscal dividends but had to come at the expense of other programs, from acknowledged tax increases, or from de facto bracket-creep tax increases. Another alternative for the federal government was financing new and expanded programs through continuously larger budget deficits. But that alternative too was not painless, since it was believed in the 1970s that an annual budget deficit of even $50 billion carried unacceptable inflationary effects.

Despite continued budget deficits through the Nixon, Ford, and Carter administrations ranging from a low of $8 billion in fiscal 1974 to highs of $70.5 and $72.7 billion in 1976 and 1980,[13] the Reagan administration went into office in 1981 with a commitment to a major increase in defense spending and a major cut in individual and corporate income taxes. Part of the Reagan justification for the tax cuts was that it would in fact cost nothing with respect to the deficit, since the extra income kept by individuals and corporations would according to supply-side economic theory stimulate enough new economic activity to generate more new revenues than the revenues forgone by the tax cut. Politically neutral technical experts at the Congressional Budget Office and the staff of the Joint Committee on Taxes forecast in 1981, however, a massive loss of revenues, beginning at $37.7 billion in 1982 and climbing to $267.7 billion in 1986.[14]

In short, through its tax cuts and its increased defense spending, the Reagan administration created unprecedented large budget deficits — an average of $193 billion a year over its eight years. It tripled the size of the national debt inherited from President Carter and all his predecessors from $994 billion to $2.8 trillion by 1988[15] and produced in Washington a mentality of being constantly broke. The GRH and BEA reinforced that outlook by prohibiting any increases in a

[13] *Budget of the United States Government, Fiscal Year 1992, Part 7, Historical Tables* (Washington, DC: U.S. Government Printing Office, 1992), Table 1.1.

[14] Gregory B. Mills and John L. Palmer, eds., *Federal Budget Policy in the 1980s* (Washington, DC: Urban Institute, 1984).

[15] *Budget, Historical Tables*, Table 1.1.

spending program without compensating decreases in other programs or finding new sources of revenues. Proposed cutbacks and eliminations of social welfare programs, not spending increases and new initiatives, became the Washington agenda in the discussion of federal domestic programs. Victories in Congress for supporters of federal aid became simply saving a program from termination or having it take a smaller cut than that proposed by the Reagan or Bush administration as opposed to improving or expanding a program's quality. In this austere climate of opinion, even pro-aid Democrats went along with some cuts in order not to appear fiscally irresponsible against a backdrop of $200 to $300 billion annual deficits.

Political Factors

The importance of the party affiliation of the president and of the distribution of party strength in the two houses of Congress comes from the fact that since the 1930s, Democrats in Congress (with the exception of the southern Democrats) and Democratic presidents have supported the expansion of the federal government's role in social welfare programs for the poor and grant programs for distressed local and state governments. Republicans in Congress (with some exceptions among eastern Republicans) and Republican presidents have not.[16]

The most important political consideration for the prospects of increased city aid is whether there will ever again be a liberal, pro-city Democratic president serving with Congresses that will have heavy Democratic majorities and whether Democrats will be as pro-city as in the past. This prospect depends on whether the elections to the presidency in 1980 and 1984 of Ronald Reagan and in 1988 of George Bush reflect that a new long-term Republican electoral majority for the presidency has emerged, committed to ideological conservatism and to a reduced federal role in domestic affairs in principle and unrelated to short-term budgetary stringencies.

In the past three decades a twofold population trend has weakened the political strength of the urban East and Midwest. Within metropolitan areas, the older cities have been losing population to their suburbs. Within the nation, the East and Midwest have been losing population to the South and West. In 1990, only 30 percent of all Americans lived in central cities, while a smaller 18 percent lived in really large central cities of 250,000 or more. A full 48 percent of Americans lived in the outside-central-city or suburban portions of metropolitan areas, and 22 percent lived outside of metropolitan areas entirely.[17] Furthermore, the percentage of the white population that lived in central cities in 1990 was even

[16] See Demetrios Caraley, "Congressional Politics and Urban Aid," *Political Science Quarterly* 91 (Spring 1976): 19–45.
[17] Calculated from U.S. Bureau of the Census, Current Population Reports, Series P-60, No. 175, *Poverty in the United States: 1990* (Washington, DC: U.S. Government Printing Office, 1991), Table 1.

lower — 26 percent — meaning that 74 percent of the politically and economically dominant population lived in suburbs and rural areas. On the other hand, majorities of the black population — 56 percent — and of the Hispanic population — 52 percent — lived in central cities and experienced directly various degrees of city distress.[18]

The decline in the proportion of the population living in large cities results in a steadily decreasing number of members in the House of Representatives who represent central city districts. In the 95th, 96th, and 97th Congresses (1977–1982) only 105 districts (or 24 percent) — not even a plurality of districts — was predominantly central city. 125 (or 29 percent) were predominantly suburban, 132 (or 30 percent) rural, and 73 (or 17 percent) mixed. In the 98th Congress (1983–1984) after the reapportionment of the House to reflect the 1980 census, the number of the districts that remained predominantly central city dropped to only 94 (or 22 percent), while the predominantly suburban districts increased to 137 (or 31 percent). Of the remaining districts, 85 (or 20 percent) were rural and 118 (or 27 percent) were mixed. Even among the seats held by northern Democrats before the 1982 reapportionment, the 70 districts that were predominantly suburban slightly exceeded in number the 66 that were predominantly central city. There were also thirty-five northern Democratic constituencies that were predominantly rural. As a result of the 1990 census and the required decennial reapportionment, the 103d Congress, to be elected in 1992, will have a still smaller number of members from central cities.

In the 95th, 96th, and 97th Congresses, the suburban northern Democrats were almost as supportive of pro-city positions (averaging 88 percent) as were the central-city northern Democrats (90 percent). Even the rural northern Democrats' votes were substantially pro-city (80 percent).[19] How long northern Democratic House members from suburban and rural constituencies will continue to share the policy outlook of the Democratic central-city representatives, who are ceasing to be the dominant contingent in the northern Democratic membership, is an open question. But it is difficult to conceive of a rise in the Democratic suburban and rural level of pro-city support, so the probability is that the level will drop.

Some signs of things to come may be the House and Senate floor votes in 1988 that tried to restore some appropriations for Urban Development Action Grants, after the appropriations committees had cut them out entirely. In the House a small majority of Democrats voted for an amendment to restore some funds — 51 percent (northern Democrats 66 percent, southern Democrats 19 percent). But

[18] Calculated from ibid., Table 8.

[19] This analysis is based on a long-term study of congressional voting behavior and urban programs during the Carter, Reagan, and Bush administrations. Findings were previously reported in Demetrios Caraley, "Carter, Congress, and the Cities" in Dale Rogers Marshall, ed., *Urban Policy Making*, (Beverly Hills, CA: Sage Publications, 1979), 71–98; and Demetrios Caraley and Yvette Schlussel, "Congress and Reagan's New Federalism," *Publius: The Journal of Federalism* 16 (Winter 1986): 49–79.

a majority of Republicans plus a minority of Democrats were able to outvote it and keep UDAGs dead. In the Senate not even a majority but only 48 percent of all Democrats (60 percent of northern Democrats and 24 percent of southern Democrats) voted to restore funds for UDAGs.[20] When general revenue sharing was killed in committee in 1985, there was not even an attempt to save the program by Democratic-sponsored floor amendments.

The decline in the proportion of the population living in the Northeast and Midwest has resulted in a decreasing number of representatives from those regions. As a result of the 1980 census, the states in the East and Midwest lost, and those in the South and West gained, seventeen seats. The losers were New York (five seats), Illinois, Pennsylvania, and Ohio (two seats each), Michigan, New Jersey, Indiana, Missouri, Massachusetts, and South Dakota (one seat each). The gainers were Florida (four seats), Texas (three seats), California (two seats), New Mexico, Arizona, Colorado, Utah, Oregon, Tennessee, Nevada, and Washington (one seat each).

Within states the major central-city losers were St. Louis, Chicago, Detroit, Pittsburgh, Philadelphia, Jersey City, Newark, and New York City. While such sunbelt central cities as Phoenix, Albuquerque, San Antonio, Houston, and San Jose gained seats, sunbelt suburban areas captured the most representatives – a net of twenty-three seats, eight in Florida alone. (It should be noted that even greater losses than those of central cities were suffered by rural areas both in the snowbelt's Midwest and in most states of the sunbelt.) In short, the loss of seats were in the East and Midwest, which gave a relatively high level of support to programs of poor persons and poor cities. The gains were in the West and South, where except for the western Democrats there have been only low levels of support.

As a result of the 1990 census, the Northeast and Midwest will again lose seats while the South and West will gain, for a net change of 16. The winners will be California (seven seats). Florida (four seats), Texas (three), and Washington, Georgia, Arizona, and North Carolina (one seat each). The biggest losers are the Northeast's and Midwest's urban states: New York (three); Illinois, Michigan, Ohio, and Pennsylvania (two each for a total of eight); and New Jersey and Massachusetts (one each). Other states that will lose one seat each are Kansas, Iowa, Kentucky, Louisiana, Montana, and West Virginia.

Because the Senate is never reapportioned, the impact of present population trends is more difficult to nail down. Senators in general, even Democratic senators from states with large cities, will inevitably have to recognize the increasingly suburban character of their overall constituencies. According to the 1980 census, after three decades of suburbanization, in only one state – New York – did the combined populations of all central cities of over 50,000 constitute a majority of

---

[20] CQ House Vote #196 and CQ Senate Vote #244, *Congressional Quarterly Almanac, 100th Congress, 2d Session, 1988* (Washington, DC: Congressional Quarterly Service, 1989).

the population. On the other hand, in 1980 eleven states—Massachusetts, Florida, Rhode Island, New Jersey, Illinois, Delaware, Maryland, Wyoming, Utah, Nevada, and California—had majorities of their populations in suburban areas including some small suburban cities. Politically, therefore, senators are not able to afford the reputation of being out-and-out champions of large cities and of the disproportionately large concentrations of poor and blacks who live there.

Finally, the increasing suburbanization and the westward and southward flow of the population affects the intensity of presidential leadership in favor of increased federal aid to its poor and its large cities. In a nation in which after each decennial census, fewer electoral votes come from the East and Midwest and where suburban populations are increasingly in a position to outvote the residents of large cities, presidents will not find it electorally profitable to assign policy and budgetary priorities to programs that can be perceived as basically benefiting those cities and the poor who live there. Democratic presidents, whose traditional followings have included the poor and the black and others who live in large cities, will be caught in a double bind, no doubt finding it much harder to ignore the needs of those city dwellers since they constitute the bedrock of Democratic presidential strength and are essential for capturing the Democratic presidential nomination.

In 1976, for example, President Carter's victory depended on the almost two-to-one majorities or better he received in such cities as New York, Boston, Newark, Philadelphia, Cleveland, Chicago, Detroit, Minneapolis, St. Louis, Oakland, and Baltimore. Substantial parts of those majorities came from black voters, who were estimated as having cast 90 percent of their votes for Carter nationally. The large majorities built up in New York City, Philadelphia, Pittsburgh, Cleveland, Toledo, Milwaukee, St. Louis, and Kansas City accounted for Carter's statewide margins of victory in New York, Pennsylvania, Ohio, Wisconsin, and Missouri, without which he would not have had the electoral votes to win the presidency.[21] When Carter sought reelection in 1980, he again needed and sought strong support among large-city and black electorates and again received very large majorities in such cities as New York (70 percent), Chicago (72 percent), Philadelphia (63 percent), Detroit (82 percent), Baltimore (77 percent), San Francisco (62 percent), Boston (62 percent), New Orleans (59 percent), St. Louis (69 percent). Yet because of the large-scale erosion of his support outside of central cities, in no case except Baltimore and Maryland did Carter's large city-wide majorities enable him to carry the state and its electoral votes.[22]

Walter Mondale in 1984 also cultivated large-city and black constituencies, even though that opened him to the charge that he was catering to special interests.

[21] Calculated from Richard M. Scammon and Alice V. McGillivray, *America Votes 12, 1976*, (Washington, DC: Congressional Quarterly, 1977).

[22] Calculated from Scammon and McGillivray, *American Votes 14, 1980*.

But Mondale, too, while succeeding in amassing large majorities in many big cities—for example, New York (61 percent), Chicago (65 percent), Detroit (81 percent), Baltimore (72 percent), San Francisco (68 percent), and St. Louis (65 percent)—nevertheless lost every state with large cities except his home state of Minnesota.[23]

In 1988, Michael Dukakis, who at no time in his campaign proposed increased federal aid for poor cities and poor people, won some states—Hawaii, Massachusetts, New York, Oregon, Rhode Island, Washington State, and Wisconsin—by scoring large majorities in their largest cities. Yet Dukakis lost other states—California, Connecticut, Illinois, Louisiana, Maryland, Michigan, Missouri, New Jersey, Ohio, and Pennsylvania—despite the majorities he won in their largest cities; these majorities were not, however, as large as Carter's or Mondale's, which may reflect his ignoring urban needs in his campaign.[24]

PUBLIC PHILOSOPHY IN ELITE AND PUBLIC OPINION

There is the possibility of an even more fundamental, long-term threat to resumption of a benevolent bailer-out federalism. This would be the case if there has developed a new public philosophy among political elites and in broad public opinion that opposes efforts by the federal government to redistribute resources from persons, government jurisdictions, and geographic areas of relative affluence to those of relative poverty and distress in order to reduce wide disparities within the nation. Such a philosophy may be reaching not only Republican but also Democratic members of Congress and Democratic aspirants to the presidency. Notwithstanding the conventional wisdom that there is essentially no turnover in Congress, only 163 of 435 members of the House and 50 of the 100 senators serving in 1991-1992 also served as long ago as the last years of the Carter administration—1979-1980—and therefore have personal recollection of being part of a body that considered it normal to help needy governmental jurisdictions and poor people.

Certainly nothing in the 1984 and 1988 elections suggested that many Americans were demanding that cuts in federal aid to local and state governments and social welfare spending be restored, despite government statistics and other studies showing a rise in the percentage of the population in poverty. To the extent that they took domestic policy into account, most Americans seemed willing, in exchange for renewed economic growth and tax cuts, to tolerate a disproportionately large share of growth going to families with income in the highest quintile. They also seemed to tolerate a permanent lowering of the economic floor below which the conditions of the poor and the services of large city governments had not been allowed to drop in the 1970s.

---

[23] Calculated from Scammon and McGillivray, *America Votes 16, 1984.*
[24] Calculated from Scammon and McGillivray, *America Votes 18, 1988.*

Another part of such a new sink-or-swim public philosophy would be an acceptance by Americans of the view that localities and states have to operate on their own, regardless of how meager their economic base might be relative to the service and program needs of their citizens. This would be so despite the fact that some jurisdictions with terrible conditions might be imposing higher taxes than those with the best conditions.

Will the Bush administration quickly succeed in restoring—as the Reagan administration had maintained from 1982 to 1988—economic growth leading to at least the perception of improvement in standards of living for middle-class Americans? If it should do this and continue to prevent general tax increases, the Reagan/Bush administration's policy of reducing support for the nonworking poor and reducing or eliminating aid to city and state governments might become permanently embedded in the national consensus.

IS ANOTHER SCENARIO POSSIBLE?

If on the other hand, the 1989–1992 recession drags on and continues to bring sharp economic dislocations, there may be a shift from reducing the federal benefactory role and from economic and tax policies disproportionately favoring high-income people and large corporations toward more traditional Democratic policies for dealing with recessions. Such policies would include increased federal spending to stimulate the economy and to provide public service and public works jobs for the unemployed both through direct federal spending and through grants to local and state governments in order to provide countercyclical impact. This would be difficult, even for Democrats, if the size of the budget deficit were still massive, since such spending might temporarily increase the deficit. (See Figure 6.) But a recessionary economy that does not spend for countercyclical programs also increases the deficit by reducing revenues and increasing uncontrollable spending for those brought into unemployment and poverty. Furthermore, the collapse of the Soviet Union makes possible over time substantial reductions in the defense budget and permits savings in defense beginning in fiscal year 1994 to count as pay-as-you-go increases in domestic spending. The BEA could also be amended to allow it even for the fiscal 1993 budget appropriations being considered during the 1992 congressional session.

Even then there probably would not be a climate of opinion in favor of reviving and restrengthening federal grants to city governments and other social welfare programs to the spending peak they had reached in 1978. There would be the need to be highly selective about what programs to concentrate on and thus to target federal aid both to truly needy people, and also only to truly needy local jurisdictions.

The major vehicles for delivering federal aid to local jurisdictions should be two formula grants, one a countercyclical program to trigger in and out according to some preset high level of unemployment and another program for structural fiscal distress to compensate for high levels of poverty and low taxable resources.

FIGURE 6

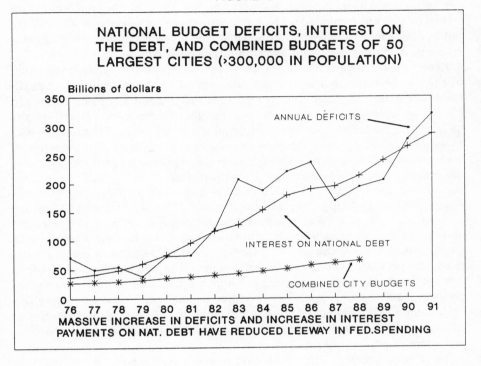

NATIONAL BUDGET DEFICITS, INTEREST ON THE DEBT, AND COMBINED BUDGETS OF 50 LARGEST CITIES (>300,000 IN POPULATION)

Billions of dollars

ANNUAL DEFICITS

INTEREST ON NATIONAL DEBT

COMBINED CITY BUDGETS

76 77 78 79 80 81 82 83 84 85 86 87 88 89 90 91

MASSIVE INCREASE IN DEFICITS AND INCREASE IN INTEREST PAYMENTS ON NAT. DEBT HAVE REDUCED LEEWAY IN FED. SPENDING

Unlike the original revenue sharing program passed in 1972 that made payments of varying size to every single general purpose local government and to all state governments, a high threshold of need or distress should be set for a jurisdiction to be eligible to receive any aid at all. Above that threshold, the sharper the distress, the deeper should be the subsidy. Traditionally, with a major exception for agricultural subsidies, Congress has not looked with favor on grant programs that do not potentially benefit a majority of congressional districts and states. But the reality of limited resources might change the mindsets of members of Congress sufficiently for them to allow targeting of those scarce resources sharply.

For this to happen, political leaders, commentators, and other opinion elites will have to articulate and reaffirm in elite and public opinion a philosophy that stresses the federal government's role as a benevolent bailer-out of last resort, somewhat like a giant insurance company, available for compensating individuals and governmental jurisdictions hit by short- or long-term emergencies beyond their powers to control.

After all, the actions of city governments did not cause the high rates of poverty, welfare dependency, violent crime, AIDS, homelessness, and the escalating cost of medical care. Nor did city governments cause the national recession that has savaged their revenues. Among all political leaders, the president has the largest capacity to command media and public attention and reshape the nation's public philosophy to have more concern for the problems of distressed city governments and the people who live within their jurisdictions.

Events, when explained in the proper framework, can also remind Americans of their self-interest in a strong and non-broke federal government, given the transitory nature of much good fortune and the vulnerability to problems and distress of persons and jurisdictions once thought to be permanently well-off and advantaged. Such events include the economic distress suffered in the mid-1980s by sunbelt cities and states because of the decline of oil prices, the protection of savers through the bailout of the savings and loan industry, the aid for repairing the damage caused by Hurricane Hugo on the East coast and by the San Francisco earthquake, the financing of the Gulf war, and the budget crises of such recently economically high-flying states as Massachusetts, Connecticut, and California.

After ten years of Reagan and Bush administration rhetoric, political leaders at some point will need to reeducate Americans to believe again that federal government programs can and have worked. Political and other opinion leaders must also persuade Americans that although it is an unpleasant fact of life to pay taxes, taxes are not some great punishment justifying massive rage against political leaders who support tax increases on the reality-based principle that there cannot be governmental services and programs without people paying taxes to fund them. To paraphrase King Lear's advice to his daughter Cordelia, Nothing will come of nothing: think again.

There must emerge political leadership to point out the paradox and inconsistency of arguing, as President Bush did in his 1991 State of the Union message, that government bureaucracies cannot be trusted to achieve desirable domestic goals and values but foreign policy organs and military forces — these bureaucracies somehow are not called that — can. There is another important paradox and inconsistency to which leaders must call attention. We have shown by deed that we can train minority youth from big city slums to operate, maintain, and repair the most complicated military weapons and equipment; yet many political leaders still argue it is impossible to train such youth in skills that will bring them good jobs in the civilian economy and that it is a waste of money to fund programs that try to do so.

Fortunately for the overall good of the nation, in the United States poor people and highly distressed local government jurisdictions are only a minority. This would be a surprise to James Madison who was worrying in *The Federalist* No. 10 about a tyranny by a majority faction of poor against a minority of the wealthy and about the expropriation of the rich by the poor. Madison could not have conceived of the present situation where any tyranny is one of an insensitive majority of well-off or well-enough-off that ignores the minority which is poor. If a democracy is to remain stable, the majority must be humane enough to take care of minorities who have serious problems and who because of those problems and lack of numbers will never have political strength to impose their own policy solutions through their own political power. The ultimate power of a desperate minority that feels permanently abandoned and lives without hope is an escalation of violence, crime, drug use, begging, and out-of-wedlock children — all already much too high. While this behavior is primarily self-destructive, it also hurts city governments by making large cities less and less attractive to those who would choose to live in them but have the economic capacity to move, even if reluctantly, to more attractive locales.

Realistically, the bottom line is this: For the majority in America to feel generous enough to sacrifice part of its income as taxes to ameliorate the conditions of poor cities and poor people not just as an antirecession expedient, two things have to happen. The economic condition of that majority would have to be improving sharply and the president must be urging the majority to want to help. The economic growth required is more than the selective kind of the Reagan years, which delivered real improvements in the standard of living only to the top quintile of earners in the population.[25] Generosity toward poor people and needy city governments requires truly vigorous economic growth that will bring tangible and substantial improvements in the standard of living of those earners in the middle three quintiles who have been working harder and harder in the past ten years just to stay even.*

[25] See Committee on Ways and Means, U.S. House of Representatives, *Overview of Entitlement Programs: 1991 Green Book: Background Material and Data on Programs within the Jurisdiction of the Committee on Ways and Means* (Washington DC: U.S. Government Printing Office, 1991), 1204, Table 35.

* This article is a revised and condensed version of a paper delivered at the 1991 Annual Meeting of the American Political Science Association in Washington, DC. I thank Scott Adler, Vilma Caraley, Michael Delli Carpini, Melissa Elstein, Anne Newland, Richard Pious, Judith Russell, and Robert Shapiro for reading and commenting on drafts of this article. I also thank Scott Adler, Judy Aks, Melissa Elstein, and Priya Nanda for various kinds of research assistance.

APPENDIX

City or Suburban Ring S = suburban ring	Median Family Income	Percent Population in Poverty	Median Income per Percent of Poverty
Newark	$11,989	32.8	$366
El PasoS	$12,584	26.1	$482
Atlanta	$13,591	27.5	$494
Miami	$13,355	24.5	$545
New Orleans	$15,003	26.4	$568
Baltimore	$15,721	22.9	$687
Birmingham	$15,210	22.0	$691
St. Louis	$15,265	21.8	$700
Norfolk	$14,779	20.7	$714
Cleveland	$15,991	22.1	$724
El Paso	$15,746	21.2	$743
Buffalo	$15,432	20.7	$746
San Antonio	$15,859	20.9	$759
Memphis	$16,921	21.8	$776
Detroit	$17,033	21.9	$778
Boston	$16,062	20.2	$795
Philadelphia	$16,388	20.6	$796
Tampa	$15,350	18.7	$821
New York	$16,818	20.0	$841
Cincinnati	$16,800	19.7	$853
Chicago	$18,776	20.3	$925
Oakland	$17,651	18.5	$954
AlbuquerqueS	$16,227	16.8	$966
Washington, DC	$19,099	18.6	$1,027
Pittsburgh	$17,499	16.5	$1,061
Jacksonville	$17,646	16.0	$1,103
Columbus	$18,612	16.5	$1,128
Tucson	$17,395	14.7	$1,183
Norfolk — Virg.BeachS	$18,391	15.5	$1,187
Los Angeles	$19,467	16.4	$1,187
Akron	$18,031	15.0	$1,202
Austin	$19,531	15.8	$1,236
Fort Worth city	$18,237	13.9	$1,312
MemphisS	$20,686	15.4	$1,343
Long Beach	$19,650	14.2	$1,384
Dallas city	$19,703	14.2	$1,388
Milwaukee	$19,738	13.8	$1,430
JacksonvilleS	$18,546	12.8	$1,449
Minneapolis	$19,737	13.5	$1,462
Toledo	$20,220	13.6	$1,487
Portland	$19,501	13.0	$1,500
Kansas City	$20,034	13.2	$1,518
San Francisco	$20,911	13.7	$1,526
Nashville	$19,366	12.6	$1,537
MiamiS	$20,203	12.5	$1,616
Albuquerque	$20,061	12.4	$1,618
San Diego	$20,133	12.4	$1,624

continued

APPENDIX (continued)

City or Suburban Ring S = suburban ring	Median Family income	Percent Population in Poverty	Median Income per Percent of Poverty
Oklahoma City	$19,565	12.0	$1,630
Charlotte	$20,258	12.4	$1,634
BirminghamS	$20,159	11.8	$1,708
Houston	$21,881	12.7	$1,723
Omaha	$20,458	11.4	$1,795
Indianapolis	$20,715	11.5	$1,801
TampaS	$16,841	9.3	$1,811
Phoenix	$20,365	11.1	$1,835
Tulsa	$19,615	10.4	$1,886
St. Paul	$20,743	10.9	$1,903
NashvilleS	$19,987	10.4	$1,922
AustinS	$22,189	11.4	$1,946
Seattle	$22,096	11.2	$1,973
LA—Long BeachS	$22,182	11.2	$1,981
San DiegoS	$20,429	10.3	$1,983
Tulsa	$20,956	10.4	$2,015
Wichita	$20,893	10.2	$2,048
TucsonS	$21,525	10.4	$2,070
PhoenixS	$20,605	9.9	$2,081
CharlotteS	$19,630	9.1	$2,157
San AntonioS	$21,386	9.8	$2,182
New OrleansS	$21,775	9.9	$2,199
Oklahoma CityS	$20,488	9.0	$2,276
Honolulu	$23,712	10.0	$2,371
Virginia Beach	$21,809	8.9	$2,450
HonoluluS	$23,422	9.1	$2,574
AtlantaS	$22,694	8.3	$2,734
St. LouisS	$23,050	7.6	$3,033
San Jose	$25,598	8.2	$3,122
ToledoS	$23,273	7.3	$3,188
PittsburghS	$22,024	6.9	$3,192
PortlandS	$23,004	7.2	$3,195
PhiladelphiaS	$23,722	7.1	$3,341
CincinnatiS	$22,888	6.8	$3,366
Kansas CityS	$23,507	6.8	$3,457
Dallas—FortWorthS	$23,633	6.7	$3,527
OmahaS	$22,273	6.3	$3,535
BostonS	$24,300	6.8	$3,574
San Francisco—OaklS	$26,347	7.3	$3,609
BuffaloS	$22,255	6.1	$3,648
ColumbusS	$22,898	6.2	$3,693
AkronS	$23,340	6.3	$3,705
ClevelandS	$25,409	6.8	$3,737
HoustonS	$26,749	7.1	$3,767
WichitaS	$22,815	6.0	$3,803
IndianapolisS	$23,228	6.1	$3,808
NewarkS	$26,640	6.4	$4,163
SeattleS	$25,693	6.1	$4,213

continued

APPENDIX (continued)

City or Suburban Ring S = suburban ring	Median Family income	Percent Population in Poverty	Median Income per Percent of Poverty
BaltimoreS	$24,804	5.6	$4,429
San JoseS	$27,898	6.1	$4,573
DetroitS	$26,888	5.7	$4,717
New YorkS	$27,443	5.6	$4,901
Washington,DC,S	$29,563	5.5	$5,375
ChicagoS	$27,762	4.7	$5,907
Minneapoilis—St.PaulS	$26,093	4.4	$5,930
MilwaukeeS	$26,596	3.4	$7,822

The Urban Underclass and the Poverty Paradox

PAUL E. PETERSON

The urban underclass is at once a characterization of a fragment of American society, a statement about the interconnections among diverse social problems, and an attempt to theorize about the paradox of poverty in an affluent society. The term is powerful because it calls attention to the conjunction between the characters of individuals and the impersonal forces of the larger social and political order. "Class" is the least interesting half of the word. Although it implies a relationship between one social group and another, the terms of that relationship are left undefined until combined with the familiar word "under." This transformation of a preposition into an adjective has none of the sturdiness of "working," the banality of "middle," or the remoteness of "upper." Instead, "under" suggests the lowly, passive, and submissive, yet at the same time the disreputable, dangerous, disruptive, dark, evil, and even hellish. And apart from these personal attributes, it suggests subjection, subordination, and deprivation. All these meanings are perhaps best brought together in Richard Wagner's *The Ring of the Nibelung*. Wotan goes under the earth to wrest the ring from the malicious Alberich, who had used it to enslave a vile and debased subhuman population.

Because of these diverse meanings, underclass is a word that can be used by conservatives, liberals, and radicals alike. It is a fitting term for conservatives who wish to identify those people who are unable to care for themselves or

PAUL E. PETERSON, Henry Shattuck Professor of Government at Harvard University, is director of Harvard's Center for American Political Studies. He is coauthor of numerous books including most recently *Welfare Magnets: A New Case for a National Standard* and, as coeditor and contributor, *The Urban Underclass.*

31

their families or are prone to antisocial behavior. But underclass, like lumpen proletariat, is also a suitable concept for those who, like Karl Marx, want to identify a group shaped and dominated by a society's economic and political forces but who have no productive role. And underclass is acceptable to some liberals who somewhat ambiguously refuse to choose between these contrasting images but who nonetheless wish to distinguish between the mainstream of working-class and middle-class America and those who seem separate from or marginal to that society. But, above all, the concept has been called back into the social science lexicon because it offers an explanation for the paradox of poverty in an otherwise affluent society that seems to have made strenuous efforts to eradicate this problem.

Two recent analyses of the urban underclass, Charles Murray's *Losing Ground* (1984) and William Wilson's *The Truly Disadvantaged* (1987), have generated the most vigorous research effort on the poverty paradox since the proliferation of urban studies spawned by the civil rights movement during the 1960s. Indeed, this renaissance of social science investigation into the connection between the urban underclass and the paradox of poverty in the late 1980s is, on the whole, simply a picking up of the intellectual pieces that were left scattered in the early 1970s by the acrimonious debate over the existence and nature of the culture of poverty, Daniel Moynihan's study of *The Negro Family* issued by the Labor Department, and the Nixon administration's family assistance plan.[1] The objectivity of research, the effect on scholarship of the racial background of social science investigators, and the hidden agendas of protagonists in the debates all became a matter of considerable disputation. Amidst this turmoil, college students and younger scholars turned their attention elsewhere, foundation and government agencies reoriented their research priorities, and universities closed down their urban studies programs. The research and analysis commented upon in this article is just one sign among many that at least for the moment the urban studies tide has begun to flow back in.

THE PARADOX OF CONTINUING POVERTY

When Lyndon Johnson declared the War on Poverty in 1964, he had good reason to believe that the federal government could succeed in ridding itself of the paradox of widespread poverty in the world's wealthiest country. The poverty rate in the United States had been declining steadily since 1940 even without any self-declared government effort to address it. In 1940 some 34 percent of the

---

[1] Charles A. Murray, *Losing Ground: American Social Policy, 1950–80* (New York: Basic Books, 1984); William Julius Wilson, *The Truly Disadvantaged: The Inner City, the Underclass, and Public Policy* (Chicago: University of Chicago Press, 1987); Office of Policy Planning and Research, *The Negro Family: The Case for National Action* (Washington, DC: Department of Labor, 1965); on the controversy, see Lee Rainwater and William L. Yancy, *The Moynihan Report and the Politics of Controversy* (Cambridge, MA: MIT Press, 1967).

population was living in poverty; by 1960 this had decreased to 15 percent and by 1970 to 11 percent. Among black Americans the decrease had been even steeper: from 71 to 32 percent. Among Hispanics the rate fell from 55 to 23 percent.[2]

The specific battle plan drawn up by the Johnson administration for the War on Poverty failed to match the rhetorical artillery the president employed. The effort was little more than a call for citizen participation combined with a hodge-podge of hastily designed educational, job training, and neighborhood service programs that had little internal coherence and only limited financial backing. It was more important as a vehicle for involving blacks and other minorities in local political processes than as a mechanism for redistributing wealth. When the Office of Economic Opportunity, the high command for the official poverty war, was finally disbanded in the early 1970s, few noticed the difference.[3]

But a focus on the conduct of the official War on Poverty is misleading. If the war effort is understood instead as the sum total of Great Society programs enacted and enhanced during the Johnson and Nixon administrations, then the transformation of a broad range of social welfare programs in the late 1960s and early 1970s can, in comparison with previous government efforts, truly be declared a full-scale war. The elderly, for whom the poverty risk in 1960 was higher than one in three, obtained easy access to low-cost medical services and greatly improved retirement benefits. Cash assistance to the blind, deaf, and disabled was increased, funded more completely by the federal government, and indexed to changes in the cost of living. Eligibility restrictions were relaxed on aid given to needy families with dependent children, and food stamps and medical assistance were added as supplements to the cash assistance these families received. Special education programs for the disadvantaged and the handicapped were enacted. Head Start was provided to very young children, and job training programs were offered to those entering the labor market. The amount and variety of housing subsidies available to qualifying families also increased.

The most conservative way of estimating the growth of these programs is to consider the percentage of the nation's gross national product used to fund them. This estimate controls not only for inflation but also for any change in the size

---

[2] James P. Smith, "Poverty and the Family" in Gary D. Sandefur and Marta Tienda, eds., *Divided Opportunities: Minorities, Poverty, and Social Policy* (New York: Plenum, 1988), 143. Smith's measure of poverty is not quite the same as the measure used by the Bureau of the Census. It is a measure that instead weights absolute and relative definitions of poverty equally. Absolute measures would show a steeper downward trend before 1960.

[3] On the politics of the war on poverty, see James L. Sundquist, *Politics and Policy: The Eisenhower, Kennedy, and Johnson Years* (Washington, DC: The Brookings Institution, 1968), 111-154; Daniel P. Moynihan, *Maximum Feasible Misunderstanding: Community Action in the War on Poverty* (New York: Free Press, 1969); and Paul E. Peterson and J. David Greenstone, "Racial Change and Citizen Participation: The Mobilization of Low-Income Communities through Community Action" in Robert H. Haveman, ed., *A Decade of Federal Antipoverty Programs: Achievements, Failures, and Lessons* (New York: Academic Press, 1977).

of the economy that occurs as a function of growth in the size of the labor force or improved economic productivity. By this conservative measure the nation doubled its social welfare effort in the fifteen years between 1965 and 1980, increasing the share of GNP allocated to social security, welfare assistance, medical services, and food stamps from 5 to 10 percent.[4] Nor did the conservative climate and fiscal crises of the 1980s cut deeply into the size and scope of these programs. As Robert Greenstein has pointed out, the Reagan administration's efforts to cut back the welfare state was frequently checked by strong congressional supporters of existing programs.[5] Thus it might be said that as a result of its war on poverty, the nation now seems finally committed to meeting the biblical requirement that a tenth of income be set aside for those in need.

This war on poverty did not fail in any absolute sense. Although the poverty rate no longer continued to decline, it remained fairly stable at the level it had reached in the late 1960s. Among whites the official rate leveled off at about one-eighth of the population; among blacks the proportion of poor remained about one-third.[6] The poverty rate among older Americans continued to decline. Whereas one-quarter of those aged sixty-five or older had an income below the poverty line in 1970, only one-eighth did in 1987. Social security programs had been extended to include virtually all workers, benefit levels had been increased and indexed at a new, higher level, and medicare insured against most poverty-inducing illnesses. For this group at least, the effort to eradicate poverty had been a resounding success.

Yet in recent years there has been a gnawing sense that poverty, instead of disappearing, has become worse. Not only has the poverty rate for the population as a whole stabilized at around 13 percent, but the risk of becoming poor has increased in disconcerting ways. First, the official poverty rate among Hispanics increased from 28 to 39 percent between 1972 and 1987. It is not clear, however, how much of this apparent change actually occurred. The Bureau of the Census broadened its definition of Hispanic during this period, making comparisons over time suspect. In addition, it is not clear whether any increases that have occurred have been caused by changes that have taken place within the states. Both the legal and illegal immigration of many low-income Latinos from Mexico, Puerto Rico, the Caribbean, Central America, and South America may have contributed to the increased rate. However, increases in Hispanic poverty before 1980 were as large among longer-term residents as among recent immigrants.[7]

[4] Paul E. Peterson and Mark Rom, "Lower Taxes, More Spending, and Budget Deficits" in Charles O. Jones, ed., *The Reagan Legacy: Promise and Performance* (Chatham, NJ: Chatham House, 1988), 217.

[5] Robert Greenstein, "Universal and Targeted Approaches to Relieving Poverty: An Alternative View" in Christopher Jencks and Paul E. Peterson, eds., *The Urban Underclass* (Washington, DC: Brookings Institution, 1991).

[6] For whites it was 9.9 percent in 1970, 10.2 percent in 1980, and 10.5 percent in 1987; for blacks the percentages were 33.5, 32.5, and 33.1.

[7] Proceedings from the National Council of La Raza's Poverty Project Roundtable, *Hispanic*

TABLE 1

Households with Incomes below the Poverty Line, Selected Years, 1960–87 (Percent)

Year	Central City	Suburb	Nonmetropolitan
1960	13.7	9.6	28.2
1970	9.8	5.3	14.8
1980	14.0	6.5	12.1
1987	15.4	6.5	13.8

Sources: Bureau of the Census, "Characteristics of the Low Income Population, 1971," Series P-60, no. 86 (Washington, DC: Department of Commerce, 1972); Bureau of the Census, *Statistical Abstract of the United States: 1982–83* (Washington, DC: Department of Commerce, 1982); Bureau of the Census, "Poverty in the United States, 1987," Series P-60, no. 163 (Washington, DC: Department of Commerce, 1989).

Whether that remained the case in the 1980s, when the number of immigrants increased sharply, is not yet clear. It is thus not certain to what extent the poverty rate has increased among Hispanics who are not recent immigrants to the United States.

Young families have also experienced a steadily increasing chance of being poor. Although the poverty rate among the elderly was cut by one-half between 1970 and 1986, the probability that a child under the age of eighteen would be living in a poor family increased from 15 to 20 percent.

The heightened risk of poverty has shifted from people in rural areas to those living in central cities. In 1960 about 28 percent of the rural households were poor, as compared with 14 percent in the nation's central cities and 10 percent in the suburbs. By 1987 the rate in rural America had fallen to 14 percent, while in the central cities it had climbed sharply from its low of 10 percent in 1970 to 15 percent (see Table 1). This change, it should be stressed, was not the result of any movement in the overall population from rural America to the central cities. In fact, the percentage of the nation's nonpoor population living in central cities was smaller in the late 1980s than in 1960.

Finally, the poor today are living in female-headed families more often than ever before. Whereas 25 percent of the poor were living in female-headed families in 1960, by 1980 about 35 percent were, and by 1987 perhaps 40 percent were. That female-headed families were somewhat more likely to be poor in 1987 than they were in 1970 (an increase from 50 to 55 percent) provides part of the explanation. But more important was the increase in the percentage of all families that were headed by women. As Christopher Jencks has reported, the percentage of female-headed families has increased rapidly among all racial and occupational groups.[8] Between 1970 and 1987 the percentage among whites increased from 8 to 13 percent and among blacks from 28 to 42 percent.

Poverty: How Much Does Immigration Explain? (Washington, DC: National Council of La Raza, 1989).

[8] Christopher Jencks, "Is the American Underclass Growing?" in Jencks and Peterson, eds., *The Urban Underclass.*

In short, the poverty paradox continues even after a major increase in the government's commitment to the welfare state. And not only has the overall poverty rate refused to fall in the 1970s and 1980s in the way that it had in earlier decades, but the risk of poverty grew greater among Hispanics, children, residents of urban areas, and those living in female-headed families (itself a growing percentage of the population).

Nor is it just the recent trends in poverty rates that are disconcerting. The poverty paradox is even more apparent when the United States is compared with other industrial societies. With the U.S. government's official measure of poverty as a standard, comparative data were collected for eight industrial countries — Australia, Canada, Norway, Sweden, Switzerland, the United Kingdom, the United States, and West Germany — for 1979-82. Australia had a slightly higher poverty rate than the United States, while the United Kingdom's rate was 1 percentage point less. But the average poverty rate in the other countries was 5 points lower. The differences were even more dramatic when the rates of children in poverty were calculated: the United States scored higher (that is, worse) than did any other country. Its rate was only slightly higher than Australia's, but it was more than 6 percentage points higher than the rate in the United Kingdom and 10 percentage points higher than the average of the other five countries. Only among the elderly did the poverty rate in the United States not appear exceptional; it ranked fourth after the United Kingdom, Australia, and Norway, and was only slightly higher than the rate in West Germany. In other words, cross-national comparisons reinforce the impression one obtains by examining changes in the incidence of poverty within the United States over time. The poverty rate in this affluent society seems exceptionally high, and young people are especially at risk.[9]

THE UNDERCLASS-POVERTY CONNECTION

The relationship between this poverty paradox and the urban underclass has been a subject of considerable debate. Many poor people are clearly not members of any underclass. The elderly poor, widows, orphans, the severely sick and disabled, and the simply unlucky can find themselves suddenly plunged into poverty without warning. Similarly, many people who engage in activities said to be characteristic of the underclass are hardly poor. Indeed, some of the most celebrated instances of an underclass style of life — laziness, unreliability, unrestrained attachment to fancy clothes and high fashion, episodic romantic attachments, drug addiction, and alcohol abuse — are to be found among the very rich.

---

[9] Timothy Smeeding, Barbara Boyle Torrey, and Martin Rein, "Patterns of Income and Poverty: The Economic Status of Children and the Elderly in Eight Countries" in John L. Palmer, Timothy Smeeding, and Barbara Boyle Torrey, eds., *The Vulnerables* (Washington, DC: Urban Institute, 1988), 96–97. International comparisons of poverty levels are not easily made. I report here the indicators of absolute, not relative, poverty. If relative measures were used, the United States would look even worse.

Indeed, for some analysts the poverty paradox is only one manifestation of a much more general deterioration in American society and culture. The major problem is the way in which a spreading underclass culture is undermining the country's productive capacity, family life, social integration, and, ultimately, its political stability.[10] Other analysts see virtually no relationship between the poverty paradox and the existence of an urban underclass. Often they object to using the word underclass, and if they accept the concept, they argue that an underclass, to the extent that one exists, is small, heterogeneous, and not growing. They argue that it constitutes no more than a minor portion of the low-income population, and that overall poverty levels have little to do with the activities of this segment of the population.[11]

From these varying views on the urban underclass, one can differentiate four quite separate explanations for the poverty paradox: the incomplete extension of the welfare state, the culture of poverty, the perverse incentives provided by welfare assistance, and the disproportionate effects of changes in the international economy on the core areas of cities. Each explanation implicitly or explicitly addresses the way in which the urban underclass has contributed to a poverty paradox, and each offers policy recommendations designed to resolve that paradox.

An Inadequate Welfare State

The standard interpretation, at least in liberal intellectual circles, is that the United States has always been an inegalitarian society in which the myth of equal opportunity has obscured a reality of submerged class conflict, racial discrimination, and tolerance of economic inequality. Compared with European societies, the United States has never had a strong labor movement, a vigorous socialist

---

[10] On these themes, see Lawrence M. Mead, *Beyond Entitlement: The Social Obligations of Citizenship* (New York: Free Press, 1986); Allan Bloom, *The Closing of the American Mind: How Higher Education Has Failed Democracy and Impoverished the Souls of Today's Students* (New York: Simon and Schuster, 1987); and Charles A. Murray, *In Pursuit of Happiness and Good Government* (New York: Simon and Schuster, 1987). Earlier versions of these themes can be found in Emile Durkheim, *Suicide: A Study in Sociology* (Glencoe, IL: Free Press, 1951); Daniel Bell, ed., *The Radical Right: The New American Right*, expanded and updated (Garden City, NY: Doubleday, 1963); William Kornhauser, *The Politics of Mass Society* (Glencoe, IL: Free Press, 1959); David Riesman, *The Lonely Crowd: A Study of the Changing American Character* (Garden City, NY: Doubleday, 1953).

[11] Various estimates of the size of the underclass population have emphasized that it is much smaller than the poverty population taken as a whole. See Erol R. Ricketts and Isabel V. Sawhill, "Defining and Measuring the Underclass," *Journal of Policy Analysis and Management* 7 (Winter 1988): 316–325; Robert D. Reischauer, "The Size and Characteristics of the Underclass" (Paper prepared for the Research Conference of the American Public Policy and Management Association, 1987); Terry K. Adams, Greg J. Duncan, and Willard L. Rodgers, "The Persistence of Poverty" in Fred R. Harris and Roger W. Wilkins, eds., *Quiet Riots: Race and Poverty in the United States* (New York: Pantheon, 1988).

party, or a coherent set of national bureaucratic institutions that could administer an integrated welfare state.[12] Americans have instead relied on great natural resources, a decentralized governmental system, a large internal private market, and dynamic economic growth to resolve their social tensions. Extremes of wealth and poverty have emerged side by side, and although some efforts to ameliorate these extremes developed in the wake of the Great Depression of the 1930s and the civil disorders of the 1960s, the country is too committed to individual liberty, too suspicious of big government, and too divided by race and ethnicity to redistribute wealth in such a way as to meet the needs of the poor adequately.

Although the United States made greater progress toward creating a welfare state during the Great Society years than at any other time in its history, the argument continues, the result is still a patchwork of programs and institutions that fails to provide for the needs of the poor in a comprehensive manner. The most elaborate and expensive of Great Society innovations were the elaboration of the social security program and the institution of medicare, both of which addressed the economic and social needs of the elderly. Not surprisingly, it is precisely this group for which the appellation poverty paradox seems no longer appropriate. Theda Skocpol has pointed out that social innovation was much more modest for other demographic groups.[13] Although the "deserving" poor — the blind, deaf, and disabled — were placed within a new, nationally funded program that materially improved their welfare, the government was still reluctant to address the needs of the "undeserving" poor — those who many people thought could and should earn a living for themselves. Aid to families with dependent children remained a program administered by the states. When the federal government supplemented this cash assistance with food stamps, the cash assistance provided by state governments declined, leaving poor families no better off than they had been.[14] "Undeserving" men and women in households without dependent children were eligible only for state general assistance programs, which varied greatly from one part of the country to the next and in most places provided only the most token assistance. The amount of this assistance also declined in value

[12] Stephen Skowronek, *Building a New American State: The Expansion of National Administrative Capacities, 1877–1920* (New York: Cambridge University Press, 1982); Martin Shefter, "Party Bureaucracy and Political Change in the United States" in Louis Maisel and Joseph Cooper, eds., *Political Parties: Development and Decay* (Beverly Hills, CA: Sage, 1978); Seymour Martin Lipset, "Why No Socialism in the United States?" in Seweryn Bialer and Sophia Sluzar, eds., *Sources of Contemporary Radicalism* (Boulder, CO: Westview Press, 1977): Louis Hartz, *The Liberal Tradition in America: An Interpretation of American Political Thought since the Revolution* (New York: Harcourt Brace, 1955); Margaret Weir, Ann Shola Orloff, and Theda Skocpol, eds., *The Politics of Social Policy in the United States* (Princeton, NJ: Princeton University Press, 1988).

[13] Theda Skocpol, "Targeting within Universalism: Politically Viable Policies to Combat Poverty in the United States" in Jencks and Peterson, eds., *The Urban Underclass.*

[14] Paul E. Peterson and Mark Rom, *Welfare Magnets: A New Case for a National Standard* (Washington, DC: Brookings Institution, 1990).

when federally funded food stamps became available.[15] Admittedly, medicaid helped reduce the extreme disparity in medical services between the middle class and the poor, but housing subsidies reached only a small minority, and increased educational services were too marginal and too fragmented to have much effect.

For the most part the liberal view attributes the poverty paradox to the inadequate development of the welfare state rather than to any changes in society or to specific characteristics of an urban underclass. But there is one strand of thinking within the liberal tradition that at least has implications for understanding the urban class phenomenon — the discussion of social rights and citizenship that has evolved out of the writings of the British social theorist, T. H. Marshall. From this perspective, the United States has a larger, more threatening underclass than most European countries because it has done so little to incorporate marginal groups into the social and political mainstream. The United States has a dual economy, a social world divided along racial and ethnic lines, and large numbers of people who are politically apathetic and uninvolved. Any society that does not treat all its citizens as valued members of the political community encourages marginal citizens to think of themselves as political outsiders who share in neither the benefits nor the responsibilities of the social and political community. If an underclass exists, it is because the state has created a group of outcasts that are denied their social and political rights.

There are at least three major pieces of evidence that support the liberal view: the welfare state in the United States is much less uniform and comprehensive than it is in many European countries; the elderly have done much better in the past two decades than have other social groups; and the changes in public policy wrought by the Great Society have been less significant than has often been claimed. But if these pieces of evidence support the liberal interpretation, another points in another direction. Poverty in the United States had been declining steadily between 1940 and 1960, two decades in which the welfare state expanded hardly at all. Yet when the welfare state expanded in the 1970s, progress toward eliminating poverty came to a halt. What is more, poverty increased among young families and inner-city residents.

The Culture of Poverty

The cultural explanation, perhaps the classic statement of the relationship between the underclass and the poverty paradox, holds that the style of life to which the urban poor has become attached is self-perpetuating. Street life in the ghetto is exhilarating — at least in the short run. In a world where jobs are dull, arduous, or difficult to obtain and hold, it is more fun to hang out, make love, listen to and tell exaggerated stories of love and danger, plan parties and escapades, and

---

[15] Peter H. Rossi, *Down and Out in America: The Origins of Homelessness* (Chicago: University of Chicago Press, 1989), 190–194.

exhibit one's latest purchases or conquests. Gangs provide young people thrills, protection, mutual support, friendship, prestige, and enough income to allow them to buy fashionable clothes, alcohol, and drugs. When men cannot earn enough to support their families adequately, they avoid enduring relationships with their female companions. Women respond by becoming self-reliant, domineering, and mutually supportive. But without an adult male figure in the household, they are unable to protect their children from the alluring street life that promises short-term excitement, if not much hope for a prosperous future.[16]

There is little consensus on the origins of the culture of poverty in American society. Some theorists have attributed it to the inequalities of economic power in the larger society, others to processes of urbanization that undermined the mutual interdependence of family members characteristic of traditional societies. John Ogbu has recently used an imaginative reconstruction of the cultural thesis to account for the contrasting experiences of various ethnic groups in American society.[17] Those groups—American blacks being the extreme case—who were compelled to come to or were forcefully incorporated into the United States and, once there, were subjected to poverty, discrimination, and slavery, constructed for themselves a conflictual understanding of the country's social and political institutions. Members of these forcefully incorporated groups explained personal disappointments and affronts as the product of broad social forces—class dominance, racial prejudice and discrimination, cultural exclusiveness—over which they, as individuals, had little control. It was hopeless to fight the system; instead, one might as well rip off and enjoy as big a piece of it as one could. As New Yorkers would say, "Take a bite of the Big Apple." But this explanation of their experiences, Ogbu suggests, would often become self-fulfilling—both for the individual minority member and the group as a whole. The more one rejects the system, the less one is willing to study or work and the more one is rejected by the societal mainstream.

Voluntary immigrants to America experienced many of the same disappointments, affronts, and rejections, but when they compared their experience in the United States with their experience in their homeland, they found opportunity much greater in the United States. They thus explained their limited success as

---

[16] This summary of the anthropological descriptions of poverty draws on Ulf Hannerz, *Soulside: Inquiries into Ghetto Culture and Community* (New York: Columbia University Press, 1969); Oscar Lewis, *The Children of Sanchez: Autobiography of a Mexican Family* (New York: Random House, 1961); Oscar Lewis, *La Vida: A Puerto Rican Family in the Culture of Poverty—San Juan and New York* (New York: Random House, 1966); Elliot Liebow, *Tally's Corner: A Study of Negro Streetcorner Men* (Boston: Little, Brown, 1967); and Lee Rainwater, *Behind Ghetto Walls: Black Families in a Federal Slum* (Chicago: Aldine Press, 1970).

[17] John U. Ogbu, *Minority Education and Caste: The American System in Cross-Cultural Perspective* (New York: Academic Press, 1978); Ogbu, "Diversity and Equity in Public Education: Community Forces and Minority School Adjustment and Performance" in Roy Haskins and Duncan MacRae, eds., *Policies for America's Public Schools: Teachers, Equity, and Indicators* (Norwood, NJ: Ablex Publishing, 1988).

a function of their own shortcomings, and they believed that if their children acquired the advantages of language and education they could succeed in the new world. These voluntary immigrants worked hard, told their children to take advantage of the opportunities available to them, and, once again, often found their prophecy self-fulfilling.

Whatever the causes of ghetto social practices, anthropological studies of the culture of poverty continue to provide troubling accounts of urban underclass life. Elijah Anderson shows the processes by which teenage girls decide to keep their babies to term and raise them, the joys a young child brings to a single parent, and the sorrows and troubles that later emerge. David Greenstone discusses the ways in which these commitments to street life can be understood both as a rational response to immediate circumstances and as a product of a distinctive cultural milieu. He then suggests, along lines similar to those developed by Ogbu, that only by reducing the distance and conflict between mainstream institutions and ghetto culture can policy makers find the mechanisms for transforming it.[18]

If the emphasis on a cultural milieu helps explain immediate choices in poor urban neighborhoods, it is by itself too static a concept to be a satisfactory explanation for the poverty paradox. Indeed, many of those who describe the culture of poverty locate its origins in social relationships in the wider society, whether these be characterized in terms of class conflict, racial discrimination, cultural distance, or social dislocation. At its best, the explanation warns against expecting rapid change in urban neighborhoods in response to broader economic and political change. At its worst it blames the victims for their problems. In all cases, it is most satisfying when linked to other, more structural interpretations.

Perverse Government Incentives

The third interpretation of the relationship between the underclass and poverty, propounded most compellingly by Charles Murray, identifies the Great Society programs as the most important structural factor affecting inner-city culture. While accepting the description of ghetto life elaborated by cultural anthropologists, Murray claims that members of the urban underclass, far from being irrationally bound by a cultural milieu that is as self-debilitating as it is unchangeable, are quite rational in the way they live their lives. He attributes the increase in male unemployment and female-headed households not to a spreading underclass culture but, ironically enough, to the Great Society programs that were expected to eliminate the poverty paradox.[19] Murray argues that the increasing size and

[18] Elijah Anderson, "Neighborhood Effects on Teenage Pregnancy" in Jencks and Peterson, eds., *The Urban Underclass*; J. David Greenstone, "Culture, Rationality, and the Underclass" in ibid.

[19] Murray, *Losing Ground*. I am using Murray's argument as shorthand for a broader literature advancing a similar line of interpretation. See Mead, *Beyond Entitlement*; Nathan Glazer, *The Limits of Social Policy* (Cambridge, MA: Harvard University Press, 1988); Edward C. Banfield, "Welfare: A Crisis without 'Solutions,'" *Public Interest* 16 (Summer 1969): 89–101; Leslie Lenkowsky, *Politics, Economics, and Welfare Reform: The Failure of the Negative Income Tax in Britain and the United*

availability of cash assistance, disability insurance, food stamps, medicaid insurance, housing subsidies, and other government aids to the poor inadvertently created a new set of incentives for marginal members of American society. It was no longer necessary to work in order to survive; indeed, full-time employment in an unpleasant, entry-level position at times yielded less after-tax, take-home pay than the income one could receive in benefits from a multiplicity of government programs. And marriage could be economically painful. The old shibboleth that two could live more cheaply than one no longer held. Instead, a single woman with children could receive more from the government than from the earnings of her potential husband. It was better — and more fun — for both if they lived apart; she could share her welfare check with him, and he could earn through episodic or part-time employment enough to sustain an adventurous street life. The result was an increase in the poverty rate in the later years of the 1970s.

Murray's explanation resonated well with the political climate of the early 1980s. Americans were suspicious of big government, the welfare state, and the political demands made by minority spokespersons. Murray's analysis blamed government for the rising percentages of children born out of wedlock, the rising percentages of unemployed young males, the seemingly pervasive crime, drugs, and violence in cities, and the continuing sharp racial tensions in American life. If most Americans were unwilling to dismantle the welfare state altogether, they certainly accepted limits on its further expansion.

Murray's critique has nonetheless been subjected to relentless criticism.[20] Some have argued that the work ethic is deeply ingrained in all parts of American society and that the dignity that comes from an earned income is something most people strongly prefer to welfare assistance. They have pointed out that most studies shown little, if any, effect of welfare assistance on willingness to work. Neither do they show much effect of welfare benefit levels on the incidence of out-of-wedlock births.[21] Others have argued that inasmuch as cash assistance to welfare recipients was diminishing in terms of real dollars throughout the 1970s, it was peculiar for Murray to argue that increases in these benefits could be

---

States (Washington, DC: American Enterprise Institute for Public Policy Research, 1986); Martin Anderson, *Welfare: The Political Economy of Welfare Reform in the United States* (Stanford, CA: Hoover Institution Press, 1978).

[20] See Sheldon Danziger and Peter Gottschalk, "The Poverty of Losing Ground," *Challenge* 28 (May–June 1985): 32–38; and David T. Ellwood and Lawrence H. Summers, "Is Welfare Really the Problem?" *Public Interest* 83 (Spring 1986): 57–78

[21] Sara McLanahan, Irwin Garfinkel, and Dorothy Watson, "Family Structure, Poverty, and the Underclass" in Michael G. H. McGeary and Laurence E. Lynn, Jr., eds., *Urban Change and Poverty* (Washington, DC: National Academy Press, 1988); David T. Ellwood and Mary Jo Bane, "The Impact of AFDC on Family Structure and Living Arrangements" in Ronald G. Ehrenberg, ed., *Research in Labor Economics* 7 (Greenwich, CT: JAI Press, 1985), 137–207; Kristin Moore, *Policy Determinants of Teenage Childbearing* (Washington, DC: Urban Institute, 1980); but see Robert D. Plotnick, "Welfare and Out-of-Wedlock Childbearing: Evidence from the 1980s" (Paper prepared for the Conference on the Urban Underclass, Northwestern University, 1989).

causing poverty to increase. As Greg Duncan and Saul Hoffman show, the income loss to a young woman who has a child out of wedlock or does not finish high school has actually increased in recent years.[22] Still others have taken issue with the finding that the poverty rate was in fact increasing, noting that the apparent increases could be accounted for by errors in the way changes in the cost of living were being measured.

In defending his interpretation against these criticisms, Murray has pointed out that whatever the measurement problems are, it is certainly clear that the poverty paradox is not withering away. He has argued, moreover, that efforts to discredit his analysis are based on studies that focus on small variations in welfare policy from one state to another. More important than minor variations, he has claimed, is the major national increase in the level of welfare provided in the late 1960s as well as the greater ease with which the poor could receive it. If cash assistance diminished after 1975, the loss has been offset by the food stamp program, medicaid, housing assistance, and other benefit programs.[23]

The Inner City in a Changing Economy

It was in this context that a fourth interpretation of the poverty paradox was developed by William Julius Wilson. In a series of essays that resulted in *The Truly Disadvantaged*, he developed an explanation for continuing poverty that accepted the accuracy of anthropological studies of the urban underclass but explained its existence not as the result of government handouts, but as the social by-product of a changing economy whose uneven impact was leaving inner cities with extraordinarily high levels of unemployment.

Wilson's thesis contains the following propositions:

• In the face of increasing competition from foreign countries, the United States has been moving from a unionized, oligopolistic, manufacturing economy to a more competitive, less unionized, service economy in which hourly earnings are falling while skill requirements are rising.

• These changes are having a disproportionate effect on urban minorities because the loss of manufacturing jobs has been greatest within large cities, and most of the new, high-technology service industries are locating in smaller cities or on the fringes of the metropolitan area. Urban minorities do not have ready access to the new jobs because the jobs are difficult to reach and educational requirements are high.

• As a result, the percentage of urban, working-age minority men who are employed in stable, reasonably well paid jobs has fallen dramatically.

---

[22] Greg J. Duncan and Saul D. Hoffman, "Teenage Underclass Behavior and Subsequent Poverty: Have the Rules Changed?" in Jencks and Peterson, eds., *The Urban Underclass.*

[23] Charles A. Murray, "Have the Poor Been 'Losing Ground'?" *Political Science Quarterly* 100 (Fall 1985): 427–445; and Murray, "No, Welfare Isn't Really the Problem," *Public Interest* 84 (Summer 1986): 3–11.

• Without a decent job, men are undesirable marriage partners, and the number of female-headed households has as a result increased rapidly.

• These changes have been aggravated by the increasing social isolation of the inner-city poor caused by the outward migration of middle-class whites and blacks, who are moving to suburbs in pursuit of jobs, better houses, and more effective schools.

• Thus there are growing concentrations of low-income minorities in the inner cities, within which dysfunctional social behavior becomes contagious. Lacking middle-class adult role models, local places of employment, adequate public services, or community institutions that support traditional family values, these core areas become breeding places for sexual promiscuity, crime, violence, drug addiction, and alcohol abuse. It is here that one finds the people who are properly called the urban underclass, because they are isolated from the mainstream social, occupational, and political institutions of the society.

• To counteract these trends, Wilson advocates policies that will guarantee a full-employment economy; federal policies that provide unemployment insurance, family allowances, and other social services to all citizens; greater race and class desegregation within metropolitan areas; and revitalization of community institutions in the urban core.

RESEARCH RELEVANT TO *THE TRULY DISADVANTAGED*

Recent research and analyses reflect and respond to these diverse explanations for the continuing paradox of poverty. Although implicit and explicit references are made to all four interpretations, the one given the most attention is Wilson's theory of the way the changing U.S. economy has affected those living within the inner cities. The findings reported here and in other recent studies allow scholars to expand and qualify Wilson's hypotheses in a number of ways.

First, as Wilson hypothesized, it is becoming increasingly evident that changes in the U.S. economy are affecting the economic well-being of young black men. The annual earnings of young men between the ages of twenty-five and twenty-nine declined by 20 percent between 1973 and 1986. Among blacks the decline was 28 percent. Among those without a high school education the decline was 36 percent.[24] These changes are a function of decreases in both male employment and the hourly earnings paid to young men.

It is unlikely that the cause of this dramatic change in the earnings received by young, less educated minority men is simply that they are no longer as willing and able to work as before. For one thing, the decline in the earnings received by all young men suggests that something more than individual initiative is at

---

[24] Andrew Sum, Neal Fogg, and Robert Taggart, "Withered Dreams: The Decline in the Economic Fortunes of Young, Non-College Educated Male Adults and Their Families" (Paper prepared for the William T. Grant Foundation Commission on Family, Work, and Citizenship, 1988), 43, B-2.

issue. And as Marta Tienda and Haya Stier show, most working-age adults in the poorest neighborhoods of Chicago either are working, are seeking work, or say that they would work if they could find a job. Of course, reporting a willingness to work in a survey is different from actually bearing the heavy work, discomforts, and annoyances that typically accompany what is euphemistically called an entry-level position. But as Joleen Kirschenman and Kathryn Neckerman document, many employers hiring people for low-paid positions use racial background, minority status, place of residence, and such other indicators of social class as personal appearance, speech patterns, and family references as cues for predicting job performance.[25]

Yet neither the use of racial cues by employers nor the unpredictability of the work habits of young inner-city men kept unemployment rates from falling dramatically in Boston when the area enjoyed a prolonged economic boom. As Richard Freeman shows, the rates fell faster in the core areas of Boston than they did in the metropolitan area as a whole. And Paul Osterman finds that the poverty rate in these core areas of Boston also fell much below the national average. Similarly, black unemployment decreases at a much faster rate than white unemployment when the national economy is in the boom phase of the business cycle. For example, when the white unemployment rate fell by 4 percentage points between 1983 and 1988, the black unemployment rate fell by nearly 7 points.[26]

The findings on the economic behavior of urban firms and inner-city residents complement one another. Young, poorly educated minority men are the last to be hired, but when the economic situation creates a labor shortage, employers will hire workers from core areas of the city. The corollary, of course, is that minorities are also the first to be fired when the business cycle turns downward. When white unemployment levels climbed 4 points between 1977 and 1983, black rates rose by 8 points.

These sharp short-term fluctuations in the demand for minority workers provide a clue for understanding the decline during the past two decades in the employment rates and national average hourly earnings among young, poorly educated minority men. Very likely, the decline is the result not of changes in the quality of the labor supplied by these people but of the increased competition they face in the labor market. This competition has come from various sources. Foreign workers have become more direct competitors with workers in the United States as international trade flows have increased and companies have the option of expanding operations either in the United States or overseas. Wage levels in

[25] Marta Tienda and Haya Stier, "Joblessness and Shiftlessness: Labor Force Activity in Chicago's Inner City" in Jencks and Peterson, eds., *The Urban Underclass;* Joleen Kirschenman and Kathryn M. Neckerman, "'We'd Love to Hire Them, But . . .': The Meaning of Race for Employers" in ibid.
[26] Richard B. Freeman, "Employment and Earnings of Disadvantaged Young Men in a Labor Shortage Economy" in ibid.; Paul Osterman, "Gains from Growth? The Impact of Full Employment on Poverty in Boston" in ibid.

developing countries are much lower than those in the United States, dampening the price business is willing to pay American workers. Other sources of increased competition have been internal to the United States: the rising number of legal and illegal immigrants, the increasing percentage of women participating in the labor force, and the particularly large size of the age cohort entering the labor market in the late 1970s and early 1980s. Ascertaining the exact impact of these internal sources of competition is complicated because the new workers also became new consumers who increase the demand for goods and services. But among all three groups the supply of entry-level workers increased more rapidly than the supply of more skilled, better educated, and more experienced workers. Under these circumstances the competition for beginning positions was particularly intense, depressing earnings and opportunities at the lower end of the occupational spectrum.

Had productivity rates increased as rapidly in the 1970s and 1980s as they did in the 1950s and 1960s, the increase in the labor supply might have been easier to absorb without an adverse effect on unemployment rates and worker earnings. As it was, the impact of the larger labor supply was felt keenly by young men. Women made gains because they were remaining in the labor market longer and because their relative position had been so inferior. Older workers were protected by seniority privileges and union agreements designed when labor competition was less intense. The most highly skilled workers enjoyed strong demand for their services because the economy was growing fastest in the technologically sophisticated sectors. The losers were young, poorly educated minority men.

The change in their earnings prospects may well have affected the marriage prospects of inner-city minority men. Unemployment rates are always lower for married than for unmarried men, whether because married men feel they need to work or because working men are more likely to marry.[27] Although it is probably a little of both, the weight to be attributed to each cause is not easily ascertained. Robert Mare and Christopher Winship nonetheless show that the decline in male earnings is the most important identifiable factor adversely affecting marriage rates.[28]

But although the changing earning prospects of young men compromise their marriageability, one should not attempt to explain the increase in the percentage of female-headed households from this development alone. Mare and Winship show that the effects of employment on marriage are only one part of the story. And as Christopher Jencks points out, the increase in female-headed households in the past twenty years is occurring among blacks, whites, and Hispanics, among the middle class as well as the poor. Divorce, single-parent families, and out-of-

[27] In 1989 the unemployment rate among married men was less than 3.5 percent at a time when overall unemployment rates were above 5 percent, "Married and Jobless" (figure), *Wall Street Journal*, 27 April 1990.

[28] Robert D. Mare and Christopher Winship, "Socioeconomic Change and the Decline of Marriage for Blacks and Whites" in Jencks and Peterson, eds., *The Urban Underclass*.

wedlock births are becoming more or less accepted practices in many parts of the United States. The trend leaves too many children with impaired financial support, inadequate adult supervision and instruction, compromised security, fewer alternatives for establishing intergenerational relationships, and fewer adult role models. The most powerful force contributing to the formation of the urban underclass, perversely enough, may be the changing values of mainstream American society, in which the virtues of family stability, mutual support, and religiously based commitment to the marriage vow no longer command the deference they once did.[29]

But however unfortunate some of its consequences, the trend is understandable. Women are becoming more self-sufficient. And the institution of the family seems less necessary because it is being supplemented or replaced by schools, day care centers, social security, health insurance, and the numerous other social services of modern society. Jencks ruminates that the only place a strong two-parent family may be critically important is the inner city, where the family is necessary to offset the powerful allure of the street. But however one assesses this change in American society, one must acknowledge that the socioeconomic forces shaping family life are not limited to the worsening economic position of young men.[30]

Not only is the changing economic and social structure of the United States affecting the urban underclass, but the concentration of poor within the nation's inner cities may also contribute to the problem. Both Jonathan Crane and Susan Mayer provide new data to show that living in a community or attending a school with disproportionate numbers of poor people or minorities increases the chance that an adolescent will drop out or have a child out of wedlock. In both studies this finding holds even after the young person's family background is taken into account. Nor are the ill effects of poverty concentrations limited to teenage years. James Rosenbaum and Susan Popkin show that when poor women move to the suburbs, their job opportunities are better. Because these results reflect the experience of poor families who had little choice in whether they were assigned to inner-city or suburban public housing, the finding that where you live affects your economic opportunities is particularly striking.[31]

But if concentrations of poverty have a detectable economic consequence, the political consequences are less clear. Jeffrey Berry, Kent Portney, and Ken Thomson find that living in a poor neighborhood has little effect on a person's political attitudes and behavior. Poor people living in poor neighborhoods are

[29] Jencks, "Is American Underclass Growing?" in ibid.
[30] Ibid.
[31] Jonathan Crane, "Effects of Neighborhoods on Dropping Out of School and Teenage Childbearing" in ibid.; Susan E. Mayer, "How Much Does a High School's Racial and Socioeconomic Mix Affect Graduation and Teenage Fertility Rates?" in ibid.; James E. Rosenbaum and Susan J. Popkin, "Employment and Earnings of Low-Income Blacks Who Move to Middle-Class Suburbs" in ibid.

no more cynical or distrustful or likely to withdraw from the political process than poor living in middle-class neighborhoods.[32]

Whatever the consequences of concentrated poverty, there is little evidence that the poor are any more isolated than they have been in the past. Reynolds Farley's analysis of population changes in metropolitan areas between 1970 and 1980 shows that there has been virtually no change in the degree of income segregation within either the black or the white community in most of them. (There was a slight decrease in the degree of racial segregation.) Other studies have shown that in some large cities — Chicago, New York, Philadelphia, Detroit, and a few others in the Northeast — the proportion of poor people who live in neighborhoods that are extremely poor has increased. This seems to result, however, mainly from a general increase in poverty levels in these metropolitan areas rather than from any changes in the extent to which residents are segregating themselves by income.[33]

These results do not in any way diminish the seriousness of the problem of an urban underclass, but they suggest that one should be careful in making claims about the extent to which the situation is growing worse. On the contrary, Christopher Jencks shows that according to a number of indicators the underclass is shrinking. A higher percentage of the minority population is receiving high school diplomas, a smaller percentage of teenagers is having babies out of wedlock, both blacks and whites are experiencing fewer crimes committed against them, and the use of drugs is declining. Perhaps it is not so much that the situation is deteriorating as that Americans' social expectations are rising.[34]

In his article in this issue of *Political Science Quarterly*, William Julius Wilson dismisses some of these data as irrelevant to the theory he developed in *The Truly Disadvantaged*. In an important clarification of his theory, Wilson now states that the cause of the urban underclass is the simultaneous presence of economic marginality and extreme social isolation. Poverty within the inner city is debilitating when it is intensely concentrated, a condition particularly prevalent within large cities. Changes in an indicator of class segregation, such as the one used by Reynolds Farley, do not capture changes in the size of the underclass because they do not capture the extent to which extreme isolation is increasing.[35] To bolster his argument, Wilson points out that the numbers of poor people living

[32] Jeffrey M. Berry, Kent E. Portney, and Ken Thomson, "The Political Behavior of Poor People" in ibid.

[33] It may be, however, that poverty became more concentrated after 1980; it will be possible to ascertain this once the 1990 census data are released.

[34] Jencks, "Is American Underclass Growing?" in Jencks and Peterson, *The Urban Underclass.*

[35] Wilson suggests that the degree of isolation among those already socially isolated may increase without any change in the degree of isolation of the median poor person. All the change is occurring among people below the median. Because Farley examined changes only in the median, he missed the changes occurring at the bottom extreme of the distribution. In my view, this is possible but unlikely. See Reynolds Farley, "Residential Segregation of Social and Economic Groups among Blacks, 1970–1980" in ibid.

in extremely poor neighborhoods — those in which 40 percent or more of the population are poor — increased between 1970 and 1980. The upward trend is especially evident in the largest American cities.

It is precisely the living and working conditions in these extremely isolated neighborhoods that require understanding and analysis, Wilson argues. Tests of the theory in other settings are beside the point. When Berry, Portney, and Thomson did not find significant political differences between the poor living in poor and nonpoor neighborhoods, it was because they were neither studying the largest cities of the industrial belt nor limiting their analysis to extremely impoverished neighborhoods.[36] Jonathan Crane's study is much more persuasive to Wilson, because Crane shows that neighborhood effects on dropping out of high school and experiencing an out-of-wedlock birth are especially powerful when poverty levels escalate above a critical threshold.[37]

Studies that use national samples and examine overall trends are rejected by Wilson as atheoretical, inappropriate efforts to look at an urban underclass defined as economically marginal and extremely isolated socially. If theory is to guide future research, that research must focus its attention on inner-city poverty in the largest cities. To highlight his now even greater emphasis on the conjunction of economic and extreme social factors, Wilson suggests that it may be more appropriate to speak of the ghetto poor rather than the urban underclass. The new term makes clear exactly whom Wilson is speaking about — and, perhaps more important, whom he is not speaking about.

There can be little doubt that Wilson has strengthened his theory by narrowing its focus to those neighborhoods in which poverty is particularly concentrated. Yet there are costs as well as gains to narrowing the explanatory focus this way. At best the reformulated theory applies to only a small portion of the poverty population. Little more than 1 percent of the U.S. population in 1980 lived in metropolitan census tracts in which the population was more than 40 percent poor. The percentage of poor people who lived in such neighborhoods was less than 9 percent; 21 percent of poor blacks and 16 percent of poor Hispanics lived in such neighborhoods. Nor does the reformulated theory account for changes that occurred in the 1970s. The increase in the ghettoization of poor black people living in metropolitan areas was only 1 percent and that of Hispanics decreased by 5 percent.[38] The extent to which ghettoization is occurring varies dramatically

---

[36] Wilson's methodological criticism of Berry, Portney, and Thomson reveals the way in which his ideas are evolving, for in his own study of a sample of Chicago parents, he included all those living in neighborhoods in which poverty levels were 20 percent or more. (See Tienda and Stier, "Joblessness and Shiftlessness" in Jencks and Peterson, *The Urban Underclass*.) It would seem that Wilson would now want to focus any analysis on more extremely isolated neighborhoods.

[37] Crane, "Effects of Neighborhoods" in Jencks and Peterson, *The Urban Underclass*.

[38] The reader may wonder how these figures can be consistent with the fact that the number of poor people living in extremely poor neighborhoods increased by 30 percent. The answer is twofold. First, because poverty was moving from rural to urban areas, the numbers of poor living in extremely poor urban neighborhoods was rising right along with the number of poor living in less poor neighbor-

among regions. According to Paul Jargowsky and Mary Jo Bane, the percentages of poor people living in these isolated communities fell in the South and West while increasing in the Northeast and Midwest. Most of the increases in the population living in extremely poor neighborhoods between 1970 and 1980 occurred in just five cities — New York, Chicago, Philadelphia, Newark, and Detroit. Such increases seem to be strongly correlated with increases in the overall level of poverty in a specific metropolitan area. Very little, if any, can be attributed to increasing class segregation within the black community. Unless the 1990 census reveals that poverty became much more concentrated in the 1980s than it did in the 1970s, a theory in which increasing class segregation and extreme social isolation play a central role will have limited ability to explain contemporary processes of social change.[39]

Wilson's theory originally promised to provide an explanation for the poverty paradox — the perpetuation of poverty in the 1970s and 1980s when many had expected it would gradually diminish. In its more circumscribed form, the theory may still tell us important things about a very visible, politically significant portion of the population — blacks living in the largest central cities of the rustbelt. As Wilson points out, it is here that racial tensions are the greatest and where the images that help shape national discourse are most readily retrieved. But even if his theory, as clarified, helps account for the behavior of a politically salient segment of the population, it makes only a modest contribution to our understanding of the poverty paradox.

Any theory that promises to explain the connection between the poverty paradox and the urban underclass must apply more widely than just to places where poverty is extremely concentrated. Such a theory, it seems to me, needs to focus on three facets of contemporary life that Wilson and others have identified as critical — the increasing numbers of female-headed households, the declining earnings and labor force participation of young men from minority backgrounds, and the shift in poverty from rural areas to central cities (not the shift within metropolitan areas from neighborhoods that are less poor to ones that are more poor). Wilson's original formulation has stimulated debate and research because it identified connections among these three phenomena. But except under the extreme conditions that Wilson now hypothesizes, these factors may not be as closely linked as his theory has implied. The sources for the changes in the economic opportunities for young black men are not just the decline in the number of jobs within the manufacturing sector. The rise in the percentage of female-headed households is not caused just by the changing employment

---

hoods. In other words, it was not so much ghettoization that was occurring as a shift in poverty from rural to urban America (see Table 1). Second, inasmuch as only a small percentage of the poor lived in such neighborhoods in 1970, a large percentage increase between 1970 and 1980 still changed by only a small amount the overall percentage of the metropolitan poor that was socially isolated.

[39] Paul A. Jargowsky and Mary Jo Bane, "Ghetto Poverty in the United States, 1970–1980" in Jencks and Peterson, *The Urban Underclass*.

opportunities of young men. The shift of poverty from rural to urban settings is not simply the result of the decentralization of industry and commerce. The problem is more complex, more difficult to disentangle, and less susceptible to any one solution.

If there is no single, simple explanation, certain policy conclusions can nonetheless be drawn from the four interpretations I have summarized. Wilson is correct in emphasizing that unless the United States remains strong, growing, and economically competitive, nothing is likely to reduce the poverty rate significantly. But the experience of the 1980s shows that a steadily growing economy will not by itself eliminate the poverty paradox. In addition, as liberal theorists point out, the income transfer system needs to be restructured so that government responds to the needs of working-age adults and families in as humane a way, as it does to the needs of the elderly. As both Theda Skocpol and Robert Greenstein suggest, this will require a much more centralized, comprehensive, and integrated welfare system than the nation currently has.

Adopting such a policy does not entail the rejection of Charles Murray's argument that our present welfare system discourages participation in the mainstream economy. There is something wrong about a health care system that provides assistance to the nonworking indigent but will not help those in low-paid jobs where employers do not provide health insurance. There is also something wrong about a system in which the movement from welfare to work must be abrupt and expensive. An integrated, comprehensive national welfare policy could provide a more flexible public response to those who move in and out of low-skilled, low-paid employment.

Finally, the United States needs a much more flexible and adaptable educational system in the core areas of cities, a system that can enhance the country's human capital, strengthen the institutional position of the family, and reduce the alienation between minority youth and the mainstream institutions of society. The current expensive, bureaucratically controlled, hierarchical, rule-bound, stratified, gang-infested system of urban education needs to be drastically changed. We need to redesign our urban school systems to give families more choice and more control, provide harbors for young people seeking to escape the neighborhood peer culture, and create a learning environment that respects the culture of the low-income, minority community. If the civil rights movement wants to shed its middle-class bias and address the critical problems of the poor that became of increasing concern to Martin Luther King, it should make educational choice for urban residents and an integrated welfare system its most important concerns.*

---

* This article is adapted and updated from Christopher Jencks and Paul E. Peterson, eds., *The Urban Underclass* (Washington, DC: The Brookings Institution, 1991).

Another Look at
The Truly Disadvantaged

WILLIAM JULIUS WILSON

In the aftermath of the controversy generated in 1965 by the Moynihan report on the black family, empirical research on inner-city poverty and other social dislocations ground to a halt. In the past few years, however, such research activity has revived as media reports and debates among academics have captured public interest in the growing problems of urban ghettos. Like the 1960s discussions of the causes and consequences of urban poverty that focused on the Moynihan report and on Oscar Lewis's work on the culture of poverty, much of the new discourse is contentious and acrimonious. My book, *The Truly Disadvantaged*, has become a point of reference in this controversy and, as is too often true of controversies, a good deal of the discussion is based on inaccurate interpretations of the arguments set forth.[1]

[1] Office of Policy Planning and Research, *The Negro Family: The Case for National Action* (Washington, DC: Department of Labor, 1965); Oscar Lewis, *The Children of Sanchez: Autobiography of a Mexican Family* (New York: Random House, 1961); Oscar Lewis, *La Vida: A Puerto Rican Family in the Culture of Poverty — San Juan and New York* (New York: Random House, 1966); Oscar Lewis, *Five Families: Mexican Case Studies in the Culture of Poverty* (New York: Basic Books, 1959); Oscar Lewis, "The Culture of Poverty" in Daniel Patrick Moynihan, ed., *On Understanding Poverty: Perspectives from the Social Sciences* (New York: Basic Books, 1968); William Julius Wilson, *The Truly Disadvantaged: The Inner City, the Underclass, and Public Policy* (Chicago:

WILLIAM JULIUS WILSON is Lucy Flower University Professor of Sociology and Public Policy at the University of Chicago. He is past president of the American Sociological Association, a MacArthur Prize Fellow, and a member of the National Academy of Sciences, the American Academy of Arts and Sciences, and the American Philosophical Society. His book, *The Truly Disadvantaged*, has generated renewed discussion of the connection between the urban underclass and poverty in large cities.

53

A worthy goal of any author is to write so as not to be misunderstood. But even the most carefully phrased statements on the underclass are unlikely to escape misinterpretation because, as Jennifer Hochschild has pointed out, the issues in this instance are "so complicated and politically sensitive that analysts have an apparently almost irresistible tendency to focus on that part of the problem that fits their own preconceptions and to deny or ignore those parts that violate their preconceptions."[2] Because the comments of my critics feature systematic empirical research and thoughtful formulations of concepts, however, my arguments tend to be carefully and accurately discussed. The few misinterpretations are probably caused by the lack of clarity with which my ideas were originally stated. Indeed, these misinterpretations could have been avoided if I had presented a more explicit statement of my theory, the hypotheses embedded in the theory, and the conditions that must be present before they can be tested. Accordingly, to put the rest of my discussion here in proper focus, I will first recapitulate the major arguments advanced in *The Truly Disadvantaged* and present the formal structure of the theoretical framework. I will then assess the empirical, conceptual, and policy arguments that directly or indirectly address the major hypotheses in my book.

A SUMMARY OF *THE TRULY DISADVANTAGED*

I argue in *The Truly Disadvantaged* that historical discrimination and a migration to large metropolises that kept the urban minority population relatively young created a problem of weak labor force attachment among urban blacks and, especially since 1970, made them particularly vulnerable to the industrial and geographic changes in the economy. The shift from goods-producing to service-producing industries, the increasing polarization of the labor market into low-wage and high-wage sectors, innovations in technology, the relocation of manufacturing industries out of central cities, and periodic recessions have forced up the rate of black joblessness (unemployment and nonparticipation in the labor market), despite the passage of antidiscrimination legislation and the creation of affirmative action programs. The rise in joblessness has in turn helped trigger an increase in the concentrations of poor people, a growing number of poor single-parent families, and an increase in welfare dependency. These problems have been especially evident in the ghetto neighborhoods of large cities, not only because the most impoverished minority populations live there but also because

---

University of Chicago Press, 1987). For a comparative discussion of these two controversies, see William Julius Wilson, "The American Underclass: Inner-City Ghettos and the Norms of Citizenship (Godkin lecture, John F. Kennedy School of Government, Harvard University, 1988); and Lee Rainwater and William L. Yancy, *The Moynihan Report and the Politics of Controversy* (Cambridge, MA: MIT Press, 1967).

[2] Jennifer L. Hochschild, "The Politics of the Estranged Poor," *Ethics* 101 (April 1991): 572.

the neighborhoods have become less diversified in a way that has severely worsened the impact of the continuing economic changes.

Especially since 1970, inner-city neighborhoods have experienced an outmigration of working- and middle-class families previously confined to them by the restrictive covenants of higher-status city neighborhoods and suburbs. Combined with the increase in the number of poor caused by rising joblessness, this outmigration has sharply concentrated the poverty in inner-city neighborhoods. The number with poverty rates that exceed 40 percent — a threshold definition of "extreme poverty" neighborhoods — has risen precipitously. And the dwindling presence of middle- and working-class households has also removed an important social buffer that once deflected the full impact of the kind of prolonged high levels of joblessness in these neighborhoods that has stemmed from uneven economic growth and periodic recessions.

In earlier decades, not only were most of the adults in ghetto neighborhoods employed, but black working and middle classes brought stability. They invested economic and social resources in the neighborhoods, patronized the churches, stores, banks, and community organizations, sent their children to the local schools, reinforced societal norms and values, and made it meaningful for lower-class blacks in these segregated enclaves to envision the possibility of some upward mobility.

However, today the ghetto features a population, the underclass, whose primary predicament is joblessness reinforced by growing social isolation. Outmigration has decreased the contact between groups of different class and racial backgrounds and thereby concentrated the adverse effects of living in impoverished neighborhoods. These concentration effects, reflected, for example, in the residents' self-limiting social dispositions, are created by inadequate access to jobs and job networks, the lack of involvement in quality schools, the unavailability of suitable marriage partners, and the lack of exposure to informal mainstream social networks and conventional role models.

Accordingly, *The Truly Disadvantaged* argued that the factors associated with the recent increases in social dislocation in the ghetto are complex. They cannot be reduced to the easy explanations of a "culture of poverty" that have been advanced by those on the right, or of racism, posited by those on the left. Although the ghetto is a product of historical discrimination and although present-day discrimination has undoubtedly contributed to the deepening social and economic woes of its residents, to understand the sharp increase in these problems requires the specification of a complex web of other factors, including shifts in the American economy.

THE FORMAL STRUCTURE OF THE THEORETICAL FRAMEWORK

This summary of *The Truly Disadvantaged* does not make explicit the fact that social-structural, social-psychological, and cultural variables are integrated into my theoretical framework.[3] A more formal statement of this framework is that a structure of inequality has evolved which is linked to contemporary behavior in the inner city by a combination of constraints, opportunities, and social psychology.

The exogenous factors, representing the sources of the racial concentration of urban poverty, include racial discrimination, changes in the economy that have relocated industries and restructured occupations, and political processes (anti-bias legislation and affirmative action programs) that have had the unanticipated consequence of widening class divisions among urban blacks. The endogenous determinants created by these exogenous factors include such demographic variables as urban migration, age structures, and the pool of marriageable men, and economic factors such as the distribution of employment and income. These variables are important for understanding the experiences of all low-income urban groups, not just the ghetto underclass.

The endogenous determinants further include social isolation, which is unique to the social environment of the underclass. Social isolation deprives residents of inner-city neighborhoods not only of resources and conventional role models, whose former presence buffered the effects of neighborhood joblessness, but also of the kind of cultural learning from mainstream social networks that facilitates social and economic advancement in modern industrial society. The lack of neighborhood material resources, the relative absence of conventional role models, and the circumscribed cultural learning produce outcomes, or concentration effects, that restrict social mobility. Some of these outcomes are structural (lack of labor force attachment and access to informal job networks), and some are social-psychological (negative social dispositions, limited aspirations, and casual work habits).

From the point of view of the accumulation of scientific knowledge, it is important to keep these theoretical issues in mind to establish clearly the empirical, conceptual, and theoretical contributions of the authors who further understanding of the underclass phenomenon.

THE ECONOMY AND WEAK LABOR FORCE ATTACHMENT IN THE INNER CITY

In my attempt in *The Truly Disadvantaged* to examine empirically the problem of the growing concentration of poverty, I used census tracts as proxies for nonpoverty and inner-city areas. The latter was divided into poverty, high-poverty, and extreme poverty neighborhoods. Most of my analysis of concentrated poverty focused on areas of extreme poverty, that is, those in which at least 40 percent of the people are poor. More recent studies have followed this

---

[3] In the ensuing discussion in this section, I benefited from the formal explication of *The Truly Disadvantaged* in Morris Zelditch, Jr., "Levels in the Logic of Macro-Historical Explanation" (Paper presented at the annual meeting of the American Sociological Association, 1989).

lead by defining ghettos as those areas with poverty rates of at least 40 percent. The ghetto poor are therefore identified as those among the poor in the inner city who reside in these neighborhoods of extreme poverty.[4]

Paul Jargowsky and Mary Jo Bane have shown that the proportion of the poor who reside in ghetto neighborhoods varies dramatically by race. Whereas only 2 percent of the non-Hispanic white poor lived in ghettos in 1980, some 21 percent of black poor and 16 percent of Hispanic poor resided there. And almost a third of all metropolitan blacks lived in a ghetto in 1980. Sixty-five percent of the 2.4 million ghetto poor in the United States are black, 22 percent Hispanic, and 13 percent non-Hispanic and other races. Thus to speak of the ghetto poor in the United States is to refer primarily to blacks and Hispanics. This has both descriptive and theoretical significance.

What is not revealed in *The Truly Disadvantaged* and what is clearly spelled out by Jargowsky and Bane is that the increase of ghetto poverty occurred mainly in only two regions of the country: the Midwest and the Northeast. Moreover, ten cities accounted for three-fourths of the total rise of ghetto poverty during the 1970s. One-third of the increase was accounted for solely by New York City, and one-half by New York and Chicago together. By adding Philadelphia, Newark, and Detroit, two-thirds of the total increase is accounted for. The others in the top ten were Columbus, Ohio; Atlanta; Baltimore; Buffalo; and Paterson, New Jersey. Of the 195 standard metropolitan areas in 1970 that recorded some ghetto poverty, 88 experienced decreases in the number of ghetto poor by 1980. Those with the largest decreases were Texas cities with significant declines in Hispanic ghetto poverty and southern cities with sharp drops in black ghetto poverty.

---

[4] See Loïc J. D. Wacquant and William Julius Wilson, "Poverty, Joblessness and the Social Transformation of the Inner City" in Phoebe H. Cottingham and David T. Ellwood, eds., *Welfare Policy for the 1990s* (Cambridge, MA: Harvard University Press, 1989); and Paul A. Jargowsky and Mary Jo Bane, "Ghetto Poverty in the United States, 1970–1980" in Christopher Jencks and Paul E. Peterson, *The Urban Underclass* (Washington, DC: Brookings Institution, 1991). In discussing the correspondence between ghetto neighborhoods and extreme poverty census tracts in Chicago, Wacquant and Wilson state, "Extreme-poverty neighborhoods comprise tracts with at least 40 percent of their residents in poverty in 1980. These tracts make up the historic heart of Chicago's black ghetto: over 82 percent of the respondents in this category inhabit the west and south sides of the city, in areas most of which have been all black for half a century and more, and an additional 13 percent live in immediately adjacent tracts. Thus when we counterpose extreme-poverty areas with low-poverty areas, we are in effect comparing ghetto neighborhoods with other black areas, most of which are moderately poor, that are not part of Chicago's traditional black belt" (p. 16). Jargowsky and Bane use the same rationale on a national level: "Visits to several cities confirmed that the 40 percent criterion came very close to identifying areas that looked like ghettos in terms of their housing conditions. Moreover, the areas selected by the 40 percent criterion corresponded rather closely with the neighborhoods that city officials and local Census Bureau officials considered ghettos." Of course, not all the people who reside in ghettos are poor. In the ten largest American cities as of 1970, the number of Hispanic residents (poor and nonpoor) residing in ghettos areas tripled between 1970 and 1980; the number of blacks doubled.

The focus of *The Truly Disadvantaged*, however, was on the increase in ghetto poverty. The questions are why did this increase occur and why was most of it confined to the large industrial metropolises of the Northeast and Midwest? Because these two regions experienced massive industrial restructuring and loss of blue-collar jobs. Cities of the frostbelt suffered overall employment decline because "growth in their predominantly information-processing industries could not numerically compensate for substantial losses in their more traditional industrial sectors, especially manufacturing."[5] Cities in the sunbelt experienced job growth in all major sectors of the economy (manufacturing, retail and wholesale, white-collar services, and blue-collar services) between 1970 and 1986.

In *The Truly Disadvantaged* I maintained that one result of these changes for many urban blacks has been a growing mismatch between the location of employment and residence in the inner city. Although studies based on data collected before 1970 did not show consistent or convincing effects on black employment as the result of this spatial mismatch, the employment of inner-city blacks relative to suburban ones has clearly deteriorated since then.[6] Recent research conducted mainly by urban and labor economists strongly shows that the decentralization of employment is continuing and that employment in manufacturing, most of which is already suburbanized, has decreased in central cities, particularly in the Northeast and Midwest. Blacks living in central cities have less access to employment, as measured by the ratio of jobs to people and the average travel time to and from work, than do central-city whites. Unlike most other groups of workers, less educated central-city blacks receive lower wages in the central city than less educated suburban blacks. And the decline in earnings of central-city blacks is positively associated with the extent of metropolitan job decentralization.[7]

But are the differences in employment between city and suburban blacks mainly the result of changes in the location of jobs? It is possible that in recent years the migration of blacks to the suburbs has become much more selective than in earlier years, so much so that the changes attributed to job location are really caused by this selective migration.[8] The pattern of black migration to the suburbs in the 1970s was similar to that of whites during the 1950s and 1960s in the sense that it was concentrated among the more educated and younger city residents.[9]

[5] John D. Kasarda, "Structural Factors Affecting the Location and Timing of Urban Underclass Growth," *Urban Geography* 11 (May–June 1990): 241.

[6] Harry J. Holzer, "The Spatial Mismatch Hypothesis: What Has the Evidence Shown?" (Paper presented at a conference on *The Truly Disadvantaged*, Northwestern University, October 1990). For a study based on earlier data, see David T. Ellwood, "The Spatial Mismatch Hypothesis: Are there Teenage Jobs Missing in the Ghetto?" in Richard B. Freeman and Harry J. Holzer, eds., *The Black Youth Employment Crisis* (Chicago: University of Chicago Press, 1986).

[7] Holzer, "Spacial Mismatch Hypothesis."

[8] Christopher Jencks and Susan E. Mayer, "Residential Segregation, Job Proximity, and Black Job Opportunities: The Impirical Status of the Spatial Mismatch Hypothesis" (Working paper for Center for Urban Affairs and Policy Research, Northwestern University, 1989).

[9] William Frey, "Mover Destination Selectivity and the Changing Suburbanization of Whites and

However, in the 1970s this was even more true for blacks, creating a situation in which the education and income gaps between city and suburban blacks seemed to expand and that between city and suburban whites seemed to contract.[10] Accordingly, if one were to control for personal and family characteristics, how much of the employment gap between city and suburbs would remain?

This question was addressed in the study by James E. Rosenbaum and Susan J. Popkin of the Gautreaux program in Chicago.[11] The design of the program permitted them to contrast systematically the employment experiences of a group of low-income blacks who had been assigned private apartments in the suburbs with the experiences of a control group with similar demographic characteristics and employment histories who had been assigned private apartments in the city. The authors' findings support the spatial mismatch hypothesis. After controlling for personal characteristics (including family background, family circumstances, human capital, motivation, and length of time since the respondent first moved to the Gautreaux program — all before the move — and education after moving), they found that those who moved to apartments in the suburbs were significantly more likely than those moving to apartments in the city to have a job after the move. When asked what makes it easier to obtain employment in the suburbs, nearly all the respondents mentioned the availability of jobs.

The occupational advancement of the more disadvantaged urban minority members has also been severely curtailed by industrial restructuring. John Kasarda's research demonstrates that "the bottom fell out in urban industrial demand for poorly educated blacks," particularly in the goods-producing industries, in northeastern and midwestern cities.[12] And data collected from the Chicago Urban Poverty and Family Life Survey show that efforts by out-of-school inner-city black men to obtain blue-collar jobs in the industries in which their fathers had been employed have been hampered by industrial restructuring. "The most common occupation reported by the cohort of respondents at ages 19 to 28 changed from operative and assembler jobs among the oldest cohorts to service jobs (waiters and janitors) among the youngest cohort."[13]

Finally, a recent study shows that although black employment in New York City declined by 84,000 in durable and nondurable goods manufacturing — industries whose workers have lower levels of education — from 1970 to 1987, black employment increased by 104,000 in public administration and professional ser-

---

Blacks," *Demography* 22 (May 1985): 223–243; Eunice S. Grier and George Grier, "Minorities in Suburbia: A Mid-1980s Update" (Report prepared for the Urban Institute Symposium on Residential Mobility and Minority Incomes, April 1988).

[10] Holzer, "Spatial Mismatch Hypothesis."

[11] James E. Rosenbaum and Susan J. Popkin, "Employment and Earnings of Low-Income Blacks Who Move to Middle-Class Suburbs" in Jencks and Peterson, eds., *The Urban Underclass*.

[12] John D. Kasarda, "Urban Industrial Transition and the Underclass," *Annals of the American Academy of Political and Social Science* 501 (January 1989): 35

[13] Mark Testa and Marilyn Krogh, "The Effect of Employment on Marriage among Black Males in Inner-City Chicago" (Unpublished ms., University of Chicago, 1989).

vices—industries whose workers are more highly educated.[14] Thus, if industrial restructuring has reduced opportunities for the least educated blacks, it may have improved opportunities for those more highly educated.

As I pointed out in *The Truly Disadvantaged*, manufacturing industries have been a major source of black employment in the twentieth century. Unfortunately, these industries are particularly sensitive to a slack economy, and blacks lost a considerable number of jobs during the recession-plagued decade of the 1970s.[15] A unique test of my argument that many of the employment problems among disadvantaged inner-city youths are the direct result of job losses in local labor markets was provided by Richard Freeman.[16] Examining the employment situation of disadvantaged black youths from 1983 to 1987 in metropolitan areas that had achieved the tightest labor markets by 1987, Freeman found that despite the social problems that beset these youths and "despite the 1980s twist in the American labor market against the less skilled, tight labor markets substantially improved the economic position of these workers." Although jobless rates remain high among disadvantaged minority youths, dramatic progress occurred during the economic recovery of the late 1980s in the metropolitan areas with the tightest labor markets.

If a tight labor market reduces joblessness among the disadvantaged, it also effectively reduces poverty, as Paul Osterman clearly shows.[17] When Boston experienced full employment in the 1980s, not only was there a significant drop in poverty, but a high percentage of the poor had jobs. However, the strong economy did not significantly affect the prevalence of single-parent families. Was the period that Osterman observed (1980 to 1988) of sufficient length to allow for changes in family formation as a response to changes in the economy to emerge? Changes in employment and poverty are likely to appear much sooner following changes in the economy than changes in family formation, because the latter not only represents a more indirect relationship to the economy but a more complex and subtle process of human experience as well.

The relationship between employment and marriage received more detailed attention from Robert Mare and Christopher Winship.[18] They found only modest support for the hypothesis, emphasized in *The Truly Disadvantaged*, that associates the sharp rise in poor single-parent families with the declining employment status of young black men. "Changes in the employment of young black men,"

---

[14] Thomas Bailey, "Black Employment Opportunities" in Charles Brecher and Raymond D. Horton, eds., *Setting Municipal Priorities, 1990* (New York: New York University Press, 1989).

[15] For a good discussion of this problem, see Frank Levy, *Dollars and Dreams: The Changing American Income Distribution* (New York: Russell Sage Foundation, 1987).

[16] Richard B. Freeman, "Employment and Earnings of Disadvantaged Men in a Labor Shortage Economy" in Jencks and Peterson, eds., *The Urban Underclass.*

[17] Paul Osterman, "Gains from Growth? The Impact of Full Employment on Poverty in Boston" in ibid.

[18] Robert D. Mare and Christopher Winship, "Socioeconomic Change and the Decline of Marriage for Blacks and Whites" in ibid.

they concluded, "explain approximately 20 percent of the decline in their marriage rates since 1960." Their results are based on national surveys. But unlike *The Truly Disadvantaged*, their writing makes no effort to examine regional differences that may reflect the impact of changes in the industrial economies in the Northeast and Midwest.

The data that would be most relevant for understanding the relationship between employment and marriage among the underclass are those collected from inner cities. Since the publication of *The Truly Disadvantaged*, this relationship has been examined more closely with data from the inner-city neighborhoods of Chicago as a part of the Urban Poverty and Family Life Study. A recent paper by Mark Testa based on these data shows that black men in inner-city Chicago who have stable work are twice as likely to marry as black men who are jobless and are not in school or in the military.[19]

However, Testa's study also shows that the decline in marriage among inner-city blacks is not simply a function of the proportion of jobless men. Because the disparity in marriage rates between employed and jobless black men was smaller for older cohorts, it is reasonable to consider the effects of weaker social strictures against out-of-wedlock births. "In earlier years," he comments, "the social stigma of illegitimacy counterbalanced economic considerations in the decision to marry. As the norms of legitimacy weakened, marriage rates dropped precipitously among chronically jobless men as couples no longer felt obliged to legitimate the birth of a child for social reasons."[20]

In *The Truly Disadvantaged* I related the increasing jobless rate among black men to geographic, industrial, and other shifts in the economy. This hypothesis has drawn criticism because some observers believed that the focus on impersonal economic forces overlooked willful acts of employment discrimination against racial minorities.[21] Although empirical research on such discrimination is scarce, data from the Chicago Urban Poverty and Family Life Study's survey of employers, as reported by Joleen Kirschenman and Kathryn Neckerman, suggest that inner-city blacks, particularly black men, do indeed face negative attitudes from employers. They report that many employers consider inner-city workers, especially young black men, to be uneducated, uncooperative, and unstable. Accordingly, employers may practice what economists call statistical discrimination, making judgments about an applicant's productivity, which are often too difficult or too expensive to measure, on the basis of his or her race, ethnic, or class background.[22] Although only a few employers explicitly expressed racist

---

[19] Mark Testa, "Joblessness and Absent Fatherhood in the Inner City" (Paper presented at the annual meeting of the American Sociological Association, 1990).

[20] Ibid., 22.

[21] Bailey, "Black Employment Opportunities"; and Hochschild, "Politics of Estranged Poor."

[22] See also Kathryn M. Neckerman and Joleen Kirschenman, "Statistical Discrimination and Inner-City Workers: An Investigation of Employers' Hiring Decisions" (Paper presented at the annual meeting of the American Sociological Association, 1990).

attitudes or a categorical loathing of blacks, many did in fact practice statistical discrimination by screening out black job applicants because of their social class, public school education, and inner-city residence. These factors also served as proxies for judgments about productivity.

As the research of Richard Freeman suggests, however, the practice of statistical discrimination will vary according to the tightness of the labor market.[23] It therefore ought not be analyzed without reference to the overall state of the local or national economy. In a tight labor market, job vacancies are more prevalent, unemployment is of shorter duration, and wages are higher. The pool of potential workers expands because an increase in job opportunities not only lowers unemployment but also draws into the labor force those workers who respond to fading job prospects in slack markets by dropping out of the labor force altogether. Accordingly, the status of disadvantaged minorities improves in a tight labor market because unemployment is reduced, better jobs are available, and wages are higher. In contrast, in a slack labor market employers are — indeed, can afford to be — more selective in recruiting and in granting promotions. They inflate job prerequisites and the importance of experience. In such an economic climate, the level of employer discrimination rises and disadvantaged minorities suffer disproportionately.[24]

Although basic economic transformations and changes in labor markets are important for understanding the life experiences of the urban minority poor, *The Truly Disadvantaged* also argued that the out-migration of higher-income residents from certain parts of the inner city resulted in a higher concentration of residents in ghetto neighborhoods. This contention has been controversial. Douglas Massey and Mitchell Eggers, for instance, have found that the increase of segregation among black social classes during the 1970s was not sufficient to account for the rise in concentrated urban black poverty. They argue that because of persisting segregation, higher-income blacks have been less able than the privileged of other groups to separate themselves from the poor.[25] Accordingly, an increase in the poverty rate of a highly segregated group will be automatically accompanied by an increase in the concentration of poverty. Reynolds Farley reaches the same conclusion. "Wilson's conclusion that poor blacks in Chicago lived in proportionally more impoverished neighborhoods in 1980 than in 1970 . . . is accurate . . . but the situation occurred because of overall increases in black poverty rather than because of higher levels of social class residential segregation or a new outmigration of prosperous blacks.[26] However, Paul Jargowsky and

[23] Freeman, "Employment and Earnings of Disadvantaged Men" in Jencks and Peterson, eds., *The Urban Underclass.*

[24] James Tobin, "On Improving the Economic Status of the Negro," *Daedalus* 94 (1965): 878–898.

[25] Douglas S. Massey and Mitchell L. Eggers, "The Ecology of Inequality: Minorities and the Concentration of Poverty, 1970–1980," *American Journal of Sociology* 95 (March 1990): 1153–88.

[26] Reynolds Farley, "Residential Segregation of Social and Economic Groups among Blacks, 1970–1980" in Jencks and Peterson, eds., *The Urban Underclass.*

Mary Jo Bane turn down the argument that changes in poverty rates alone explain changes in ghetto poverty.[27]

The conflicting findings and conclusions correspond with different measures of concentrated poverty. Massey and Eggers and Farley use an index of segregation to calculate the probability of intraclass contact among groups in metropolitan areas.[28] Although this measure provides a unique description of the overall level of concentrated poverty in standard metropolitan statistical areas [SMSAs], it does not identify particular neighborhoods that are ghettos and others that are not. Focusing on Philadelphia, Cleveland, Milwaukee, and Memphis, they designate ghetto and nonghetto neighborhoods and report a significant geographic spreading of ghetto neighborhoods from 1970 to 1980. Areas that had become ghettos by 1980 had been mixed-income tracts in 1970, although they were contiguous to areas identified as ghettos. These results support the hypothesis that a major factor in the growth of ghetto poverty has been the exodus of the nonpoor from mixed income areas: "the poor were leaving as well, but the nonpoor left faster, leaving behind a group of people in 1980 that was poorer than in 1970."[29]

These results also contradict Paul Peterson's argument that "very little, if any [of the increase in the number of poor people living in extremely poor neighborhoods] can be attributed to increasing class segregation within the black community."[30] On the contrary, the data suggest that the increase of segregation among black social classes was one of several major factors that accounted for the growth of ghetto poverty. As Jargowsky and Bane point out, "In none [of the four cities] was the process a simple matter of the poor moving into ghetto areas or the nonpoor moving out. Nor can the situation in any city be described as one in which people basically stayed put but that changes in the poverty rate caused more areas to be pushed over the 40 percent line. Instead there was a general pattern of dispersion—probably part of a longer historical trend—interacting with changes in the poverty rate and continuing high levels of racial segregation." As the population spread out from areas of mixed income, Jargowsky and Bane go on to state, the next ring, mostly areas that were white and nonpoor, became the home of a "larger proportion of the black and poor population. The white nonpoor left these areas, which also lost population overall."[31] Thus the black middle-class out-migration was not followed by a significant rise of black interclass segregation in neighborhoods where the middle class relocated.

Unfortunately, the geographic spread of ghetto poverty cannot be captured in

[27] Jargowsky and Bane, "Ghetto Poverty in the United States, 1970–1980" in ibid.

[28] Massey and Eggers, "Ecology of Inequality"; Farley, Residential Segregation" in Jencks and Peterson, eds., *The Urban Underclass.*

[29] Jargowsky and Bane, "Ghetto Poverty" in Jencks and Peterson, eds., *The Urban Underclass.*

[30] Paul E. Peterson, "The Urban Underclass and the Poverty Paradox" in ibid.

[31] Jargowsky and Bane, "Ghetto Poverty" in ibid. For a comprehensive study that presents similar findings, see Claudia J. Coulton, Julian Chow, and Shanta Pandey, *An Analysis of Poverty and Related Conditions in Cleveland Area Neighborhoods* (Cleveland: Center for Urban Poverty and Social Change, Case Western Reserve University, 1990).

studies that focus on the concentration of poverty in SMSAs based on a segregation index. Although the studies by Farley and Massey and Eggers are important for understanding the significance of racial segregation in accounting for changes in the concentration of metropolitan poverty, they do not provide an appropriate test of the hypothesis that associates the increase of ghetto poverty with the out-migration of higher-income blacks from certain inner-city neighborhoods.

SOCIAL ENVIRONMENT AND LABOR FORCE ATTACHMENT IN THE INNER CITY

The exodus of higher-income blacks was not only a factor in the growth of ghetto poverty. It also deprived these neighborhoods of structural resources, such as social buffers to minimize the effects of growing joblessness, and cultural resources, such as conventional role models for neighborhood children, therefore further contributing to the economic marginality of the underclass.

In *The Truly Disadvantaged* I argued that the central problem of the underclass is joblessness reinforced by increasing social isolation in impoverished neighborhoods, as reflected, for example, in the residents' declining access to job information network systems. Martha Van Haitsma, in important conceptual writing, has more sharply delineated the relationship between the social environment and experiences in the labor market by distinguishing those persons with weak attachment to the labor force whose social context "tends to maintain or further weaken this attachment."[32] I would like to include this more explicit notion in my framework by equating the social context with the neighborhood.

Unlike the usage of Marta Tienda and Haya Stier, the term weak labor force attachment as used here does not imply a willingness or desire to work.[33] Rather, I view weak labor force attachment as a structural concept set in a theoretical framework that explains the vulnerability of certain groups to joblessness. In other words, the concept signifies the marginal position of some people in the labor force because of limited job opportunities or limited access to the informal job network systems. From a theoretical standpoint there are two major sources of weak labor force attachment: macrostructural processes in the larger society, particularly the economy, and the individual's social environment. The former has been discussed; let me now briefly focus on the latter.

To understand the unique position of the underclass, it is important to understand the association between attachment to the labor force and the neighborhood

[32] Martha Van Haitsma, "A Contextual Definition of the Underclass," *Focus* 12 (Spring–Summer 1989): 28.

[33] Marta Tienda and Haya Stier, "Joblessness and Shiftlessness: Labor Force Activity in Chicago's Inner City" in Jencks and Peterson, eds., *The Urban Underclass*. The concept of weak labor force attachment initially received systematic attention in the work of Sara McLanahan and Irwin Garfinkle, "Single Mothers, the Underclass, and Social Policy," *Annals of the American Academy of Political and Social Science* 501 (January 1989): 92–104.

context. As Martha Van Haitsma points out, "environments with few opportunities for stable and legitimate employment and many opportunities for other types of income-generating activities, particularly those which are incompatible with regular employment," perpetuate weak labor force attachment.[34] Poor people who reside in neighborhoods that foster or support strong labor force attachment are in a much different social context than those with similar educations and occupational skills living in neighborhoods that promote or reinforce weak labor force attachment. Thus neighborhoods that have few legitimate employment opportunities, inadequate job information networks, and poor schools not only give rise to weak labor force attachment but also raise the likelihood that people will turn to illegal or deviant activities for income, thereby further weakening their attachment to the legitimate labor market. A jobless family in such a neighborhood is influenced by the behavior, beliefs, orientations, and social perceptions of other disadvantaged families disproportionately concentrated in the neighborhood. To capture this process I used the term "concentration effects," that is, the effects of living in an overwhelmingly impoverished environment.

Four recent papers address the hypothesis on concentration effects. Elijah Anderson's research in a ghetto neighborhood of Philadelphia provides ethnographic support by showing how a young woman's proximity to and degree of integration with certain neighborhood peer groups can significantly increase her chances of becoming pregnant.[35] Jonathan Crane, relying on evidence from a unique data set (the neighborhood characteristics file from the 1970 Public Use Microdata Sample), provides quantitative support for the hypothesis by showing that neighborhood influence on teenage childbearing and dropping out among both blacks and whites was substantial in inner cities.[36] Consistent with the arguments developed in *The Truly Disadvantaged*, Crane found that "neighborhood effects are much larger at the bottom of the neighborhood distribution than elsewhere." And Susan Mayer supports the hypothesis with data from the High School and Beyond Survey. She finds that teenagers attending schools of low socioeconomic status are more likely to give birth out of wedlock than those with the same socioeconomic background who attend schools of higher socioeconomic status.[37]

In their paper on the political behavior of poor people, Jeffrey Berry, Kent Portney, and Ken Thomson present evidence that does not support the concentration-effects hypothesis.[38] It is important to note, however, that the cities they

[34] Van Haitsma, "Contextual Definition of Underclass," 29.

[35] Elijah Anderson, "Neighborhood Effects on Teenage Pregnancy" in Jencks and Peterson, eds., *The Urban Underclass*.

[36] Jonathan Crane, "Effects of Neighborhoods on Dropping Out of School and Teenage Childbearing" in ibid.

[37] Susan E. Mayer, "How Much Does a High School's Racial and Socioeconomic Mix Affect Graduation and Teenage Fertility Rates?" in ibid.

[38] Jeffrey M. Berry, Kent E. Portney, and Ken Thomson, "The Political Behavior of Poor People" in ibid.

selected for analysis included virtually no neighborhoods with a poverty level of 40 percent or more. Although their study used a poverty line below that of the official poverty line, the absence of extreme poverty or ghetto neighborhoods qualifies their conclusion that the concentration of poor blacks does not lead to distinctive patterns of political behavior.

It would also be interesting and important to replicate the study by Greg Duncan and Saul Hoffman in areas of extreme poverty.[39] On the basis of national data from the Michigan Panel Study of Income Dynamics, they found that raising welfare benefit levels increased slightly the chances that a teenager would have a child out of wedlock and would receive AFDC (Aid to Families with Dependent Children). Nonwelfare opportunities decreased the chances, and the effect was much stronger. The teenagers most likely to bear a child, they find, are those with the least to lose. This view is supported in Anderson's study: "Those who cannot go on to college, who lack an outlook, who fail to find a husband with whom they can pursue the dream and become upwardly mobile, appear to adapt to the situation of closed mobility they see before them." And as Crane's research demonstrates, this is far more likely to happen in an impoverished inner-city neighborhood than in one that is less poor. That is one of many reasons why the neighborhood environment is crucial to my definition of the underclass.[40]

SOCIAL THEORY AND THE CONCEPT OF THE UNDERCLASS

In my formulation the concept of underclass derives its meaning from a theoretical framework that links structural, social-psychological, and cultural arguments. David Greenstone has thus misinterpreted the theoretical discussion in *The Truly Disadvantaged* when he argues that my analysis settles on one fundamental opposition: underclass behavior must be attributed either to responses to an economic predicament or to the cultural commitments to dysfunctional and irrational values.[41] Simplistic either-or notions of culture and social structure impede the development of a broader theoretical context in which to examine questions recently raised by the ongoing debate on the underclass.

In early studies of the inner city, some observers argued that ghetto-specific behaviors were unique adaptations to the restricted opportunities of the disadvantaged in American society, not a different system of values.[42] Although they

---

[39] Greg J. Duncan and Saul D. Hoffman, "Teenage Underclass Behavior and Subsequent Poverty: Have the Rules Changed?" in ibid.

[40] Crane, "Effects of Neighborhoods on Dropping Out" in ibid.

[41] J. David Greenstone, "Culture, Rationality, and the Underclass" in ibid.

[42] Kenneth B. Clark, *Dark Ghetto: Dilemmas of Social Power* (New York: Harper and Row, 1965); Lee Rainwater, "Crucible of Identity: The Negro Lower-Class Family," *Daedalus* 95 (Winter 1966): 176–216; Rainwater, *Behind Ghetto Walls: Black Families in a Federal Slum* (Chicago: Aldine Press, 1967); Ulf Hannerz, *Soulside: Inquiries into Ghetto Culture and Community* (New York: Columbia University Press, 1969).

discussed the influence of culture — that is, the extent to which people follow their inclinations as they have been developed by learning from other members of the community — they did not argue that the influence takes on a life of its own or is autonomous in the ghetto. In other words, these authors demonstrated the possibility of seeing the importance of macrostructural constraints (that is, of avoiding the extreme assumption of a culture of poverty) while still recognizing the value of a more subtle cultural analysis of life in poverty. The question Ulf Hannerz raised twenty years ago remains an important research hypothesis today. Is there a fundamental difference between "a person who is alone in being exposed to certain macrostructural constraints" and a person "who is influenced both by these constraints and by the behavior of others who are affected by them."[43]

What distinguishes members of the underclass from those of other economically disadvantaged groups is that their marginal economic position or weak attachment to the labor force is uniquely reinforced by the neighborhood or social milieu. For this reason Christopher Jencks's discussion of the concept of the underclass is not relevant.[44] Although he has elegantly and impressively laid out the various ways that one can view the underclass, his typology has no underlying theoretical significance. He argues that what we now call the underclass bears a striking resemblance to what sociologists used to call the lower class. This is not true for the formulation developed in *The Truly Disadvantaged* and further elaborated here. Indeed, I know of no previous studies that attempted to define lower class in terms of the dual problem of marginal economic position and social isolation in highly concentrated poverty areas, an important distinction that cannot be captured by using the standard designation "lower class." In America the problems this definition of the underclass connotes are more likely to be found in the inner-city ghettos.

Jencks argues that my definition of the underclass also turns out to mean a largely nonwhite population because I emphasize location. However, in my usage, the concept can be theoretically applied not only to all racial and ethnic groups, but also to different societies. In the United States the concept will more often refer to minorities because the white poor seldom live in extreme poverty or ghetto areas. However, there is nothing in the definition that restricts its application to nonwhites. Moreover, in other societies the combination of weak labor force attachment and social isolation may exist in certain urban environments without the same level of concentrated poverty inherent in American ghettos. For example, there is evidence that the long-term jobless in inner cities in the Netherlands have experienced sharply decreasing contact with conventional groups and institutions in the larger society despite levels of class and ethnic segregation far lower than those of American inner cities. This development has prompted some Dutch social scientists to discuss the formation of an underclass

[43] Hannerz, *Soulside*, 184.
[44] Christopher Jencks, "Is the American Underclass Growing?" in Jencks and Peterson, eds., *The Urban Underclass*.

in the Netherlands in precisely the theoretical terms I outlined in *The Truly Disadvantaged*.[45]

Unless the concept of underclass is defined as a part of a theoretical framework, as I have done, its meaning will become hopelessly polluted and, as Herbert Gans has warned, will be used increasingly to discredit the urban minority poor.[46] Indeed, one of my concerns is that because of the atheoretical way that the concept is often defined by scholars and nonscholars alike, its use has become exceedingly controversial, so much so that the debate has often obscured the important theoretical and empirical issues outlined here.[47] The crucial question is whether a theoretically defined concept of underclass, which is by its very nature complex, will be overshadowed in the long run by nonsystematic, arbitrary, and atheoretical usages that often end up as code words or ideological slogans, particularly in journalistic descriptions of inner-city behavior. If this proves true, research scholars ought to give serious consideration to dropping the term and carefully selecting another that also allows one to describe and highlight the important theoretical linkage between a disadvantaged group's position in the labor market and its social environment.

THE UNDERCLASS AND PUBLIC POLICY

The growing concentration of poverty and social isolation of the inner cities has implications not only for the quality of life and patterns of social interaction in impoverished urban neighborhoods, but for the larger urban environment as well. None of these cities can escape the deleterious consequences of the social transformation of the inner city and the growth of an underclass.

The problem is not simply the fiscal burden created by the sharp deterioration of aggregate family income or the erosion of the municipal tax base caused by the growth in the number of "high-cost" citizens at the very time that large and increasing numbers of higher-income families have abandoned the cities. The deterioration of ghetto neighborhoods has also sapped the vitality of local busi-

[45] See, for example, Kees Schuyt, "The New Emerging Underclass in Europe: The Experience of Long-Term Unemployment in Dutch Inner Cities" (Paper presented at the Leiden Workshop on Modern Poverty, Unemployment, and the Emergence of a Dutch Underclass, University of Leiden, Netherlands, August 1990); Robert C. Kloosterman, "The Making of the Dutch Underclass? A Labour Market View" (Paper presented at ibid.); Godfried Engbersen, "Modern Poverty in the Netherlands" (Paper presented at ibid.); also see Godfried Engbersen, Kees Schuyt, and Jaap Timmer, "Cultures of Unemployment: Long-Term Unemployment in Dutch Inner Cities" (Paper presented at ibid.).

[46] Herbert J. Gans, "Deconstructing the Underclass: The Term's Danger as a Planning Concept," *Journal of the American Planning Association* 56 (Summer 1990): 271–349.

[47] See also William Julius Wilson, "Social Theory and Public-Agenda Research: The Challenge of Studying Inner-City Social Dislocations" (Presidential address, annual meeting of the American Sociological Association, 1990).

nesses and other institutions, and it has led to fewer and shabbier movie theaters, bowling alleys, restaurants, public parks and playgrounds, and other recreational facilities. Residents of inner-city neighborhoods are therefore often compelled to seek leisure activity in other areas of the city, where they come into brief contact with citizens of different racial, ethnic, or class backgrounds. Sharp differences in cultural style and patterns of interaction that reflect the social isolation of neighborhood networks often lead to clashes. Both the white and minority classes have complained bitterly about how certain conveniently located areas of the central city have deteriorated following the influx of inner-city residents. The complaints have inevitably come to be directed at the underclass itself.

Meanwhile, racial tensions between poor blacks and working-class whites reflect an even more serious consequence of the social transformation of the inner city. Working-class whites, like inner-city minorities, have felt the full impact of the urban fiscal crisis in the United States. Unlike middle-class whites, they have been forced by financial exigencies to remain in the poorer parts of the cities and suffer the strains of crime, poorer services, and higher taxes. Unlike the more affluent whites who choose to remain in the wealthier sections of the cities, they cannot easily escape the problems of deteriorating public schools by sending their children to private schools, a problem made worse by the sharp decrease in the numbers of urban parochial schools. Thus, in recent years, the racial struggle for power and privilege in the cities has been essentially a struggle between the have-nots over access to and control of decent housing and decent neighborhoods.

Working-class whites are more likely than middle-class whites to express their hostility in blatantly racist terms and behavior, sometimes manifested in acts of violence such as the recent killing of a young black man in the white ethnic neighborhood of Bensonhurst in New York City, and they are less likely to distinguish between the middle-class and disadvantaged minorities. Middle-class whites are more subtle in their expressions of hostility and are more likely to direct their racial antagonisms specifically toward poor minorities.

The increasing antagonism has been further aggravated by a conservative political atmosphere, particularly during the Reagan presidency, that has not only reinforced the dominant American belief system that poverty is a reflection of individual inadequacy but has discouraged efforts for new and stronger social programs to address the growing problems of urban inequality.

These changes in the racial and political climate in America have profound implications for the way to address the problems of race and class in the inner cities. I am therefore reminded of the words of the late black economist, Vivian Henderson, who wrote, "The economic future of blacks in the United States is bound up with that of the rest of the nation. Policies, programs, and politics designed in the future to cope with the problems of the poor and victimized will also yield benefits to blacks. In contrast, any efforts to treat blacks separately from the rest of the nation are likely to lead to frustration, heightened racial animosities, and a waste of the country's resources and the precious resources of black people."[48]

I agree with Henderson. In the coming years the best political strategy for those committed to racial justice is to place more emphasis on race-neutral programs that would not only address the plight of the disadvantaged among minorities but would apply to all groups in America. After all, Americans across racial and class lines continue to be concerned about increased unemployment, decreased job security, deteriorating real wages, poorer public education, escalating medical and hospital costs, the lack of good child care, and more crime and drug trafficking in their neighborhoods. Because these problems are more highly concentrated in the inner cities as a result of cumulative effects of decades of racial subjugation, programs that aggressively address them will disproportionately benefit the underclass.

Theda Skocpol and Robert Greenstein ought to be considered in this context.[49] The issue is not simply the degree to which universal or targeted programs can sustain political support. The important question is whether costly programs perceived to be targeted to minorities can be generated and adequately supported in the present climate of budgetary constraint and racial antagonism. Although many social programs did indeed survive the Reagan budget cuts, they are hardly sufficient to address the manifold problems gripping the ghetto. We must generate new initiatives if we are indeed to move significant numbers of American citizens out of the underclass. Whether we follow Skocpol's program of targeting within universalism or Greenstein's argument that a mixture of universal and targeted approaches will likely be necessary to achieve a significant impact, the real challenge is to develop programs that not only meaningfully address the problems of the underclass but that draw broad support.

This was my concern when I wrote *The Truly Disadvantaged* and argued for improving the life chances of truly disadvantaged groups such as the ghetto underclass by emphasizing programs to which the more advantaged groups of all races and class backgrounds can positively relate. I now believe that this is best achieved not simply through a combination of targeted and universal initiatives, but through targeted and universal initiatives that are clearly race neutral.*

[48] Vivian Henderson, "Race, Economics, and Public Policy," *Crisis* 82 (Fall 1975): 50–55.

[49] Theda Skocpol, "Targeting within Universalism: Politically Viable Policies to Combat Poverty in the United States" in Jencks and Peterson, *The Urban Underclass*; Robert Greenstein, "Universal and Targeted Approaches to Relieving Poverty: An Alternative View" in ibid.

* This article is adapted and updated from Christopher Jencks and Paul E. Peterson, eds., *The Urban Underclass* (Washington, DC: The Brookings Institution, 1991).

Health Care Market Reform in Congress: The Uncertain Path from Proposal to Policy

THOMAS R. OLIVER

In 1980 Ronald Reagan swept into the presidency on a wave of antigovernment sentiment after promising deregulation, decentralization, and restoration of individual responsibility and opportunity. This pro-competitive, antiregulatory temperament was captured in legislative proposals to stimulate competition in the financing and delivery of health services.[1] In the 96th and 97th Congresses from 1979 to 1983, several bills were introduced to create financial incentives to expand consumer choice in purchasing health services, induce greater price competition among health care professionals and institutions, improve efficiency in the organization and delivery of services, and ultimately lower the costs of health care.

The moment appeared ripe for an earnest attempt at structural reform of the health care system: national health care expenditures continued to increase at a pace well above the costs of other consumer goods and services, with hospital expenditures leading the way. The highly regulatory hospital cost containment program offered by President Jimmy Carter had gone down to defeat in 1979.

---

[1] A 1983 article in this journal noted the ascent of health care market reform onto the American political agenda and examined the underlying theory and key provisions of the leading proposals. See Bonita A. Wlodkowski, "Caveat Emptor in Health Care," *Political Science Quarterly* 98 (Spring 1983): 35–45.

THOMAS R. OLIVER is assistant professor in the Policy Studies Program at the University of Maryland Graduate School, Baltimore. He has published on policy innovation in community and state health care systems.

The pro-competitive measures seemed to offer a rational, comprehensive alternative for policy makers anxious to deal with soaring health costs and federal budget deficits. Finally, pro-competition advocates occupied key positions in both the Congress and the administration.

Yet nothing came of these pro-competitive proposals that promised to enhance consumer choice and save individuals and the government billions of dollars at the expense of a bloated health care industry. Instead, in March 1983 Congress enacted a new prospective reimbursement system to regulate hospital payments under the Medicare program. This payment system amounted to direct price-setting by the federal government — in the eyes of many, the antithesis of the ideal of market-oriented, pluralistic reform.

How can one explain this rapid turn of events in the legislative policy process? This article utilizes the models of congressional decision making proposed by John W. Kingdon[2] to trace the rise and fall of health care competition proposals on the political agenda. In his earlier model, Kingdon outlined the goals that guide legislators' voting behavior and the cognitive process that members of Congress use to arrive at policy decisions. In his subsequent study on agenda setting and formulation of policy alternatives, he argued that legislators apply the same process they use in voting to other earlier decision points in the policy making process. In particular, these models emphasize the importance of consensus in creating impetus for legislative action and explain why, lacking consensus or other overriding support in the policy environment, many issues and policy alternatives never receive serious consideration in congressional committees and executive policy councils.[3]

In this view, proposals for broad market reform were rejected in favor of Medicare rate regulation, because of conflicting forces in the policy-making environment. Ultimately, there was no consensus on wide-scale market reform. In light of legislators' goals and three sets of environmental constraints — interest group opposition, lack of public opinion support, and abandonment of pro-competition positions in the executive branch — it can be understood why Congress opted to focus on short-term measures to control federal health expenditures rather than to follow free-market ideology.

THE POLICY PROBLEM: CONTROL OF HEALTH CARE COSTS

Health care reform is an issue that during the 1960s and early 1970s achieved great prominence on the congressional agenda. Americans perceived that despite the presence of the most sophisticated health care technologies in the world, there were significant shortcomings in the distribution, quality, and efficiency of their

---

[2] John W. Kingdon, "Models of Legislative Voting," *Journal of Politics* 39 (August 1977): 563–95; John W. Kingdon, *Agendas, Alternatives, and Public Policies* (Boston: Little, Brown, 1984).
[3] Kingdon, *Agendas, Alternatives, and Public Policies*, 157–59.

health services. To meet these shortcomings, Congress authorized a number of programs — subsidies for hospital construction and modernization, hospital and medical insurance for the elderly, education and training grants for the health professions, physician peer review, medical assistance for the poor, developmental grants for comprehensive prepaid medical care organizations, and state and regional health services planning.

In a sense, each of these programs was part of the groundwork for a comprehensive national health insurance (NHI) system. Policy makers felt that once the large gaps in the system were closed, the next logical extension in social welfare policy would be publicly financed health insurance for all individuals and families. This was the idea underlying the proposals of leaders in congressional health policy such as Edward Kennedy, the ranking Democrat on the health subcommittee of the Senate Labor and Human Resources Committee, and Wilbur Mills, former chairman of the powerful Ways and Means Committee overseeing the Medicare and Medicaid programs.

Unfortunately, while public programs improved the quality and equitable distribution of health services, the costs of health care began an inflationary spiral that continues to the present. Policy analysts and politicians failed to understand how expanding insurance coverage would increase the use of health services; how new technological developments would raise the unit costs of medical diagnosis and treatment; and, most importantly, how perverse economic incentives for health care providers and consumers alike would stimulate excessive production and consumption of health services.[4] The resulting increases in the use and intensity of health care produced an inflation in costs that far outpaced price increases in the general economy. Per capita spending on personal health services rose from $181 in 1965 to $1,090 in 1981. In that same period, national health expenditures increased from 6.2 to 9.8 percent of the gross national product.[5]

By the late 1970s and early 1980s, rising governmental outlays for health programs not only jeopardized plans for universal NHI but also came to be perceived as significant obstacles to a balanced federal budget.[6] Two policy options to curb the growth of the health care sector emerged in Congress at this time. The first approach was to establish guidelines for hospital rate increases. Hospital services, which accounted for over 40 percent of all personal health care expenditures and were experiencing a spectacular price inflation of over 15 percent per year, were

---

[4] Aaron Wildavsky's analysis of the "political pathology of health policy" concluded that governmental subsidies for medical care had resulted in uncritical investment in high medical technology with minimal returns to the health of Americans. Aaron Wildavsky, "Doing Better and Feeling Worse: The Political Pathology of Health Policy" in John Knowles, ed., *Doing Better and Feeling Worse* (New York: Norton, 1977), 105–24.

[5] Robert M. Gibson and Daniel R. Waldo, "National Health Expenditures, 1981," *Health Care Financing Review* 4 (September 1982): 23.

[6] Linda E. Demkovich, "Competition's Coming On," *National Journal*, 12 July 1980, 1152. This concern is also discussed in Kingdon, *Agendas, Alternatives, and Public Policies*, 179–80.

an obvious target for regulatory action. Yet even a weakened version of the hospital cost containment bill offered by the Carter administration was soundly defeated in 1979.[7] The technical and administrative complexity of the proposed legislation made it unsalable in the face of intensive lobbying from the health care industry.[8] Along with universal NHI, the regulatory approach did not fit with the basic political requirements of the times.[9]

What was needed was a policy alternative that recognized "the need to hold down the costs appearing on the federal budget, the need to allow private insurers to retain a major role in health care, and the need to limit the size and scope of government activity."[10] An attractive option to regulation, according to many analysts, was market-oriented reform — the introduction of a systematic set of new incentives to encourage greater competition among health care providers, improve efficiency in the organization and delivery of health services, and in the long run control the escalation of health care costs. The market reform alternative presented an opportunity to simultaneously exploit the "problem window" created by chronic health care cost inflation to the "political window" opened by the incoming Reagan administration's pro-market stance. The following section summarizes the rationale and policy objectives of the pro-competition proposals — attempts to formulate good public policy in an era of deregulation.

PRINCIPLES OF HEALTH CARE MARKET REFORM

The market approach to cost containment attempted to overcome four failures in the traditional system of health care financing and services. First, individuals have little motivation to forgo consumption of health services when they are covered by comprehensive, tax-free insurance for even routine procedures and when they share little or no costs of each additional service. Second, the traditional fee-for-service payment mechanism rewards health professionals for providing more, not fewer, medical tests and treatments. This economic incentive reinforces professional norms for high quality care. Third, the lack of consumer knowledge and information about medical care creates a dependence on the health professional; in effect, the provider controls both the demand and the supply of services and hence the costs of those services. Finally, most payments to hospitals and professionals are based on the costs of care rather than on competitive prices, so efficiency is not rewarded in most services.

These failures, advocates of competition argued, affect the decisions that individuals make in consuming health services. There are two types of decisions: the first is the decision to seek treatment at the time of illness, and the second is

---

[7] Alain C. Enthoven, *Health Plan* (Reading, MA: Addison-Wesley, 1980), 98.

[8] Paul J. Feldstein and Glenn Melnick, "Congressional Voting Behavior on Hospital Legislation: An Exploratory Study," *Journal of Health Politics, Policy and Law* 8 (Winter 1984): 686–701.

[9] Kingdon, *Agendas, Alternatives, and Public Policies*, 153–57.

[10] Enthoven, *Health Plan*, 161.

the purchase or selection of a health insurance plan. Accordingly, two general approaches were proposed to control costs through price competition.

The first approach was to force people to share more of the costs of each procedure or service they receive. Patients were then expected to seek care in less expensive settings or forgo services that they believe will have only a small benefit. The main problem with this strategy was that it is extremely difficult to provide the health care consumer with complete information on the costs, risks, and benefits of various health services in various settings. Furthermore, in the case of acute illness the patient is in no position to weigh this information but instead is likely to seek the best medical care available. In reality, the physician or other health professional will usually be the proxy for the patient in deciding what volume and timing of medical treatments are appropriate. And a physician paid on a fee-for-service basis is in a position to benefit both the patient and him or herself by doing more at the expense of the "medical commons."[11]

The second approach emphasized competition between alternative delivery systems and traditional fee-for-service medical practices. Individuals were to be offered several choices of insurance plans with different benefits, cost-sharing requirements, and premiums, and often with different participating physicians and hospitals. They would select the package best suited to their needs, conscious of both the scope and price of each plan. This approach channels the purchasing power of the consumer through the plans, which then are responsible for assuring that an appropriate level of services is provided to their subscribers. In order to compete on the basis of price, the plans must control the services they deliver so that costs do not exceed the fixed revenues paid by subscribers. They are able to do this by reducing the amount of high-cost services such as hospital care and increasing the volume of ambulatory services and preventive care. Under competitive conditions, prepaid health plans such as health maintenance organizations were shown to cost 10 to 40 percent less than conventional, fee-for-service medical care.[12]

LEGISLATIVE PROPOSALS AND POLICY OBJECTIVES

This vision of organized health care competition was embodied in economist Alain Enthoven's Consumer Choice Health Plan, which served as the prototype for most of the pro-competition bills introduced in the 96th and 97th Congresses.[13] The specific legislative components of the pro-competition strategy

[11] James F. Blumstein and Frank A. Sloan, "Redefining Government's Role in Health Care: Is a Dose of Competition What the Doctor Should Order?," *Vanderbilt Law Review* 34 (May 1981): 857, 869.

[12] Harold S. Luft, "How Do Health Maintenance Organizations Achieve Their 'Savings'?" *New England Journal of Medicine* 298 (15 June 1978): 1336–43; Harold S. Luft, "Assessing the Evidence on HMO Performance," *Milbank Memorial Fund Quarterly* 58 (Fall 1980): 501–36; Harold S. Luft, *Health Maintenance Organizations: Dimensions of Performance* (New York: Wiley, 1981).

[13] The Consumer Choice Health Plan, originally commissioned but then rejected by Secretary of

included: reducing or eliminating the tax deductions for health insurance premiums by employers and the excludability of health benefits from employees' taxable income; providing multiple choice of health plans for employees, Medicare and Medicaid beneficiaries; requiring an equal contribution of the employer or government toward the purchase of these plans regardless of the costs of the plans.

The pro-competition proposals had several policy objectives. First, they were primarily concerned with long-term, system-wide reform.[14] They addressed not only the pressing issue of increasing health care costs, but also the underlying organizational and financial characteristics of health services that give rise to cost inflation. In this respect, competition advocates explicitly rejected short-term programs aimed at trimming budget deficits. David Stockman, a proponent of market reform first as a congressman and later as director of the Office of Management and Budget, claimed the catalyst for his bill was the irrationality and unworkability of the original hospital cost containment legislation.[15]

A second objective of the competitive strategy was to foster the development of multiple forms of health care organization and financing. Beyond the historic fee-for-service payment mechanism and indemnity insurance plans, a pluralistic system would incorporate health maintenance organizations, health care alliances, independent practice associations, preferred provider organizations, primary care networks, and other emerging entities. The goal of the pro-competition measures was to remove any organizational bias in the financing system due to tax subsidies or lack of choices in insurance plans; consumers would select among competing plans on the basis of benefits, as in the past, and on price as well.

The competitive model also intended to force the health care consumer to differentiate between high- and low-risk medical needs. Much health insurance currently covers services that are either routine or elective in nature and hence is hardly insurance in the classic sense. By eliminating tax subsidies, the pro-com-

---

HEW Joseph Califano, was first outlined in Alain C. Enthoven, "Consumer-Choice Health Plan (I): Inflation and Inequality in Health Care Today: Alternatives for Cost Control and an Analysis of Proposals for National Health Insurance," *New England Journal of Medicine* 298 (23 March 1978): 650–58; "Consumer-Choice Health Plan (II): A National Health Insurance Proposal Based on Regulated Competition," *New England Journal of Medicine* 298 (30 March 1978): 709–20. The full proposal was set forth in Enthoven, *Health Plan*. Pro-competitive proposals introduced in the 96th and 97th Congresses included S. 1485, Health Incentives Reform Act of 1979, introduced by David Durenberger; H.R. 5740, Health Cost Restraint Act of 1979, introduced by Al Ullman; H.R. 850, Health Care Reform Act of 1981, introduced by Richard Gephardt and David Stockman; S. 130, Comprehensive Health Care Reform Act, introduced by Orrin Hatch; and S. 433, Health Incentives Reform Act of 1981, introduced by David Durenberger.

[14] See Alan Murray, "Administration Urges Slash in Federal Health Care Role, Calls for 'Competitive' System," *Congressional Quarterly Weekly Report*, 7 March 1981, 417; and Wlodkowski, "Caveat Emptor in Health Care," 45.

[15] Linda E. Demkovich, "New Congressional Health Leaders — The Emphasis Is on Competition," *National Journal*, 5 July 1981, 1096–7.

petitive proposals attempted to equate a dollar's worth of health insurance with a dollar of earned (taxable) income; the consumer would thereby be encouraged to insure only high cost, unexpected services and pay for routine services out-of-pocket as he or she would for other goods and services. Alternatively, individuals would subscribe to a prepaid, comprehensive health plan, which can offer lower premiums due to its ability to reduce the use of high-cost procedures. A by-product of this policy was to encourage low-cost preventive medicine and health promotion activities.

A final objective of the competition bills was to include the elderly and the poor in the mainstream of health care. Although the Medicare and Medicaid programs would have remained as governmental responsibilities, beneficiaries would be given vouchers and allowed to enroll in a private insurance plan of their choice. This strategy would increase the access of the poor and elderly to all health care providers and lessen criticisms that a two-class system exists—criticisms that became more valid as government cut back on its payments for Medicare and Medicaid.[16]

The competition idea, both in its comprehensive form and in its component parts, had seemingly become a viable alternative as Congress considered its health policies for the 1980s. What were its realistic chances of enactment? Analysis of this question must consider the goals of individual legislators and the forces influencing their policy deliberations.

THE POLICY-MAKING ENVIRONMENT FOR PRO-COMPETITIVE LEGISLATION

Members of Congress, according to Kingdon, search for consensus in the field of forces surrounding a policy issue.[17] As proposals move onto the agenda and toward possible enactment, sources of guidance for decisions include colleagues, party leadership, clientele groups and constituency opinion, the president, executive agencies, and expert analysis.[18] Most of the time, the cues legislators receive from these sources reinforce each other. If instead of consensus they find conflict and controversy among interested parties, however, they are likely to respond to the forces linked to the goal most important to them—that of satisfying constituents, achieving intra-Washington influence, or making good public policy. This

[16] John K. Iglehart, "Medicare's Uncertain Future," *New England Journal of Medicine* 306 (27 May 1982): 1309.

[17] Kingdon, "Models of Legislative Voting," 574–79; Kingdon, *Agendas, Alternatives, and Public Policies*, 157–59.

[18] Several students of political representation and legislative decision making have identified the various outside actors influencing members of Congress. See, for example, Heinz Eulau, John C. Wahlke, William Buchanan, and Leroy C. Ferguson, "The Role of the Representative: Some Empirical Observations on the Theory of Edmund Burke," *American Political Science Review* 53 (September 1959): 744–45; Warren E. Miller and Donald E. Stokes, "Constituency Influence in Congress," *American Political Science Review* 57 (March 1963): 56; Richard F. Fenno, Jr., *Congressmen in Committees* (Boston: Little, Brown, 1973), 15; and Kingdon, "Models of Legislative Voting," 574.

section examines the field of forces facing legislators as they considered proposals to promote health care competition in the early 1980s.

Congressional Leadership in Health Policy

The most influential actors in establishing the congressional agenda and determining the fate of policy proposals appear to be the members of Congress. Kingdon noted that in hundreds of interviews with political elites inside and outside of government, 91 percent of the respondents mentioned the important role of members of Congress in moving a proposal onto the agenda for legislative action. He recounted a number of cases where individual legislators moved health issues from the planning stage to the "front burner" of congressional politics.[19] A combination of individual incentives[20] and decentralized structure[21] makes Congress a fertile ground for innovative proposals and gives individual members an inordinate influence in policy making.

Most health legislation is delegated to four committees: the Senate Labor and Human Resources, Senate Finance, House Ways and Means, and House Energy and Commerce.[22] The leadership of these committees and their respective health subcomittees serves as a focal point to assess the fate of pro-competition legislation.

Leadership changes resulting from the 1980 national election appeared to create a propitious climate for pro-competition proposals in the Senate. In the Labor and Human Resources Committee, the new Republican chairman, Orrin Hatch, dissolved the health subcommittee that had long been dominated by Edward Kennedy, a sponsor of numerous comprehensive national health insurance bills.[23] Hatch wanted control over the health issues handled in committee and served notice of a policy shift by introducing a pro-competition bill and sponsoring deregulation in the field of occupational safety and health. His health care bill, S. 130, was essentially a new version of the proposal introduced in the 96th Congress by Senator Richard Schweiker prior to his appointment as Secretary of Health and Human Services. Despite the committee reorganization, Hatch's ability to gain approval of a competition bill in the full committee was never certain. There was a large ideological gap between most of the liberal Democrats and conservative Republicans. Kennedy, the ranking minority member, still held

[19] Kingdon, *Agendas, Alternatives, and Public Policies*, 37–38.

[20] Among the studies describing legislative goals and incentives are Fenno, *Congressmen in Committees*; Kingdon, "Models of Legislative Voting"; and David R. Mayhew, *Congress: The Electoral Connection* (New Haven: Yale University Press, 1974); and Kingdon, *Agendas, Alternatives, and Public Policies*, 41–43.

[21] See Lawrence C. Dodd and Richard L. Schott, *Congress and the Administrative State* (New York: John Wiley, 1979), 65–129.

[22] Stephen E. Lawton, "Budget Reconciliation: The New Legislative Process," *New England Journal of Medicine* 305 (19 November 1981): 1299.

[23] Murray, "Administration Urges Slash in Federal Health Care Role," 416.

considerable support for his Health Care for All Americans Act, a plan for NHI that was far more comprehensive and regulatory than Hatch's proposal.[24] Also, Republicans Lowell Weicker and Robert Stafford defected to the Democratic side on enough issues to negate any partisan control in committee votes. Although Hatch was becoming known as a consensus builder and a moderate on health issues, it wasn't clear whether he wanted a pro-competition bill badly enough to push it along with the rest of his conservative social policy agenda.[25]

In the Senate Finance Committee, a pro-competitive shift also occurred in 1980. New Chairman Robert Dole replaced Russell Long, an advocate of government-financed catastrophic health insurance. Dole took a pragmatic role in the face of budget pressures: "None of us believes these [pro-competitive] proposals will provide us immediate savings. And it is immediate savings, in addition to long-term reform, that we need."[26] Avoiding the ideological underpinnings of the competition-regulation debate, Dole voiced support for the Reagan administration's proposed tax on health insurance premiums and at the same time backed a regulatory, fixed-payment scheme for hospitals in the Medicare program.[27]

Dave Durenberger, who in 1980 became the health subcommittee chairman in Finance, viewed competition as a ready policy alternative. Durenberger made health care reform his highest priority upon his election in 1978, and he introduced the first pro-competition bill in July 1979. His support for competition was rooted in his experience in Minnesota, where prior to his election he was involved in getting employers to support the local health maintenance organizations.[28] Durenberger's bill drew heavily on the adoption of competition by the Twin Cities' medical industry and stressed the ideas of consumer choice, devolution, pluralism, access, and exit. Durenberger's legislative task was made easier after the 1980 election with the defeat of subcommittee members Gaylord Nelson, Abraham Ribicoff, and former chairman Herman Talmadge, all of whom supported alternative plans for national health insurance. In addition, Jay Constantine, the staffer who for years managed the Finance Committee's health legislation and staunchly opposed competition, was gone from Capitol Hill. Following a successful reelection bid in 1982, many expected Durenberger to push Dole to consider a long-term reform measure.

In the House of Representative, the prospects for competition were more ambiguous. There were no competition advocates placed in key committee posts, and many Democratic leaders were considerably more pessimistic about the effects of stimulating health care competition.

[24] Demkovich, "Competition Coming On," 1152.
[25] Alan Ehrenhalt, ed., Politics in America: Members of Congress in Washington and at Home (Washington, DC: Congressional Quarterly Press, 1981), 1211.
[26] Linda Punch, "Congress Plans Tough Health Cuts," Modern Healthcare 14 (April 1982): 24.
[27] Iglehart, "Medicare's Uncertain Future," 1312.
[28] Demkovich, "New Congressional Health Leaders," 1095.

The pro-competition forces lost an ardent and powerful supporter in 1980 with the electoral defeat of Al Ullman, the Democratic chairman of the Committee on Ways and Means. Ullman, like Durenberger, had first-hand experience with health care competition in his home district in Oregon and had sponsored a pro-competitive bill in 1979 to apply those lessons elsewhere in the country.[29] Ullman's successor in Ways and Means, Dan Rostenkowski, placed the medical cost problem in the context of general fiscal concerns: "[T]he nation's economic recovery rests on reducing the awesome deficits set in motion last year [1981]. We don't have any choice this time about raising taxes and cutting defense. Nor can we duck the job of halting the dramatic rise of health benefits."[30] As a means to raise federal revenues, Rostenkowski showed interest in the pro-competitive strategy of limiting the tax exemption of health insurance benefits. His short-term interest, however, was protecting Medicare beneficiaries in the face of the budget-cutting proposals of the Reagan administration.[31]

The health subcommittee in Ways and Means was headed by Andrew Jacobs, who in 1980 replaced Charles Rangel as chairman. Jacobs, a fiscal conservative but fairly liberal on social and health issues, voted in favor of President Carter's hospital cost containment plan in 1979.[32] Still, he was more likely than Rangel to support, if not push, pro-competition bills: "I don't find [the competition proposals] inimical; I find them intriguing. They merit sympathetic hearings." In a *Congressional Quarterly* interview, Jacobs compared buying health care to purchasing automobiles, saying consumers should be given the incentive to become "prudent shoppers."[33] The views of Rostenkowski and Jacobs reflected the norms of fiscal responsibility and prudential policy formulation that predominate in Ways and Means and the other "control committees" in the Congress.[34] The primary role of Ways and Means in health affairs is to oversee Medicare and Medicaid, ensuring the actuarial soundness of the programs and crafting policies that command agreement on the floor of the House.

In contrast, more partisan tones emanated from the House Energy and Commerce Committee, a critical forum for pro-competitive proposals with its broad jurisdiction over health affairs. The leadership of Chairman John Dingell and Henry Waxman, head of the health subcommittee, posed a significant obstacle to competition sympathizers. Dingell's father championed national health insurance in the New Deal era, and in 1979 Dingell supported the Carter hospital cost containment bill. Waxman cosponsored several of Edward Kennedy's NHI proposals in the 1970s and became a powerful force—perhaps the most pow-

[29] Enthoven, *Health Plan*, 151–52.

[30] Punch, "Congress Plans Tough Health Cuts," 24.

[31] Iglehart, "Medicare's Uncertain Future," 1312.

[32] Ehrenhalt, *Politics in America*, 412–14.

[33] Murray, "Administration Urges Slash in Federal Health Care Role," 417.

[34] Mayhew, *Congress: The Electoral Connection*, 149–158; Fenno, *Congressmen in Committees*, 51–57.

erful—in congressional health policy formulation.[35] He voiced limited support for competition: "We like to see more market forces in the health care arena, and a system run by the private sector rather than the government."[36] Nevertheless, he believed that competition theory needs to be better defined, beyond generalizations "that mean different things to different people."[37] Waxman worried about protecting equitable access to care for high risk patients—primarily the poor and the elderly. "We may set up a system where the competition will be for the enrollment of people who are basically well . . . and [there will be] a refusal to compete for those who are primarily sick and need insurance."[38] He was clearly convinced that government regulation of health services is unavoidable.

A review of the leadership in health affairs during the 96th and 97th Congresses indicates that there was much discussion of steering policy in a pro-competitive direction but little serious legislative activity. It appears that several key members of Congress considered the competition alternative to health care regulation as good, rational policy. There were many more who considered the general idea of competition in medical services worthy of favorable publicity. Indeed, there was little outspoken criticism of competition, even from Waxman, Kennedy, and other proponents of publicly financed NHI; they paid heed to the politics of the times by introducing elements of competition into their national health insurance proposals.[39] Many aspects of the pro-competitive strategy in fact reinforced not only the conservative agenda for deregulation and market-oriented policies but appealed to liberals concerned with strengthening the hand of consumers vis-à-vis professional and institutional interests. Yet, despite the plethora of competition bills and hearings on these proposals in both the House Committee on Ways and Means and the Senate Committee on Finance, no votes were taken to push these measures through the committees to the floor. Why was there no aggressive activity within the Congress to reinforce the "position-taking"[40] in support of health care competition? A critical look at organized interests in the policy environment may yield some clues.

Interest Group Politics

In his model of congressional voting, Kingdon maintained that legislators intent on satisfying constituents consider the views not only of a geographical constituency but also of interest groups that can influence politicians' reputations and

---

[35] Ehrenhalt, *Politics in America*, 616–17.

[36] Demkovich, "New Congressional Health Leaders," 1093.

[37] Demkovich, "Competition Coming On," 1152.

[38] Murray, "Administration Urges Slash in Federal Health Care Role," 417.

[39] Enthoven, *Health Plan*, 164.

[40] This term was used by Mayhew to describe one of several electorally useful activities of members of Congress. According to Mayhew, members often take public positions on issues to gain favorable publicity and constituent support, but rarely back up their position taking with serious legislative activity. Mayhew, *Congress: The Electoral Connection*, 61–62.

electoral chances.[41] Organized constituencies also play a prominent role in helping set the congressional agenda: three-quarters of all interview respondents said interest groups were very important or somewhat important in determining which health issues Congress pulled from the policy stream.[42] Thus, interest groups are key actors in the policy-making process — "outside of government, but not just looking in."[43] At times, the concern with constituent interests is preeminent. Kingdon found: "[I]n view of the likelihood that important constituents will notice and disapprove of a vote out of keeping with their interests, the constituency consideration will dominate the others. If the issue is of lower salience, however, the congressman has more freedom to allow his policy views or intra-Washington considerations to control his choice."[44]

To the extent, then, that proposals for health care competition generated conflict among the constellation of forces present in the legislative process, we would expect members to choose action — or inaction — preferred by important constituencies. This section reviews the positions that influential clientele groups in congressional committee politics took on the pro-competitive proposals. Surprisingly, almost all groups viewed the proposals as undesirable in significant ways.

Organized Labor

In the past, unions and other employee groups supported the development of health maintenance organizations (HMOs) to increase the availability of comprehensive, prepaid health services. Thus, the consumer choice aspects of the competition strategy were compatible with the goals of organized labor, as were plans to pay for the elderly and the poor to subscribe to comprehensive health plans.

The unions smelled a "take away" in the proposed tax law changes, however.[45] The pro-competition measures intended to discourage individuals from choosing comprehensive insurance coverage by taxing any benefits above a certain dollar amount as employee income. This contradicted the social philosophy of the labor movement. Organized labor, as Enthoven pointed out, had a longstanding commitment to universal health insurance.[46] This included a single standard of comprehensive care for everyone as a right. Competition was seen as an excuse to take back the gains made by workers in health benefits and other social insurance.

Further, the proposals would have eroded the power of union leaders negotiating for health benefits with business and industrial employers. The tax-free nature of health insurance made increases in these service benefits cheaper for

[41] Kingdon, "Models of Legislative Voting," 569–70, 582–83.
[42] Kingdon, *Agendas, Alternatives, and Public Policies*, 49.
[43] Ibid., 48–57.
[44] Kingdon, "Models of Legislative Voting," 578.
[45] Blumstein and Sloan, "Redefining Government's Role in Health Care," 863.
[46] Alain C. Enthoven, "How Interested Groups Have Responded to a Proposal for Economic Competition in Health Services," *American Economic Review* 70 (May 1980): 143.

employers than increases in wages and salaries, so these benefits had become prolific chips in the collective bargaining process. With a cap on tax-free fringe benefits, employees would prefer wage increases to expansion of health insurance coverage, so there would be no bargaining chips with which to achieve compromise victories in wage negotiations. These reasons armed both employees and their representatives against proposals tinged with competitive, free-market ideology.

Business and Industry

Business and industrial leaders lent cautious support to the general idea of competition in health services in its legislative infancy, but this backing faded rapidly. The costs of employee health benefits were a significant and growing concern for most companies.[47] In 1981, business spent about $60 billion in taxes to support Medicare and Medicaid, paid sick leave, and compliance with health and safety regulations.[48] Yet for the most part, the pro-competitive proposals were seen as an inappropriately coercive strategy by both large and small employers. In testimony before the House Ways and Means subcommittee on health affairs, the director of the Washington Business Group on Health, which represents 186 large corporations, stated:

> Let me be blunt: there is no significant support for federal legislation mandating a competition system. . . . Employers are very reluctant to support any change that would result in imputed income for employees. The objection is less pointed at health than at the broader concern for taxation of all employee benefits and the resulting employee/labor relations problems. A second concern comes from those who believe the collective bargaining system, not tax policy, should dictate the extent of employer contributions.[49]

In the eyes of business and industry, the tax cap was not an "essential" element of competition, but a means to reduce demand for health care and to increase governmental revenues.[50]

Other elements of the competition strategy were more attractive to large employers. These included providing multiple health plans for employees to choose

[47] For example, the Ford Motor Company paid out $550 million, or $290 per vehicle produced, for health services in 1980. See Jack K. Shelton, Testimony before the House Committee on Ways and Means in U.S. Congress, *Proposals to Stimulate Competition in the Financing and Delivery of Health Care*, hearings before the Subcommittee on Health of the Committee on Ways and Means, House of Representatives, 97th Congress, 1st sess., 2 October 1981 (Washington, DC: U.S. Government Printing Office [GPO], 1981), 567.

[48] Robert A. Carpenter in U.S. Congress, *Proposals to Stimulate Competition in the Financing and Delivery of Health Care*, 569.

[49] Washington Business Group on Health, statement to accompany testimony to the House Committee on Ways and Means in U.S. Congress, *Proposals to Stimulate Competition in the Financing and Delivery of Health Care*, 558, 562.

[50] Willis B. Goldbeck, ibid., 553.

from and setting equal employer contributions for each plan to discourage unnecessary choice of high-cost plans. Because of the variation in the costs of health services and the limited availability of competing plans throughout the country, however, employers favored local voluntary efforts to promote competition.[51] A significant move in this direction was the development of private coalitions of employers whose combined market power enabled them to bargain for services with health care plans and institutions in many communities.[52]

Medical Professionals

Enthoven noted a great deal of ambivalence about competition in the leadership of the American Medical Association (AMA) and among physicians in general.[53] Their priority seemed to be maintaining the status quo, as demonstrated by their lobbying against the Carter hospital cost containment plan.[54] Although the AMA, the American Society of Internal Medicine, and other physician groups endorsed certain elements of the pro-competitive strategy, they insisted that all persons must have free choice of providers of care, which many prepaid health plans do not allow due to their closed panel of participating physicians and hospitals; that competition not be extended into the Medicare and Medicaid programs; and that the application of consumer choice and tax reform be limited to employer health benefits.[55] Such limitations would have rendered pro-competitive legislation ineffective and engendered strong opposition from the business community.

Possibly the most subtle yet most threatening aspect of competition for physicians was the encroachment on their professional autonomy. "A true competitive system would require physicians to disclose more information to patients and to acknowledge the patient as the ultimate decision maker."[56] In addition, a surplus of medical doctors was already steering many physicians away from private practice and into salaried positions in competing health plans, where more attention was paid to cost containment. With the growth of the "medical-industrial complex," physicians were increasingly forced to weigh medical judgments against the cost effectiveness of available procedures and the managerial preroga-

[51] Willis B. Goldbeck, testimony before the Senate Committee on Finance in U.S. Congress, *Proposals to Stimulate Health Care Competition*, hearings before the Subcommittee on Health of the Committee on Finance, United States Senate, 96th Congress, 2nd sess., 19 March 1980 (Washington, DC: GPO, 1980), 413–14.

[52] Paul Starr, "The Laissez-Faire Elixir," *The New Republic*, 18 April 1983, 20; J. Warren Salmon, "The Competitive Health Strategy: Fighting for Your Health," *Health and Medicine* 1 (Spring 1982): 26.

[53] Enthoven, "How Interested Groups Have Responded," 146.

[54] Feldstein and Melnick, "Congressional Voting Behavior on Hospital Legislation."

[55] American Medical Association, statement to accompany testimony before the House Committee on Ways and Means in U.S. Congress, *Proposals to Stimulate Competition in the Financing and Delivery of Health Care*, 537; N. Thomas Connally in ibid., 542–43.

[56] Blumstein and Sloan, "Redefining Government's Role in Health Care," 860.

tives of large-scale medical enterprise.[57] To the extent that pro-competitive measures would rush this transformation of medicine along, they represented another venue of battle between the once-dominant "professional monopolizers" and the emergent "corporate rationalizers" over health care reform.[58]

Hospitals

The hospital industry was badly divided in its positions on pro-competition bills before the Congress.[59] Teaching hospitals and the nonprofit community hospitals, the dominant institutional providers, now faced disturbing consequences of competition. If they were forced to compete on a price basis with other institutions, they could not afford to continue worthwhile programs for teaching, research, and innovative patient care. Competitive pricing would prevent them from building the costs of these activities into their basic charges for patient care.[60] Also, many inner city and rural hospitals provided a large volume of uncompensated services for lack of any other provider of care. As with the "societal contributions" of teaching hospitals, this charity care raised the nominal costs of treating full-paying patients. Under direct price competition, therefore, the institutions meeting the historical obligation to care for the poor and uninsured would suffer even more. Hospital interests argued that provision for these uncompensated services was not adequately considered in the restructuring of health care financing envisioned by competition advocates. Thus, competition bills received some ideological support but also considerable opposition from the American Hospital Association and the Association of American Medical Colleges.[61]

The most avid supporters of medical price competition were the for-profit, or investor-owned hospitals, represented by the Federation of American Hospitals.[62] Proprietary nursing homes and prepaid group medical practices also advocated a

[57] Arnold S. Relman, "The New Medical-Industrial Complex," *New England Journal of Medicine* 303 (23 October 1980): 963–70; Paul Starr, *The Social Transformation of American Medicine* (New York: Basic Books, 1982); Blumstein and Sloan, "Redefining Government's Role in Health Care," 866.

[58] Robert R. Alford, *Health Care Politics: Ideological and Interest Group Barriers to Reform* (Chicago: University of Chicago Press, 1975), 14–15.

[59] Sheila L. Simler, "AHA Struggles to Reach Consensus," *Modern Healthcare* 14 (March 1982): 28.

[60] A paper prepared for the 1981 Private Sector Conference on Health Care Competition at Duke University estimated the cost of these "societal contributions" of academic medical centers to be over $6 billion per year. John W. Colloton, "Competition: The Threat to Teaching Hospitals" in Duncan Yaggy and William G. Anlyan, eds., *Financing Health Care: Competition Versus Regulation* (Cambridge, MA: Ballinger, 1982), 131–95.

[61] American Hospital Association, statement to accompany testimony before the House Committee on Ways and Means in U.S. Congress, *Proposals to Stimulate Competition in the Financing and Delivery of Health Care*, 168–71; Earl J. Frederick in ibid., 615–16.

[62] Michael D. Bromberg in ibid., 171–78.

pro-competition policy. The economic climate was already ripe for these entities, especially those that were part of corporate chains: they had access to capital funds, marketing expertise, and expansive market purchasing power. Their support for competition was broad, although the nursing home industry rejected most proposals concerning Medicare and Medicaid competition as disguised budget cutting by the Department of Health and Human Services.[63]

Insurers

Insurance companies, the Blue Cross and Blue Shield plans, and groups that self-insure for health services severely criticized the pro-competition proposals. Under Enthoven's Consumer Choice Health Plan, the burden of cost containment would shift heavily to insurance plans once individuals had free selection of a plan suited to their medical needs. In the insurers' view, however, the competition that would ensue would not necessarily be fair. The head of the Blue Cross hospital plans suggested that mandated competition would favor those insurers who were skilled at enrolling people whose age and health status assured low utilization of services, rather than those who were actually providing services efficiently.[64]

In fact, the growing competition among health plans was disturbing the profitable pass-through position of conventional insurers in the health care system. Under the old cost-reimbursement system, the cost increases of professional and institutional services were simply passed on to subscribers the next year. With alternative health plans able to deliver comparable services at lower prices to employers and individual subscribers, the Blues and casualty insurance companies were held responsible for curtailing the inflationary practices of hospitals and health professionals, with few if any benefits in the event of success. Despite widespread dissatisfaction with federal budget slashing in the Medicare and Medicaid programs—which shifted billions of dollars of costs to private insurance subscribers—the competition alternative was unappealing to the health insurance industry.[65]

Senior Citizens

A final, forceful constituency was the population receiving Medicare benefits. Opposition to the voucher plan of the competition proposals was voiced in congressional hearings by representatives of the American Association of Retired Persons and the Gray Panthers.[66] Their fundamental fear was that under a com-

---

[63] David C. Crowley in ibid., 668–72.
[64] Walter J. McNerney in ibid., 336.
[65] Linda E. Demkovich, "Health Insurers Favor Budget Cutting—But Not If It Means They Must Pay More," *National Journal*, 21 November 1981, 2068.
[66] James M. Hacking in U.S. Congress, *Proposals to Stimulate Competition in the Financing and Delivery of Health Care*, 386–96; Frances Klafter in ibid., 396–97.

petitive system, insurance deductibles and copayments would be raised to levels that would prohibit or discourage poorer elderly persons from seeking needed services that they are entitled to under Medicare. Also, these groups echoed Waxman's concern that insurance plans would not seek to enroll elderly or other high-risk individuals in order to keep their premiums low. Critics of the competition strategy argued that access to health care for senior citizens would decrease, not increase as intended by the legislators.[67]

Thus, the organized constituencies drawn into the debate over health care market reform, though divided, had a predominantly negative influence on the prospects for enactment. No winning coalition of interests emerged to support a pro-competitive strategy. Instead, almost all of the important clientele groups that influence national health policy had substantial misgivings about the supposedly rational solutions offered by advocates for market-oriented reform.

Given this unfavorable array of constituencies, it is not surprising that pro-competitive proposals did not receive the steadfast backing of legislators. Instead, the drafting of bills and scheduling of hearings appeared to constitute attempts by members of Congress to capitalize on a general antipathy toward government regulation; gain favorable publicity at the expense of a bloated health care system that consumed over a tenth of the average citizen's income; or raise public awareness of the competition issue to build the broad-based public support necessary to overcome interest group opposition in the decision-making process.

Public Opinion

In some cases, the salience of an issue and the intensity of support for a solution among the general public are important resources for policy makers seeking to resolve interest group hostility and policy needs.[68] Kingdon observed that in 57 percent of his interviews public opinion was ranked as an important factor in the prominence of an issue on the policy agenda.[69] The visibility of the competitive strategy, however, was limited. In a 1979 North Carolina survey, for example, only 17.5 percent of the respondents had ever heard of health maintenance organizations, a key component of the pro-competition initiatives.[70] The most salient aspects of the competition bills — taxes on employers and employees for health benefits above a certain level — were negative elements in the congressional debate.

---

[67] Daniel W. Sigelman, "Palm-Reading the Invisible Hand: A Critical Examination of Pro-Competitive Reform Proposals," *Journal of Health Politics, Policy and Law* 6 (Winter 1982): 578–620; Linda E. Demkovich, "Reagan Takes On the Elderly Again as He Seeks to Slow Medicare's Growth," *National Journal*, 12 September 1981, 1616–20.

[68] David E. Price, *Policymaking in Congressional Committees: The Impact of "Environmental Factors"* (Tucson: University of Arizona Press, 1979), 46–48.

[69] Kingdon, *Agendas, Alternatives, and Public Policies*, 69.

[70] North Carolina Division of State Budget, *1979 North Carolina Citizen Survey Data* (Raleigh, NC: Division of State Budget, 1979).

Public support for health care market reform in toto was also suspect. In congressional deliberations the presumed long-term public interest in lower health care expenses received little attention compared to the short-term costs of competition to special interests. Was this because consumer interests were never mobilized—a common fact of legislative life[71]—or because consumer interests ran counter to the market model? Victor Fuchs suggested that most Americans, contrary to economic theory, prefer comprehensive health insurance to reduce uncertainty and to avoid moral choices between medical needs and available funds during illness.[72] Only 54 percent of the persons responding to a 1982 *New York Times* poll favored the availability of cheaper but limited health insurance coverage.[73] In the Federal Employees Health Benefits Program, the primary model for consumer choice competition, only one of every nine enrollees chose to purchase low-option plans.[74] In an apt commentary on encounters between academic reason and political reality, Uwe E. Reinhardt contended:

> Remarkably, while American economists were toiling in the trenches, scoring impressive victories in the realm of thought, their fellow citizens yawned and went right on socializing this well-behaved commodity. The notion continued to spread that health care is one of those commodities to which every citizen in a civilized society is entitled regardless of ability to pay.[75]

Thus, the national mood supporting deregulation may not have extended to medical care as readily as many political observers were disposed to believe.[76] While the general climate of opinion apparently helped put the issue of health care competition on the policy agenda, it was of little help in moving specific proposals through the maze of legislative deliberation. Based on the views of the general public and health care interest groups alone, one would not expect constituency-oriented members of Congress to have pushed the pro-competition proposals toward enactment.

Partisan Politics

For a proposal to succeed in a conflictive environment where there is no majority coalition of interests or intense public support, leadership must pass from legisla-

---

[71] Michael T. Hayes, "The Semi-Sovereign Pressure Groups: A Critique of Current Theory and an Alternative Typology," *Journal of Politics* 40 (February 1978): 155–61.

[72] Victor R. Fuchs, "Economics, Health and Post-industrial Society," *Milbank Memorial Fund Quarterly* 57 (Spring 1979): 153–82

[73] Robert Reinhold, "Competition Held Key to Lower Medical Cost," *New York Times*, 1 April 1982.

[74] Sigelman, "Palm-Reading the Invisible Hand."

[75] Uwe E. Reinhardt, "Health Insurance and Cost Containment Policies: The Experience Abroad" in Mancur Olson, ed., *A New Approach to the Economics of Health Care* (Washington, DC: American Enterprise Institute, 1981), 151.

[76] Kingdon, *Agendas, Alternatives, and Public Policies*, 153–54.

tive committees to the Congress as a whole.[77] Here, the critical roles belong to political parties and the president, who can provide a counterweight to even the strongest of interest groups.[78]

When an issue commands the attention of party leadership, either in the Congress or the administration, committee routines become subordinate to partisan politics. This is likely to happen when an issue receives considerable attention in the press and in the Washington establishment and when the president places high priority on the issue and engages in extensive lobbying activities to influence congressional decisions. In that situation, legislators interested in cultivating influence defer policy judgements to party leaders.[79]

Such was not the case for health care competition. Market-oriented reform never received party-wide support from either the Republicans or Democrats. This may be due in part to the complexity and obscurity of the issue. Despite the inexorable rise in health costs nationwide, the only policies for cost containment to capture public attention were those that curtailed benefits. Another complicating factor was the mixed ideology of the reform proposals: while they mainly addressed Republican and conservative themes of restraint of government, fair market competition, and efficiency of health services, they also played to liberal themes of consumer choice and equitable treatment of the poor and elderly. Finally, there was considerable disagreement on the substantive elements of reform, even among Republicans. While most congressional bills stressed consumer choice among competing health plans, presidential advisers pushed for increased cost-sharing provisions in their proposals for Medicare and Medicaid. Without solidarity on even the most basic elements of policy design, health care competition never became a battleground for party politics, and the task of legislative leadership fell to the Reagan administration.

Policies in the Executive Branch

Amid a constellation of competing forces, executive leadership becomes a key determinant of congressional policy. "People in and around federal policy making are often preoccupied with 'the administration.' When the administration considers a given issue a top-priority item, many other participants do too. And when advocates of a given proposal find that they do not have a receptive ear in the administration, they often must downgrade their chances for a serious hearing, at least for the time being. Although it would be overstating the matter to say that the administration always dominates the government's policy agenda, the administration still figures very prominently indeed in agenda setting."[80]

[77] Theodore J. Lowi, "American Business, Public Policy, Case-Studies, and Political Theory," *World Politics* 16 (July 1964): 699.

[78] Hayes, "The Semi-Sovereign Pressure Groups," 160.

[79] Kingdon, "Models of Legislative Voting," 570, 583–85.

[80] Kingdon, *Agendas, Alternatives, and Public Policies*, 23.

In Kingdon's study of agenda setting and policy making, 94 percent of the political elites interviewed cited the importance of the president, the executive office staff, or political appointees in executive agencies in steering the course of a proposed policy. These executive actors played a decisive role in twenty-two of twenty-three cases examined in the study.[81] The critical importance of the executive branch lies in its integrative capacities:

> In developing legislative proposals and priorities, the executive is less likely to focus on the demands of narrowly based groups and constituencies and more likely to perceive tradeoffs between these demands and other objectives. . . . At the same time, the executive has a superior capacity to resolve, or at least mute, conflict within its ranks and to move decisively in controversial policy areas.[82]

There were high expectations when the Reagan administration took office that a pro-competitive health policy would be pushed vigorously.[83] Two former sponsors of pro-competition plans in the Congress held high-level posts in the new administration—David Stockman as the director of the Office of Management and Budget and Richard Schweiker as the secretary of Health and Human Services (HHS). Schweiker established a task force in May 1981 to develop legislative proposals and recruited a private sector task force to advise the HHS group. In late 1981 and early 1982 the White House Cabinet Council on Human Resources reviewed a number of policy options. The Reagan administration's fiscal year 1983 budget indicated that major reforms to "introduce more price discipline into the health care market and moderate the explosive growth of health care costs" would be forthcoming.[84]

Yet, it was not until early 1983 that the administration announced its proposals to control medical costs, nearly a full year after initial plans were debated within the executive branch. The proposals represented an incremental reform of the existing system, if not a full retreat from the pro-competition agenda. The administration limited its program to a tax on employee health benefits over $840 for an individual or $2,100 for a family per year and to an increase in Medicare copayments, accompanied by a ceiling of $2,500 in personal expenses for catastrophic illness. In addition, Medicare recipients would be allowed to enroll in private health plans through the use of vouchers.[85] The 14 March 1983 *New York Times* announced: "The Reagan Administration is abandoning major components of its plan to hold down medical costs by spurring competition. . . . The plan has been opposed by major businesses, organized labor, the insurance industry and medical groups."[86] According to Starr:

[81] Ibid., 24.
[82] Price, *Policymaking in Congressional Committees*, 50.
[83] Starr, "The Laissez-Faire Elixir," 19.
[84] Janet P. Lundy, "Hospital Cost Containment," U.S. Congress, Congressional Research Service, Issue Brief IB 82072, 24 June 1982, 8.
[85] Starr, "The Laissez-Faire Elixir," 21.
[86] Robert Reinhold, "Reagan Changing Health Cost Plan," *New York Times*, 14 March 1983.

The Reagan Administration's difficulties in formulating health policy are similar to the troubles it has had in other areas of economic and social policy. A shared free-market rhetoric often conceals real differences. Not only have there been serious divisions among the policy intellectuals in health care (as there have been among monetarists and supply-siders); but the very idea of health care competition, particularly as Enthoven conceived it, was not in the least attractive to much of the health care industry. There has been a contradiction . . . between the ideological proclivities of conservatives and the pressures of interest groups that make themselves felt in the Republican Party.[87]

POLICY PRIORITIES: BUDGET RELIEF, NOT SYSTEM REFORM

Under pressure to finance budget deficits and increase military spending, the Reagan administration retreated from comprehensive structural reform of health services to a strictly fiscal policy. On the way, the end of health care cost containment came to dominate the means to achieve it. The competition strategy offered long-range savings but little in the way of immediate cost control when taken as a whole. A 1979 report by the Congressional Budget Office estimated that any savings in the first five years following enactment of a pro-competitive bill would be substantially lower than the savings under any version of cost containment regulation.[88] Furthermore, most of the anticipated savings could not be identified since they would be diffused throughout the health care system rather than located in specific programs. Thus, the market reforms offering budget relief — a cap on tax exempt health insurance and Medicare cost sharing — received more favorable attention in the administration than the consumer choice provisions.

A short-term fiscal strategy may have been more appealing to congressional leaders as well. Many of them voiced concern over the runaway costs of Medicare and Medicaid. Since 1970, Medicare payments for hospital and physician services had increased at a rate of 17.7 percent annually and were accelerating. The Congressional Budget Office projected that the hospital insurance trust fund would be depleted by 1987 or 1988.[89] The impending insolvency of the Medicare program spurred policy makers to considerably narrow their definition of the health care cost problem.

This priority on budget relief helps to explain the demise of the comprehensive program for health care competition. In hindsight, it is tempting to argue that because market reform threatened so many constituencies and promised only nebulous long-term savings, it was never a viable policy alternative. But that dismisses evidence that at one time it was considered viable and the possibility that it could at some later time again become viable. The sheer volume of legisla-

[87] Starr, "The Laissez-Faire Elixir," 21.

[88] Linda E. Demkovich, "Reagan's Cure for Health Care Ills — Keep the Government's Hands Off," *National Journal*, 13 December 1980, 2126.

[89] John E. Iglehart, "Medicare Begins Prospective Payment of Hospitals," *New England Journal of Medicine* 308 (9 June 1983): 1432.

tive activity, executive reports, and media coverage suggests that health care competition was a potent issue that for a time in the early 1980s commanded serious attention from all parties in the policy-making environment.

Even as the market reform proposals faded from the policy agenda in early 1983, the problem of health care cost control remained and in fact became more pressing, but the "problem window" in the policy stream shifted when the fiscal implications of the Reagan tax cuts and the insolvency of the Social Security trust funds came to light.[90] Still, if consumer choice competition had been the only available solution in the policy stream, it may well have been adopted. Its political downfall was guaranteed, however, when an alternative solution to health care cost containment presented itself in a timely manner. Along with interest group opposition and short-term budget constraints, the pivotal factor that sealed the fate of comprehensive market reform was the arrival of a new system to regulate hospital payments under Medicare.

CONGRESSIONAL POLICY MAKING AND THE EMERGENCE OF DRGs

The Reagan administration proposed a novel prospective payment system for hospitals under Medicare as the 98th Congress convened in January 1983. Acting with extraordinary speed, members of Congress voted to adopt the new system only two months later as part of a package of amendments to the Social Security Act.[91]

There are three compelling reasons why in such short order Congress opted to impose price regulation on hospitals in lieu of a more comprehensive reform offered by the pro-competition proposals. First, the prospective reimbursement system offered a mechanism to halt immediately the increase in Medicare hospital payments. One of the problems holding back the Carter cost containment bills was technically feasibility: there was no way at that time to compare the care delivered at one hospital with other hospitals. The 1979 proposal admitted that "data do not yet exist for classifying hospitals by type of patients cared for."[92]

---

[90] On the importance of "policy windows" of different kinds, Kingdon, *Agendas, Alternatives, and Public Policies*, 173–204.

[91] The Tax Equity and Fiscal Responsibility Act of 1982 called on the Department of Health and Human Services to develop a prospective payment plan. The outgoing Secretary of HHS, Richard E. Schweiker, submitted the HHS report to Congress on 28 December 1982. The Reagan administration formally introduced its proposal on 23 February 1983. Meanwhile, the House Ways and Means Committee and the Senate Finance Committee held hearings in early February 1983 and marked up bills in early March. The full House passed the measure on 9 March and the Senate followed on 23 March. Final passage came on 25 March, and the bill was signed into law by President Reagan on 20 April. The details of the proposals and the legislative debate are recounted in Linda E. Demkovich, "Who Says Congress Can't Move Fast? Just Ask Hospitals About Medicare," *National Journal*, 2 April 1983, 704–7; and Iglehart, "Medicare Begins Prospective Payment of Hospitals."

[92] Enthoven, *Health Plan*, 99. The importance of technical feasibility is noted by Kingdon, *Agendas, Alternatives, and Public Policies*, 138–39.

By 1983, however, a payment system based on diagnosis-related groups (DRGs) had proven to be satisfactory in a statewide experimental program begun in 1980 in New Jersey.[93] The DRG system established fixed fees for each type of case or illness. Hospitals were paid by the case, not by the quantity of services delivered, and, therefore, were encouraged to cut costs by keeping patients for shorter stays and reducing unnecessary tests and treatments. This new management technology promised what no consumer choice measures could deliver—predictable short-term savings. Tentative estimates by the Reagan administration anticipated savings to Medicare of $1.5 billion in fiscal 1984 and $20.2 billion over five years.[94]

A second factor that enabled Congress to adopt the new Medicare payment system was the vulnerability of hospitals on the issue of cost control. The hospital industry had organized a volunteer cost restraint program in December 1977 as a strategy to defeat the Carter administration proposal. This program resulted in a temporary slowdown in hospital inflation in 1978. Once the threat of legislation passed in 1980, however, the voluntary program was exposed as a mammoth failure: hospital expenses rose by 12.8 percent in 1978, 13.4 percent in 1979, and in the third quarter of 1980 reached an annual inflation rate of 17.8 percent.[95] During 1982, hospital costs increased at three times the rate of inflation in the general economy.[96] The DRG proposals, therefore, seemed well targeted. The hospital industry itself accepted the legislation, if only because the new payment system appeared less onerous than the cost-cutting provisions approved for Medicare under the 1982 Tax Equity and Fiscal Responsibility Act and set for implementation in fiscal 1984.[97]

Since the proposed payment system directly affected only hospitals, it was less likely to arouse the opposition of other interest groups active in health care politics. By further limiting its proposal to Medicare, the Reagan administration avoided the extreme controversy created by the Carter hospital cost containment plan. Changes in the Medicare program did not require significant changes in

[93] The Medicare prospective payment system was based on diagnosis-related groups, or DRGs. Each hospital patient was classified by the diagnosis of his or her medical problem. For each diagnosis, there was an established level of payment based on the average volume and costs of medical tests and treatments involved for that diagnostic category. This payment schedule was adjusted for regional variations in hospital costs and for individual hospitals involved in teaching and clinical research programs. There were a total of 467 groups or cases in the Medicare payment system, which was based on the experimental payment system developed in New Jersey under a waiver from the Health Care Financing Administration. For a history of the political development of the DRG system in New Jersey, see James A. Morone and Andrew Dunham, "The Waning of Professional Dominance: DRGs and the Hospitals," *Health Affairs* 3 (Spring 1984): 73–87.
[94] Demkovich, "Who Says Congress Can't Move Fast? Just Ask Hospitals About Medicare," 704.
[95] Karen Davis, "Regulation of Hospital Costs: The Evidence on Performance" in Duncan Yaggy and William G. Anlyan, eds., *Financing Health Care: Competition Versus Regulation* (Cambridge, MA: Ballinger, 1982), 37–65.
[96] Iglehart, "Medicare Begins Prospective Payment of Hospitals," 1429.
[97] Demkovich, "Who Says Congress Can't Move Fast? Just Ask Hospitals About Medicare," 704–5.

the private insurance industry.[98] Certainly, business and labor would be more supportive of hospital cost controls than legislative attacks on employee health benefit packages.

Because DRGs offered short-term fiscal savings and offended fewer constituencies, they were more politically attractive than pro-competitive reform. They were by no means a consensual alternative, however. Most health care groups preferred the status quo, and virtually all interests concerned with health care reform would have preferred more time to plan for such a dramatic departure from cost-based reimbursement policies.[99] The extraordinarily rapid passage of the DRG proposal through the legislative process can only be attributed to a third factor, the linkage of Medicare reform to the larger overhaul of the Social Security program in 1983.

Like Medicare, the Social Security OASDI (Old Age Survivors and Disability Insurance) fund faced depletion of its revenues; but the crisis was more immediate and on a vaster scale. Social Security reform was a political as well as fiscal imperative and commanded bipartisan attention. On 2 April 1983, the *National Journal* reported, "When Congress convened in January, social security and jobs were its top priorities. While medicare reform was important, it was clearly considered a back-burner item, House and Senate aids say, until the more pressing issues were dispensed with."[100] But the leadership and staff of the House Ways and Means Committee sensed an opportunity to tie the Medicare DRG proposal to "one of the greatest legislative engines we'll ever see — the Social Security bill."[101] They pressed HHS to complete the administration's formal prospective payment proposal and promptly crafted it into a politically acceptable compromise. Linked to the bipartisan rescue of Social Security a few weeks later, the most fundamental change in the Medicare program's seventeen-year history came into being without the usual prolonged review and debate by interest groups and legislators alike.

The legacy of DRGs illustrates a certain unpredictability in congressional agenda setting and decision making. While ordinarily the policy-making process is characterized by consensus-building, the coincidental "coupling" of problems, policy alternatives, and politics periodically provides opportunities for legislators to formulate and enact policies even in a fragmented field of political forces.[102] In this case, the Reagan administration and congressional insiders seized upon a payment system that had only a brief experimental trial in a single state and incorporated it into a $50 billion national program. Even with the phenomenal

---

[98] Insurers did argue, however, that a program limited to Medicare would allow hospitals to shift uncovered costs to private patients. Ibid., 705; Iglehart, "Medicare Begins Prospective Payment of Hospitals," 1429.

[99] Demkovich, "Who Says Congress Can't Move Fast? Just Ask Hospitals About Medicare," 705.

[100] Ibid., 704.

[101] Iglehart, "Medicare Begins Prospective Payment of Hospitals," 1430.

[102] See Kingdon, *Agendas, Alternatives, and Public Policies*, 181–88, 210–13.

speed of this transition from a speculative demonstration program into a legitimate policy option, the DRG solution arrived just in time to catch the legislative express offered by Social Security reform. Without the remarkable timing of these developments, the Medicare reform proposal would certainly have been delayed or possibly met the same fate as its pro-competitive predecessors. And the advent of DRGs, a potent new force in the health care landscape, might provide a different lesson for students of congressional policy making.

Innovation and Boundaries in American Employment Policy

MARGARET WEIR

For the thirty years that followed World War II, American presidents, in words, if not always in their actions, supported the goal of full employment. For Democrats the objective was especially salient, but, wary of the electoral repercussions, Republican politicians also highlighted employment concerns. During the later 1970s, in an economic context of sharply rising inflation, full employment receded as a political issue. And as full employment lost its place as a pivot of partisan competition, ideas arguing that government could only play a limited role in affecting employment began to set the terms for public policy.

What accounts for this change in the position of employment as a political issue, and how did ideas about limiting the government role become influential? Two major explanations, each linked to broader arguments about American exceptionalism, have been offered to account for shifts in economic policy in the late 1970s. One traces the shift to business influence, pointing to the striking political mobilization of American business and financial interests during the 1970s.[1] A second explanation highlights the role of public opinion: strong and

---

[1] The most thoroughgoing of these arguments is presented in Thomas Ferguson and Joel Rogers, *Right Turn: The Decline of the Democrats and the Future of American Politics* (New York: Hill and Wang, 1986).

MARGARET WEIR is senior fellow at the Brookings Institution. She is the author of *Politics and Jobs: The Boundaries of Employment Policy in the United States*. Her current research examines the political isolation of cities in the United States.

widespread opposition to inflation joined with antipathy to federal power to overwhelm negative sentiments about unemployment.[2]

Although substantial evidence exists to back up each claim, this article argues that the role of business and public opinion cannot be properly understood unless the debates about employment policy in the late 1970s are seen as the final stage of a policy sequence that began in the 1940s. To understand why full employment lost its force as a political issue, we need to understand why alternative policies that revise and enhance government's role attracted so little support.

I examine two episodes central to the development of employment policy – the transformation of Keynesian policy ideas after the 1940s and the War on Poverty. I show how three characteristics became deeply embedded in employment policy. First, American employment policy settled on a narrow definition of the problem to be solved: policy focused on "unemployment" as defined by a single aggregate number. Second, policy makers concerned with employment policy rarely conceived of their task as one of institution building. Finally, employment issues became partitioned into an economic component and a social component, each cast into a distinct orbit of politics and administration. Over time, this institutional and political segmentation limited employment policy and narrowed the possibilities for adapting policy to new political and economic conditions.

I show how the interaction of ideas and politics since the 1940s created this pattern of "bounded innovation" in which some ideas about employment policy became increasingly unlikely to influence policy. Central to this narrowing process was the creation of institutions, whose existence channeled the flow of ideas, shaped incentives for political actors, and helped to determine the political meaning of policy choices.

THE POLITICS OF BOUNDED INNOVATION

The approach I take aims to make sense of innovation as well as boundaries in American policy making. This objective directs attention to the diverse links between ideas, political institutions, political actors, networks of experts, and social interests that are often overlooked in culture- or interest-based accounts of policy making.[3] But in contrast to general theories of policy making that are not historically grounded, it also entails understanding how some avenues of

---

[2] For a sophisticated analysis of unemployment and inflation that points in this direction see Douglas Hibbs, Jr., "The Mass Public and Macroeconomic Performance: The Dynamics of Public Opinion Toward Unemployment and Inflation," *American Journal of Political Science* 23 (November 1979): 705–31. Both public opinion and business mobilization are considered as determinants of economic policy in Thomas Byrne Edsall, *The New Politics of Inequality* (New York: Norton, 1984).

[3] On culture, see Anthony King, "Ideas, Institutions and the Policies of Governments: A Comparative Analysis: Part III," *British Journal of Political Science* 3 (October 1973): 409–423. On interest explanations, see, for example, Thomas Ferguson, "From Normalcy To New Deal: Industrial Structure, Party Competition, and American Public Policy in the New Deal," *International Organization* 38 (Winter 1984): 41–93.

policy become increasingly blocked if not entirely cut off.[4] Central among the questions I ask are how do social phenomena become policy problems and how do particular understandings of problems emerge to guide policy making? How do such understandings affect the way groups identify their policy interests and in the process facilitate some alliances and discourage others?

Answering such questions requires an approach that is fundamentally historical, which looks for connections among policies over time. Such perspective is essential for understanding how opportunities for innovation arise and for assessing the range of policy possibilities open at any particular moment. Inherent in this approach is the notion that individual innovations are part of a policy sequence in which institutional development renders some interpretations of problems more persuasive and makes some prospective policies more politically viable than others.[5] In such policy sequences, decisions at one point in time can restrict subsequent possibilities by sending policy off onto particular tracks, along which ideas and interests develop and institutions and strategies adapt.[6]

To understand how a sequence develops requires examining not only the direct antecedents of innovation but also policies formally classified in other arenas, which may nonetheless shape the problem itself, thinking about the problem, or the politics of the issue. This calls for casting a broad eye over politics to understand how developments in different domains of politics and policy collide with one another to create outcomes that cannot be readily anticipated or easily controlled by individual actors. Such collisions can become turning points in a sequence by creating opportunities for political actors seeking to promote new ideas and different visions of politics.[7]

The mode of bureaucratic recruitment, the procedures that govern advancement within the federal government, and the permeability of the federal government to social groups all facilitate consideration of innovative ideas in national policy making. The American practice of recruiting government officials whose primary identification and prospects for career advancement lie in their professional expertise provides a hospitable setting for introducing new ways of looking

[4] For an influential general theory of policy making see John Kingdon, *Agendas, Alternatives, and Public Policies* (Boston: Little, Brown, 1984).

[5] On the notion of sequences, see Sidney Verba, "Sequences and Development" in Leonard Binder et al., eds., *Crises and Sequences in Political Development* (Princeton, NJ: Princeton University Press, 1971), 283–316.

[6] See the discussion in Stephen D. Krasner, "Approaches to the State: Alternative Conceptions and Historical Dynamics," *Comparative Politics* 16 (January 1984): 223–246; Stephen D. Krasner, "Sovereignty: An Institutionalist Perspective" in James Caporaso, ed., *The Elusive State: International and Comparative Perspectives* (Beverly Hills, CA: Sage Publications, 1989), 223–246; Edward G. Carmines and James A. Stimson, *Issue Evolution: Race and the Transformation of American Politics* (Princeton, NJ: Princeton University Press, 1989).

[7] These collisions are similar to the sharp changes that are envisioned by the theory of punctuated equilibrium. See Carmines and Stimson, *Issue Evolution*; and Krasner, "Sovereignty: An Institutionalist Perspective."

at problems. In contrast to systems where recruitment into government is governed by strict guidelines and conformity to established civil service norms, the American federal bureaucracy is routinely refreshed with ideas from outside government.[8] These features of American political institutions mean that a wide range of ideas have a chance of influencing American policy. Ideas that are formulated and advocated by preexisting interests as well as those devised by professional groups may find their way onto the policy agenda.

But because politicians in the United States have considerable freedom to consider and solicit a range of ideas, we must also examine the distinctive incentives that guide their choices. Two features of American politics offer clues to the conditions under which parties and presidents have evaluated policy choices. The first is the fragmented structure of national political institutions, which creates a wealth of opportunities for mobilizing opposition. The ease of mobilizing opposition encourages politicians to adopt a shortened time horizon and makes short-term coalitions the bread and butter of American policy making. Such arrangements do not encourage attention to the long-term repercussions of policy. The second feature of American politics that affects politicians' evaluations of policy is the federal system, which can create formidable political and procedural barriers. The need to negotiate the various levels of the federal system affects the way political actors decide how policy goals should be achieved or, indeed, whether they are possible at all.

The need to achieve results in the short term pushes parties and presidents to put together ad hoc coalitions around specific issues and to assemble broad public support sustained by rhetoric with wide but shallow and often vague appeal.[9] Although the support engendered by such appeals may be diffuse or ephemeral, it serves immediate political needs. Policies that depend on reforming existing institutions or building new institutional capacity are less attractive than policies that funnel distributive benefits through existing institutions, those that bypass existing institutions altogether, or those that rely on private activity that may be more easily launched. Reliance on new channels or private actors to implement policy also helps to remove obstacles posed by the federal system. Because there is little incentive to consider the long-range repercussions of policy, tactics useful in passing a policy can actually undermine the emergence of long-term political coalitions and enduring institutions needed to sustain policy direction.

Policy ideas may reach the national agenda and be selected by politicians, but unless they build supportive alliances they will be vulnerable to political attacks. Such support is often critical in allowing policy administrators to learn from their

[8] See the essays in G. Calvin MacKenzie, ed., *The In-&-Outers: Presidential Appointees and Transient Government in Washington* (Baltimore: Johns Hopkins University Press, 1987).

[9] Fred I. Greenstein, "Change and Continuity in the Modern Presidency" in Anthony King, ed., *The New American Political System* (Washington, DC: American Enterprise Institute, 1978), 65. On the use of rhetoric, see Jeffrey K. Tulis, *The Rhetorical Presidency* (Princeton, NJ: Princeton University Press, 1987).

mistakes and modify policy accordingly. It also permits policy makers to redesign policy to respond to new circumstances.

I argue that such alliances are the product of political processes, not preexisting preferences.[10] This view presumes that policy interests can be defined in different ways so that several distinct policies may be compatible with a group's interest. Potential group members do not always know their interests in a specific policy area. Moreover, existing groups may be divided or ambivalent about their policy interests. Accordingly, the process by which a group forms around support for a specific set of policy preferences cannot be taken for granted; instead, questions must be asked about why one policy is favored over another.[11]

One of the most powerful factors determining how groups define their policy interests and which alliances they enter is the organization of political institutions. The aspects of the political system that aggregate interests—in particular the party system and Congress—are central in this regard. By channeling the way groups interact in politics and policy making, these institutions greatly affect the possibilities for diverse groups to recognize common interests and construct political alliances and often determine whether such alliances are necessary.

Another factor affecting the way groups define their interests is the way a policy is packaged. Conceptualizing policy as part of a package helps to locate it within the broader framework of political conflict by identifying its relation to past policies and to other items currently on the national agenda. Such identifications can help sway definitions of interest: for example, the identification of the War on Poverty as a black program cut into white support by the late 1960s, when urban riots replaced peaceful marches. Thinking about policy in such relational terms helps make sense of patterns of support and opposition, since a single policy is unlikely to be judged simply on its own terms. Rather, it will be considered as part of a constellation of policies that seem to be related. The way a policy is packaged plays an important role in maintaining the diffuse support or acceptance necessary to protect a policy from challenge.

Politicians seek to affect these processes of group interest identification and alliance formation, but a variety of strong inertial forces limit what they can do. Interests attached to established policies can obstruct later efforts to reorganize policy along new lines.[12] The political terms on which policies are first introduced may also block later efforts to mobilize support. For example, if social support has been initially won on the basis of the effectiveness of the policy, efforts to

[10] On the need to investigate the sources of preferences, see Aaron Wildavsky, "Choosing Preferences by Constructing Institutions: A Cultural Theory of Preference Formation," *American Political Science Review* 81 (March 1987): 3–21; James G. March and Johan P. Olsen, "The New Institutionalism: Organizational Factors in Political Life," *The American Political Science Review* 78 (September 1984): 734–49.

[11] For an argument stressing the role of culture in interest construction, see Wildavsky, "Choosing Preferences by Constructing Institutions."

[12] For a discussion of this process see Gosta Esping-Andersen, *Politics Against Markets* (Princeton, NJ: Princeton University Press, 1986).

sustain support on different grounds, such as citizen's rights, will prove difficult. Likewise, initial decisions about implementation may affect later possibilities for sustaining a supportive alliance. Implementation problems can erode support for policy by giving force to arguments that unwanted side effects outweigh benefits, even if the policy is inherently desirable.

Efforts of politicians to create support for policies are also limited by events they cannot control, such as social movements, economic changes, or international political developments. Such events, often only indirectly connected to a particular policy, can nonetheless have important ramifications for the positioning of that policy. By creating a new context, such events can change the meaning of a policy, linking it with a different set of issues and tying its fate to new forces.

INNOVATING WITHIN BOUNDARIES

During the New Deal, the United States became an international leader in experimenting with new forms of government action to combat unemployment. The version of social Keynesianism articulated by Alvin Hansen, the leading American Keynesian in the 1930s and 1940s, sought to resolve the "apparent conflict between the humanitarian and social aims of the New Deal and the dictates of 'sound economics'" by tying economic stimulation to social spending and enhancing the planning capability of the federal executive.[13]

After a string of political setbacks, however, advocates of Keynesian ideas began to rethink the form their innovation should take. The defeat of the Full Employment bill in 1946, which had embodied many of the ideas of the social Keynesians (especially endorsement of spending to stimulate the economy) and its replacement with the Employment Act of 1946 (which charged the president with monitoring the economy) marked an end to the New Deal experiments with employment policy. In the years after 1946, Keynesian ideas were reworked and disseminated in a prolonged process of social learning. But the Employment Act of 1946 constrained the directions in which the ideas, institutions, and interests relevant to employment policy developed. Networks of expertise emphasizing macroeconomic approaches to employment limited the scope of employment policy. Political actors shunned the task of institution building in a domain that promised little immediate pay-off. And the key groups interested in employment policy—labor and business—elaborated alternative mechanisms rooted in the seniority system to govern employment issues.

As a consequence, employment policy began to exhibit several distinctive features: social and economic policy were sharply divided, policy focused narrowly on the rate of unemployment, and little in the way of institution building oc-

[13] Quoted in Ester Fano, "A 'Wastage of Men': Technological Progress and Unemployment in the United States," *Technology and Culture* 32 (1991): 288.

curred. These characteristics became lasting boundaries in American employment policy during the following decades despite considerable innovation as new initiatives reinforced, rather than altered, these features of policy.

Reworking Keynesian Ideas

To understand why subsequent innovations in employment policy remained within the boundaries set in the late 1940s despite innovation, we must examine how institutions relevant to employment policy helped to shape later possibilities. One of the most important ways they did this was by influencing the development and flow of ideas by encouraging research and thinking about problems along specific lines.

Much of the process by which Keynesian ideas were reworked can be understood by examining the institutional framework created by the Employment Act of 1946. The act did not write Keynesian principles into government activity the way the Full Employment bill had. Instead, systematic attention to economic matters would be assured by an annual presidential report to the Congress on the state of the economy. Presidential capacities to analyze the economy were enhanced by the establishment of a Council of Economic Advisers (CEA), a small body of advisers appointed by the president and mandated to serve him in an advisory capacity only. A companion body in Congress, the Joint Committee on the Economic Report of the President (later the Joint Economic Committee) would ensure congressional consideration of economic conditions.[14]

This set of institutions and mechanisms gave Keynesian ideas a tenuous foothold in the federal government. The most receptive entry point for such ideas was the Council of Economic Advisers, because it had a mandate to monitor the whole economy and because it recruited academic economists, among whom Keynesian ideas were spreading quickly, into short-term government service. But the CEA could only act as an advocate for these ideas if the president appointed Keynesians to the council. Even then, the council would need substantial internal strength to win battles against opposing agencies within the executive branch if discretionary action such as tax cuts were to be accepted. The experience of the CEA under Harry Truman and Dwight Eisenhower demonstrated that it would take time to build such influence.

Truman's appointees to the CEA were sympathetic to Keynesian ideas and made significant contributions to their development.[15] Nevertheless, their impact on policy was small. As a new agency that had to compete with large, well-established departments including the Treasury, the Federal Reserve, and the

---

[14] For a description of the Employment Act, see Stephen Kemp Bailey, *Congress Makes a Law* (New York: Vintage, 1950), chap. 11.

[15] On intellectual contributions see Walter Salant, "Some Intellectual Contributions of the Truman Council of Economic Advisers to Policy-Making." *History of Political Economy* 5 (Spring 1973): 36–49.

Budget Bureau, the CEA had neither the authoritative position nor the institutional strength to control policy. The CEA's early years were spent trying to sort out its status: the relationship among the three members of the council had to be thrashed out, as did the council's relationship to the president.[16]

The other major innovation of the 1946 Employment Act, the Joint Economic Committee (JEC), was more successful in building support for Keynesian ideas. In the latter half of the 1950s, it played a key role in bringing Democrats, organized labor, and economists together around a Keynesian economic agenda.[17] Because the committee's Democratic majority was dominated by liberals, it could function with a set of shared understandings about economic goals and government action that were absent from the Democratic party as a whole. Yet, the JEC was a limited tool for disseminating and organizing broad support for Keynesian ideas. It could and did schedule hearings to publicize particular perspectives, but its lack of legislative function and staffing limitations restricted its reach.

The weakness of public vehicles for advancing and adapting Keynesian ideas allowed private groups to play an important role in reshaping and winning acceptance for Keynesian principles of economic management. The model for this type of activity and a key actor in the development of Keynesian ideas was the Committee for Economic Development (CED). Launched in 1942 by forward-looking businessmen concerned that business be prepared to help shape postwar policy, the CED was a small research organization that brought together social scientists and businessmen.

Even before the war was over, the CED began to rework Keynesianism so that its most objectionable features — the potential for capricious action by the federal government and out-of-control spending policies — were removed. Instead of spending, the CED advocated reliance on automatic stabilizers — variations in government revenues and expenditures that occurred in response to economic conditions without any deliberate government action. If discretionary action were undertaken, tax cuts, not spending, were the method the CED approved.[18]

The committee's organizational form — a small, well-funded group of econo-

---

[16] See William J. Barber, "The United States: Economists in a Pluralistic Polity," *History of Political Economy* 13 (Fall 1981): 513–24.

[17] On the congressional role in economic decision making, see Victor Jones, "The Political Framework of Stabilization Policy" in Max F. Millikan, ed., *Income Stabilization for a Developing Democracy*, 604–10; Alvin Hansen, "The Reports Prepared Under the Employment Act"; and Edwin Nourse, "Taking Root (First Decade of the Employment Act)" in Gerhard Colm, ed., *The Employment Act Past and Future: A Tenth Anniversary Symposium*, National Planning Association Special Report no. 41 (Washington, DC: National Planning Association, 1956), 92–97 and 62–65.

[18] It was work by the CED's Beardsley Ruml that made possible the tax cut route. In the early 1940s, Ruml devised the withholding plan that became the basis for the American tax system, allowing tax policy to be used for stabilization purposes. On Ruml and the CED's policies see Herbert Stein, *The Fiscal Revolution in America* (Chicago: University of Chicago Press, 1969), 220–40; Robert M. Collins, *The Business Response to Keynes* (New York: Columbia University Press, 1981), chaps. 5–6.

mists working with liberal business leaders — was an ideal setting for advocacy and development of innovative economic ideas. This type of forum was far more insulated from outside pressure and from shifts in the political winds than the public institutions responsible for economic policy making. Because it was not immediately answerable to a broad business constituency, the committee could advocate policies that the majority of the business community opposed. Yet, the committee's undisputed expertise in economic matters and its ties to important business interests allowed it to launch a vigorous educational campaign that helped businesses reinterpret their economic policy interests to embrace demand management; at the same time, the CED made Keynesianism more palatable to business.[19]

If in private organizations, Keynesian ideas were being tailored to make them more acceptable to business, within the academic discipline of economics, they were being transformed into technical and theoretical problems. In the academy, economics sought to model itself on the natural sciences with a considerably narrowed agenda that excluded concerns not readily handled by prevailing models of economic behavior.[20] Increasingly, economic questions were severed from the institutional considerations that had been present in the era of institutional economics before the New Deal and in the 1930s and 1940s, when economists worked with government administrators on administrative and political innovations relevant to policy. The dominant economic ideas about employment issues thus contracted and became more technical.

The Kennedy administration's decision in 1962 to support tax cuts as a means to stimulate the economy indicated both the power that ideas could still exercise and the way those ideas had been transformed since the 1940s. Although John Kennedy did not endorse Keynesian ideas in his presidential campaign and opposed cutting taxes, his appointees to the CEA were drawn from the leading liberal Keynesian economists in the country. His choice reflected the available pool of expertise: in 1960 economists who aligned with liberal Democrats were likely to be thoroughly steeped in Keynesian ideas.[21] The selection of CEA members also reflected the emergence of a consensus among liberal economists about the relationship between economic policy, social welfare goals, and expansion of the public sector. While more generous social policies and enhanced public capacities might be attractive, economic policies should not be held captive to such goals.

Led by the energetic and persuasive Walter Heller, the CEA played the role of economic educator and advocate within and outside the Kennedy administration.

[19] Collins, *The Business Response to Keynes*, chap. 6 presents an excellent account of the CED's extensive campaigns to educate business and government officials about its views on economic policy.
[20] Ibid., 6–7; on the economics profession in the United States and the acceptance of Keynesianism, see Marc Trachtenberg, "Keynes Triumphant: A Study in the Social History of Ideas," *Knowledge and Society: Studies in the Sociology of Culture Past and Present* 4 (1983): 17–86.
[21] See the discussion in Stein, *The Fiscal Revolution in America*, 372–84.

The council enjoyed unprecedented influence under Kennedy, because of the substantial access that the president granted it and the encouragement he gave it to publicize its analysis through congressional testimony and public speeches.[22] It was also helped by the strength of the Keynesian consensus within the economics profession at the time. Heller could—and did—call upon a range of prominent economists from prestigious universities to reinforce his message.[23] His efforts ultimately paid off in 1962, when the president accepted the need for fiscal stimulus in the midst of an economic recession.

Tax cuts were the route selected. This choice reflected the doubts about the administration's ability to secure congressional approval for spending increases as well as the council's belief that tax cuts were the more efficient route.[24] The president received further encouragement to go with the tax cut strategy from the business community. The long educational project of the CED had paid off by the early 1960s in widespread business acceptance of federal deficits as a means of economic stimulus, although not all major business organizations supported cutting taxes to create those deficits. But for a president who worried about being branded antibusiness, this broad approval likely helped to tip the balance in favor of the decision to act.[25]

Even so, there was considerable congressional resistance to enacting a tax cut in a period of rising deficits. The intensive educational activities of the CED and later of Kennedy's CEA had swayed opinion at the elite level but had not conquered the realm of popular economic discourse to which Congress was more closely attuned.[26] Not just southern conservatives, but many moderate Democrats, too, worried that cutting taxes would be economically irresponsible. In fact, congressional approval of the tax cut was not assured until after President Lyndon Johnson had agreed to trim his 1965 budget request.[27] During the Ken-

[22] Erwin C. Hargrove and Samuel A. Morley, *The President and the Council of Economic Advisers* (Boulder, CO: Westview, 1984), 174, 181–82; Walter Heller, *New Dimensions of Political Economy* (Cambridge, MA: Harvard University Press, 1966), 26–27.

[23] Hargrove and Morley, *The President and the Council of Economic Advisers*, 202.

[24] Walter Heller, "Memorandum for the President Re: The Economics of the Second Stage Recovery Program," 17 March 1961, President's Office Files, File: Council of Economic Advisers, 1/61–3/61, John F. Kennedy Library, Boston, MA; "Minute on the President's Request for a Review of the Clark Community Facilities Bill and Allied Projects," 15 June 1961, File 6/1/61–6/15/61, Walter Heller Papers, John F. Kennedy Library. "Recap of Issues on Tax Cuts and the Expenditure Alternative," 16 December 1962, File: "Council of Economic Advisers," Record Group 174, National Archives, 3; see also Hargrove and Morley, *The President and the Council of Economic Advisers*, 196, 200–01.

[25] On Kennedy's relationship with business, see Hobart Rowen, *The Free Enterprisers: Kennedy, Johnson and the Business Establishment* (New York: G.P. Putnam, 1964), chap. 1; and Jim F. Heath, *John F. Kennedy and the Business Community* (Chicago: University of Chicago Press, 1969).

[26] A 1962 public opinion poll showed that 72 percent of the general public opposed a tax cut if it meant an increase in the national debt. See Heath, *John F. Kennedy and the Business Community*, 115.

[27] Hargrove and Morley, *The President and the Council of Economic Advisers*, 205–210.

nedy administration, Democratic economists had created a new language with which to justify deficits; by promoting such concepts as the full employment budget they succeeded in blunting the influence of the balanced budget ideology.[28] But continued congressional wariness raised questions about the depth of the nation's conversion.

Working with the institutional framework and the configuration of interests left by the Employment Act of 1946, Democratic politicians and their economic advisers had finally launched an activist fiscal policy twenty-six years after Franklin D. Roosevelt first proposed spending to stimulate the economy. In Andrew Shonfield's words, Americans had been the "intellectual leaders" and the "institutional laggards" in actively deploying Keynesian principles.[29] Only after a reworking of the ideas, the emergence of a strong consensus in the economics profession, and a long process of education did an administration dare to increase the deficit in order to stimulate the economy.

Limits to Innovation and the War on Poverty

During the 1960s, Democratic politicians introduced a range of innovations relevant to employment policy under the umbrella of the War on Poverty. Although these policies extended federal activity in the domain of labor market policy, they did not challenge the framework established two decades earlier. As it developed, the War on Poverty revealed the limits of that framework: efforts to expand the definition of the problem to include underemployment were stymied, the divisions between social and economic policies intensified, and little lasting institutional framework for expanding federal capacities to administer employment programs emerged. The labor market policies of the War on Poverty became remedial programs targeted at the bottom of the labor force — especially at African Americans — and remained largely unconnected to the private labor market.

Officially launched in 1964, the War on Poverty had its origins in a rather vague request several years earlier by President Kennedy to have his CEA look into the problem of poverty. The program his advisers devised over the next two years encompassed a variety of remedial service and job readiness programs that targeted the lowest end of the labor market.[30] Underpinning this strategy was the belief that macroeconomic measures would produce ample opportunities for all who were prepared to take advantage of them. The CEA devoted little attention to the relationship between poverty and underemployment, and directed thinking

---

[28] See the discussion in James Savage, *Balanced Budgets and American Politics* (Ithaca, NY: Cornell University Press, 1988), 175–79.

[29] Andrew Shonfield, *Modern Capitalism* (London: Oxford University Press, 1965), 333.

[30] For general accounts of the initiation of the War on Poverty see Allen J. Matusow, *The Unraveling of America: A History of Liberalism in the 1960s* (New York: Harper and Row, 1984), chap. 4; James L. Sundquist, *Politics and Policy: The Eisenhower, Kennedy and Johnson Years* (Washington, DC: Brookings Institution, 1968), chap. 4.

away from the relationship between poverty and the structure and operation of labor markets, and toward the problems of individuals. As Henry Aaron has noted, "perhaps the most striking characteristic of this view of the poverty cycle is the absence of any mention of the economic system within which it operates."[31]

The most innovative feature of the poverty program was the decentralized and participatory implementation framework. The federal government funneled monies directly to local communities, bypassing state and, initially at least, city authorities. The call for "maximum feasible participation" sparked the mobilization of communities to participate in administering the new programs.[32] Localities set up community action programs that created new participatory structures and oversaw the delivery of the varied services launched under the auspices of the War on Poverty.

The vagueness of the presidential directive and the dearth of academic material about poverty gave the Council of Economic Advisers considerable latitude in setting the terms for the new poverty program. The CEA's conception of the problem that policy should address — unemployment due to insufficient macroeconomic stimulation and lack of job readiness among the poor — dominated thinking about poverty and unemployment throughout the 1960s.

The influence of macroeconomists in setting the terms of the War on Poverty highlights the importance of established networks of expertise. The council's skepticism about manpower policy undermined efforts to enhance significantly the public role in job training during the 1960s. As the War on Poverty developed, efforts from within the Labor Department to expand the definition of the problem to include underemployment faced severe obstacles. Proponents of expanding policy had to fight against established theoretical perspectives as well as elaborate new criteria and categories for collecting and interpreting data. With few allies and mired in institutional rivalries, the advocates of a broader scope for employment policy did not succeed in changing established definitions.[33] Thus, although the organization of American national political institutions generally encourages consideration of a range of ideas in national policy making, the creation of institutionally-linked networks of expertise over time gives advantages to some ideas over others.

By creating a separate realm of poverty policy, the architects of the War on Poverty in the CEA reinforced the divisions between social and economic policy. Guided by a disciplinary perspective that devoted scant attention to institutions, they did little to address problems of institution building or reform. It would have been difficult for the economists on the CEA to influence institutions in any case, since the CEA was a small agency without the capacity to implement policy.

[31] Henry J. Aaron, *Politics and the Professors* (Washington DC: Brookings Institution, 1978), 20.
[32] Daniel P. Moynihan, *Maximum Feasible Misunderstanding: Community Action in the War on Poverty* (New York: Free Press, 1970).
[33] On the efforts to establish a measure for underemployment, see the discussion in *The Manpower Report of the President* (Washington, DC: GPO, 1967, 1968), 73–78 and 34–36 respectively.

The short-term perspective of politicians and particularly the president's need to push policy through quickly also helped account for the problems of institution building in employment policy and for the strengthened divisions between social and economic policy. The decision to create a separate set of agencies to implement the War on Poverty — in the process bypassing such unresponsive federal-state bureaucracies as the United States Employment Service — allowed rapid implementation of new policies, but at the same time it created obstacles for institutionalizing them. The institutional rivalries and political conflict that this route provoked placed poverty policies in constant political jeopardy. The approach embedded in the War on Poverty was far more suited to challenging existing institutions than to creating or reforming enduring institutions needed to administer employment policy.

The incentives of politicians also help account for a distinguishing feature of the War on Poverty — its racial focus. Although the poverty program was officially nonracial, the civil rights movement and later the urban riots created pressures to focus resources on African Americans. Community action agencies were pressed from below to increase the representation of blacks, and the Office of Economic Opportunity overseeing the program in Washington took on black empowerment as central to its mission.[34] And as riots began to shake northern cities, President Lyndon Johnson looked to the poverty program as a way to funnel resources into the affected black communities. The collision of the civil rights revolution with employment policy gave the poverty program a racial identification that shaped its political meaning.

The positions relevant social groups took on employment policy ratified the direction laid out by intellectual networks and political choices. Most striking was the relative lack of interest expressed by business or organized labor in extending employment policy. Although organized labor supported proposals for job training, it never viewed these programs as essential to its own well-being. And, indeed, expansions and redirections of employment policy had little to offer labor or business. Alternative arrangements secured during the New Deal and immediately after the war governed promotion and pay. Most central were the seniority system and collective bargaining; such training as existed was an internal function of the firm.[35] So long as these arrangements worked satisfactorily, neither unions nor business had much incentive to support alternative conceptions of employment policy, especially if they threatened existing arrangements. In

[34] Paul E. Peterson and J. David Greenstone, "Racial Change and Citizen Participation: The Mobilization of Low-Income Communities Through Community Action" in Robert H. Haveman, ed., *A Decade of Federal Anti-Poverty Programs: Achievements, Failures and Lessons* (Madison: University of Wisconsin Press, 1977), 248, 251–56.

[35] See Peter B. Doeringer and Michael J. Piore, *Internal Labor Markets and Manpower Analysis* (Armonk, NY: M.E. Sharpe, 1985).

this way established institutions in the domain of labor relations affected later possibilities for employment policy.

The perspectives of black Americans on employment policy developed in response to a different set of considerations. The limited focus of the War on Poverty and the failure of efforts to extend the reach of employment policy encouraged black leaders to make legal regulation — the affirmative action approach — the centerpiece of a black employment strategy. This approach, together with efforts to preserve the new jobs available to blacks in expanded federal bureaucracies, defined the most promising avenues of employment policy for African Americans.[36] Although black organizations vigorously supported broader approaches to employment when they reached the agenda, after the War on Poverty, they focused on the legal realm, where black employment problems cast as questions of rights stood a better chance of being addressed.[37]

The War on Poverty was an extraordinary episode in American politics and policy, providing a hothouse environment for experimentation. But prominent features of the poverty program as it developed had troubling consequences: the focus on the individual problems of the poor served to direct attention away from the broader economic sources of poverty; suspicion of established agencies, however well-founded, undermined possibilities for reforming existing institutions; and the racial focus of the War on Poverty limited political possibilities for enhancing existing programs or even shifting their focus.

These features of policy in the 1960s were the product of different actors who were pressing against the perceived bounds of politics and established frameworks of policy understanding. The directions in which they pushed, however, were limited by their starting points. Thus, the CEA's approach to employment policy and poverty rested on its assumptions about macroeconomic policy making; the president's enthusiasm for the poverty program stemmed from his efforts to overcome the institutional constraints on presidential policy making.

Once in place, the political meaning and policy possibilities embodied in the War on Poverty were transformed by unexpected intersections with other events. The collision of the War on Poverty with the movement for black political empowerment was central to its political fate. The sequence of policy innovation and the interaction of policy with unpredicted events deeply affected the politics of employment policy. After the War on Poverty, efforts to link poverty to employment problems faced new barriers. Policy had been carved up into two

---

[36] On the War on Poverty and public employment of African Americans, see Michael K. Brown and Steven P. Erie, "Blacks and the Legacy of the Great Society: The Economic and Political Impact of Federal Social Policy," *Public Policy* 29 (Summer 1981): 299–330.

[37] On the development of the affirmative action approach, see Hugh Davis Graham, *The Civil Rights Era: Origins and Development of National Policy* (New York: Oxford University Press, 1990), chap. 9.

realms: a politics of economic policy and a politics of poverty; no broader politics of employment united them.

IDEAS, POLITICS, AND ADMINISTRATION IN AMERICAN POLICY MAKING

During the 1970s, the United States suffered the highest rates of unemployment since the Great Depression; at the same time, the puzzling performance of the economy suggested that traditional Keynesian remedies no longer worked as they once had. In this uncertain setting, three very different perspectives contended to shape American employment policy. The first called for a larger and qualitatively different government role that would involve planning or new forms of business-labor cooperation. A second, adopted by the Carter administration, offered a blend of macroeconomic policy, jobs programs, and wage-price guidelines.

The third perspective, increasingly influential among economists and the new crop of think tanks that emerged in the 1970s, broke with the fundamental premises underlying policy for the past thirty years.[38] It argued that government action hampered the operation of the economy and asserted that the best employment policy was less government activity. Public spending and regulation, the major routes of policy development in the 1970s, were singled out as barriers to creating the economic prosperity that was the best remedy for employment problems.

The election of Ronald Reagan and the policy changes implemented during his first years in office signaled the victory of the pro-market approach. Although policy consistently fell short of the vigorous rhetoric of the Reagan administration — most notably on the subject of deficits — the character of the debate about employment qualitatively shifted during the 1980s. Debates were no longer centered around the question of *how* the government should intervene but *whether* the government should act.

To understand why the pro-market approach prevailed in the 1980s, we must consider the nature of the links that had been forged between ideas, politics, and administration in employment policy since the 1940s. The growing disjuncture among these components essential for innovation presented problems for those who wanted to extend the government role. It meant not only disrupting patterns of political-administrative interaction that had been developing for decades but also finding new ways to reorganize these elements without replicating the political and administrative problems of the past. Proponents of staying the course, on the other hand, had been weakened by a decade of puzzling economic performance. Those arguing for less government faced fewer administrative and political barriers than either alternative perspective.

[38] On the political appeal of supply-side economics see Herbert Stein, *Presidential Economics: The Making of Economic Policy from Roosevelt to Reagan and Beyond* (New York: Simon and Schuster, 1984), chap. 7.

Public Philosophies and Technical Ideas

There are two distinct ways in which the word "ideas" is used in accounts of policy making: the first meaning is captured by the concept of public philosophy.[39] It expresses broad concepts that are tied to values and moral principles and that can be represented in political debate in symbols and rhetoric. A second usage of ideas refers to a more programmatic set of statements about cause-and-effect relationships attached to a method for influencing those relationships. The language expressing programmatic ideas is the technical or professionally-rooted terminology of the expert.[40]

Although the two meanings of ideas shade over into one another and on occasion interlock, it is useful to differentiate between them, because their influence on policy and politics is distinct. Public philosophies play a central role in organizing politics, but their capacity to direct policy is limited; without ties to programmatic ideas their influence is difficult to sustain. Likewise, programmatic ideas are most influential when they are bound to a public philosophy; but these ideas must also forge links with administration. Programmatic ideas developed without reference to administration may be technically strong but are likely to be politically impotent. The influence of ideas on politics is strongest when programmatic ideas, tied to administrative means, are joined with a public philosophy; unhinged, the influence of each becomes difficult to sustain.

In American employment policy, much of the period from the 1940s to 1980 was characterized by a dissociation of programmatic ideas and public philosophy. The social Keynesianism championed by Alvin Hansen had joined a set of programmatic, administratively-rooted ideas with a broader vision about politics, most fully articulated by Roosevelt's 1944 Economic Bill of Rights. After its failure, ideas as public philosophy became increasingly disjointed from the technical policy ideas, and these ideas became increasingly divorced from administration. The growing distance of these two types of ideas and their separation from administration impoverished both.

Because programmatic ideas increasingly developed without political or administrative moorings, it became difficult for them to influence policy in any regular way. Although the expression of these ideas grew ever more sophisticated, their ability to chart new policy directions involving government action was narrowing. Research relevant to employment policy emphasized the movement of aggregate measures and microeconomic models, leaving untouched a middle ground concerned with sectors and institutions that the government was grappling to ad-

[39] See the discussion of public philosophy in Samuel H. Beer, "In Search of a New Public Philosophy" in Anthony King, ed., *The New American Political System* (Washington, DC: American Enterprise Institute, 1978), 5–44.

[40] Ideas of this sort are often the product of social research. See Carol H. Weiss, "Improving the Linkage Between Social Research and Public Policy" in Laurence E. Lynn, Jr., ed., *Knowledge and Policy: The Uncertain Connection* (Washington, DC: National Academy of Sciences, 1978), 23–81.

dress.[41] In the absence of sufficient applicable research, purely political criteria held sway. This was particularly evident in the 1970s in the federal responses to growing unemployment and inflation, ranging from wage-price guidelines to pork barrel-style public service employment.

The dissociation of the two kinds of ideas made public philosophy increasingly hollow. During the 1960s and 1970s, rhetorical appeals grew in importance, but they were unanchored in programmatic content. The War on Poverty, for example, was declared with little effort to assemble support based on a rationale for the specific policies to be undertaken.[42] The difficulty in matching politics and programmatic ideas lay behind the exhaustion of New Deal liberalism and the crisis in public philosophy that characterized the 1970s.[43] Yet, as party ties attenuated, rhetoric and symbols bore a greater burden for organizing electoral politics.

Much of Ronald Reagan's early political success can be attributed to the way he fused a bold and appealing rhetoric to a set of programmatic ideas about how the economy worked. Although widely rejected by economists, supply-side economics resonated with mainstream economists' growing disillusion with government action. Most importantly, however, supply-side economics appeared plausible, in part because it was clearly "doable" within the context of American politics and institutions. But the merging of programmatic ideas and public philosophy was more apparent than real for most policy areas during the Reagan administration. As the decade progressed, the disjuncture between rhetoric and government action on the economy grew. While the rhetoric remained firmly pro-market, policy was actually a disjointed blend of initiatives.[44] In this sense, the Reagan administration did not so much resolve as elide the problems of uniting philosophy with programmatic ideas about the economy.

The Political Problem of Positive Government

The experience of employment policy suggests that the development, access, and plausibility of ideas calling for new kinds of government capacities are handicapped by the difficulty of uniting politics, ideas, and administration in the United States.

Immediately after World War II, some supporters of a broad, more encompassing employment policy worried about precisely this problem. The political scientist E.E. Schattschneider argued that a national employment policy would

[41] See the strongly worded critique of John T. Dunlop, "Policy Decisions and Research in Economics and Industrial Relations," *Industrial and Labor Relations Review* 30 (April 1977): 275–82.

[42] See Tulis, *The Rhetorical Presidency*, 165.

[43] See Beer, "In Search of a New Public Philosophy."

[44] See Emma Rothschild, "The Real Reagan Economy," *The New York Review of Books*, 30 June 1988, 46–54; See also Benjamin M. Friedman, *Day of Reckoning: The Consequences of American Economic Policy Under Reagan and After* (New York: Random House, 1988).

be impossible without "responsible" programmatic parties. He urged that parties establish permanent research organizations that could fuse policy and politics in what he called "political planning." Stressing the inherently political nature of devising and mobilizing policy ideas, he warned that "parties simply cannot afford to rely on non-party research and publicity to do the job."[45]

Yet that is just what presidents and parties had to do in the United States. It meant that connections between politics, administration, and policy were forged in piecemeal and sporadic ways when cooperation among technical experts, interests, and government agencies could be effected or when the president threw the weight of his office behind policy innovation. In some policy areas, including social security, this union was unproblematic; in others such as medical care, it experienced partial success.

In employment policy, by contrast, the most important private interests — business and labor — had little interest in extending policy; the dominant experts paid little attention to administrative issues; and the relevant government agencies were either hostile or weak. Moreover, the president had little political interest in backing employment policy innovation so long as America remained economically strong and Keynesian policy appeared sufficient to manage unemployment. In this context, the scope of employment policy remained limited and proposals for extending it contested. Nothing in the political, intellectual, or administrative history of employment policy provided a foothold for reorienting the government's role during the 1970s, when it became clear that the older approach had broken down.

Where the difficulties of uniting politics, administration, and ideas are less severe, policies may be enacted more easily. The successes of deregulation and tax reform in the 1980s provide a telling counterexample of employment policy: in neither of these cases did ideas about reform have to contend with arguments about administrative feasibility or with opposition to building new government capacities.[46] In this context, technical ideas were able to influence policy more easily and were able to benefit from their attachment to an appealing rhetoric.

A number of analysts have portrayed the recent successes of tax reform and deregulation as evidence of the importance of ideas in policy making.[47] In each case, a strong consensus among experts allowed them to shape the terms of the policy debate and exert influence on the outcome. But what each of these instances of reform also has in common — and shares with the pro-market reforms in

---

[45] E. E. Schattschneider, "Party Government and Employment Policy," *American Political Science Review* 39 (December 1945): 1154.

[46] On tax policy see David R. Beam, Timothy J. Conlan, and Margaret T. Wrightson, "Solving the Riddle of Tax Reform: Party Competition and the Politics of Ideas," *Political Science Quarterly* 105 (Summer 1990): 193–217; on deregulation see Martha Derthick and Paul J. Quirk, *The Politics of Deregulation* (Washington, DC: Brookings Institution, 1985).

[47] See Beam, Conlan, and Wrightson, "Solving the Riddle of Tax Reform"; and Derthick and Quirk, *Politics of Deregulation*, esp. chap. 7.

employment policy as well — is administrative simplicity. Ideas that create new forms of government activity face a more difficult task. Although they might also fashion an appealing rhetoric and find political support for such concepts as fairness or opportunity, their rhetorical claims remain unconvincing; support is ephemeral if government's capacity to act is widely doubted. When there is a history of administrative failure, as in the case of employment policy, the rhetoric becomes even less likely to influence policy.

Political Possibilities and Future Employment Policy ·

What are the possibilities that American policy makers and politicians can construct an alternative approach to employment issues in the 1990s, when transformations in the international economic system and American competitiveness have become overriding concerns in public debate? I conclude by considering how new policy sequences may be launched and by sketching the features of an employment policy that combines ideas, politics, and administration in politically sustainable forms.

The start of a new policy sequence is most visible when there is a "big bang" of innovation. Yet the big bang analogy is somewhat misleading. It underestimates changes that have already prepared the way for such shifts in policy, and it overstates the degree to which policy is transformed afterwards. In fact, small changes transform policy, even in a political system in which policy shifts seem to occur all at once. Small changes not only prepare the ground for major shifts, they may also chart the direction of those transformations by providing working examples of new policy and creating new conceptions about what is possible and desirable.

During the 1980s, alterations to the economic and social environment created the potential for making small changes in employment policy that could point the way toward a fundamental reorientation in scope and mission. Support for such revitalized employment policies could be won by linking these policies with problems that have attracted broad public attention, including concern about American competitiveness, dissatisfaction with public education, and the worries about a growing underclass.[48]

The growing concern among business leaders about the quality of the American labor force and its impact on American competitiveness creates possibilities for building support for a broader, more encompassing labor market policy.[49] But

[48] See the argument of Albert O. Hirschman that "neglected" policy problems can be more easily addressed if they are attached to "privileged" policy problems that are the focus of broad public concern. Albert O. Hirschman, "Policymaking and Policy Analysis in Latin America — A Return Journey," *Essays in Trespassing: Economics to Politics and Beyond* (Cambridge, England: Cambridge University Press, 1981), 150–52.

[49] See Ray Marshall, *Unheard Voices: Labor and Economic Policy in a Competitive World* (New York: Basic Books, 1987).

to attract employer interest, employment policy would have to build much stronger ties to the private sector, attending more closely to the needs of the private economy. This does not mean, however, that policy need blindly follow the dictates of business; government could influence business goals relevant to employment policy by creating incentives to adopt some strategies rather than others. The availability of highly skilled workers, for example, may prompt movement away from a competitive strategy based on low-wage labor.

Widespread dissatisfaction with American public education provides another potential opening for expanding employment policy. The problem of school dropouts, the growth of youth unemployment, and the difficulty of making the transition from school to work all suggest the need for rethinking the institutional links between school and the labor market. Apprenticeship programs, which have attracted increasing attention, are only one of the ways in which public schools could contribute to an enhanced labor market policy. As preeminent community institutions, schools could also serve as centers of information about the labor market and programs of adult education.[50]

Finally, concern about the emergence of an American underclass has drawn attention to the links between economic change and community stability. The economic dislocations of the 1980s have highlighted the importance of local institutions in cushioning the effects of economic transitions.[51] This experience suggests the need for bottom-up community organizing strategies as an essential component of employment policy. Local organizations including community development corporations, churches, and schools can all be enlisted to increase the effectiveness and extend the reach of labor market policies.

In the context of a set of broader employment policies, such mobilization could avoid being limited by the institutional isolation that characterized organizing during the War on Poverty. A community organizing strategy builds on distinctive strengths and weaknesses of American federalism, which lacks a strong central bureaucracy but features a strong tradition of local activism. The growth of state-level administrative capacities during the 1980s together with the community-based organizations created during the 1960s may prove helpful in sustaining such local activism.[52]

These potential impulses for revitalizing employment policy suggest an approach different from the one that dominated policy in the past. They indicate the need for building stronger ties between public and private action, creating a

---

[50] For an argument in favor of creating a broad apprenticeship program in the United States, see Robert I. Lerman and Hillard Pouncy, "The Compelling Case for Youth Apprenticeships," *The Public Interest* 1001 (Fall 1990): 62–77.

[51] See William Julius Wilson, *The Truly Disadvantaged: The Inner City, the Underclass and Public Policy* (Chicago: University of Chicago Press, 1987).

[52] On the growth of state-level capacities during the 1980s, see David Osborne, *Laboratories of Democracy* (Boston: Harvard Business School Press, 1988); and R. Scott Fosler, *The New Economic Role of American States: Strategies in a Competitive World Economy* (New York: Oxford University Press, 1988).

broader scope for policy, and devoting greater attention to the institutional links that join policy areas. The resulting policy would contribute to reconciling the social and economic objectives of employment policy and would begin to address the employment needs of minorities without explicit targeting.

Reliance on macropolicy would be replaced by greater attention to the specific relationships and institutions that undergird the economy. Learning how and where the government might affect those relationships in order to influence the quantity and quality of employment is thus central to redesigning policy. Labor market policy would be expanded to serve different levels of the labor market, thereby losing its remedial character. The task of labor market policy would be more than simply addressing unemployment, its primary charge in the past. Problems of relieving bottlenecks, upgrading skills, and enhancing geographic mobility would all fall into the domain of labor market policy.[53]

This conception of employment policy calls on government to play a different role than it has in the past. It emphasizes the need of government to act as a catalyst for private activity rather than simply as a regulator or director of a separate public realm.[54] This approach channels market trends toward public goals rather than compensating for the market as in the 1960s and 1970s, or capitulating to it as in the 1980s. Increasing this type of intervention would actually strengthen the political appeal of regulatory and public-sector approaches, such as affirmative action and public employment programs; a more balanced blend of approaches would both reduce the pressure on such policies to carry the burden alone and help mitigate their status as political flashpoints. In this way, employment policy that incorporated a variety of approaches could enhance the political acceptability of policies contested during the 1960s and 1970s by changing the context within which they are evaluated.

These are some of the most promising possibilities for assembling new packages of policy: by remaking institutional links and bringing interests together in different ways, they provide the raw material for launching a new employment policy sequence.

---

[53] For an argument in favor of an employment policy organized along these lines, see Paul Osterman, *Employment Futures: Reorganization, Dislocation, and Public Policy* (New York: Oxford University Press, 1988); another argument for a broader approach to employment policy is made by Isabel Sawhill, "Rethinking Employment Policy" in D. Lee Bawden and Felicity Skidmore, eds., *Rethinking Employment Policy* (Washington, DC: Urban Institute Press, 1989), 9–36.

[54] This formulation is John T. Dunlop's. See his essay "Involving Government as a Catalyst, Not as Regulator" in William Kilberg, ed., *The Dislocated Worker, Preparing America's Workforce* (Washington, DC: Seven Locks Press, 1983), 14–17.

Sheltering the Homeless in New York City: Expansion in an Era of Government Contraction

DONNA WILSON KIRCHHEIMER

In the United States, expansion of public social functions was not expected in the 1980s. The growth trend in national social spending contracted after the Reagan administration's Omnibus Budget Reconciliation Act of 1981, which repealed certain benefits and capped the allocations for new block grants. National social expenditure later continued to increase, but the growth was principally in programs that were previously legislated and was rarely due to authorization of new social functions.

Research literature suggested it was unlikely that cities would surge forward independently to make a large and rapid addition of a social function. Studies of municipal expenditure change found that U.S. cities were historically preoccupied with their legal obligations to balance their budgets and made only conservative increments at the margin.[1] Research on urban politics asserted that the interest of a city's leadership in promoting economic activity created a bias against redistributive policies for low-income residents.[2] Moreover, when national policy ex-

---

[1] John P. Crecine, *Government Problem-Solving* (Chicago: Rand McNally, 1969).
[2] Paul E. Peterson, *City Limits* (Chicago: University of Chicago Press, 1981).

DONNA WILSON KIRCHHEIMER is associate professor of political science at the City University of New York, Lehman College. She has had over twenty years of experience in social policy development, including serving as deputy administrator for policy development in the New York City Human Resources Administration.

panded social functions historically, research characterized subnational implementation as tragic theatre in which gleaming national hopes went astray.[3]

Despite such expectations, some new social functions were assigned to U.S. government and to subnational governments during 1978–1988. Large new social responsibilities were, however, few in number, and they invite explanation. This analysis examines a significant function that the U.S. government and many state, city, and county governments (as well as thousands of private nonprofit organizations) did initiate—the financing, regulation, and provision of emergency shelter for people who were homeless.

This analysis explores the proximate political conditions that may help to explain the magnitude and speed of growth of emergency shelters at the subnational level. On the assumption that a confluence of direct political factors would be necessary to account for large expansion, the analysis tests a series of hypotheses. These are: bureaucratic momentum, the political opportunity structure, the political culture, the policy regime, the political interest structure, media agenda, and authoritative bargaining arenas. To evaluate these multiple factors, the analysis focuses on a single site. It draws on the case of emergency shelter for the homeless in New York City during 1978–1988. New York City was a harbinger of the national increase in homeless people and of expansion of emergency shelters in other cities.

EMERGENCY SHELTERS IN NEW YORK CITY

The growth in New York City expenditures for emergency shelters was sudden and large, not at all the type of incremental creep that was thought to typify urban expenditure change. From 1978 to 1985, the city's annual spending increased from $8 million to over $100 million for operating and capital improvements for shelter services for homeless single men and women. Additionally, new city budget allocation for emergency shelter for homeless families started after 1982 and increased to $100 million by 1985.

New York City government had on a small scale provided temporary shelter to the homeless for about a century, but significant changes during 1978–1988 transformed it into a new function. First, during that period, the average nightly census exceeded 2,000 persons for the first time since the Depression. In the Depression, the municipal lodging house overflowed until the Works Progress Administration supported new annexes for almost 10,000 people nightly in 1936. A half century later, the nightly census boomed again and reached over 10,000 single men and women in winter 1986–1987. Second, use of shelters climbed through the 1980s, while peak Depression use dropped after 1936 to only 300 per night in World War II. Third, homeless families appeared in large numbers; they quintupled from under

---

[3] Jeffrey L. Pressman and Aaron B. Wildavsky, *Implementation*, 3d ed. (Berkeley: University of California Press, 1984).

1,000 per night before 1982 to about 5,000 (including 12,000 children) in 1987. Fourth, the period of stay elongated in the 1980s. Families remained in shelters an average of thirteen months in 1986. Many single men and women were repeat users, although many shelters prohibited return to the same bed every night. Fifth, the number of shelters mushroomed. Shelters for single men and women increased from three in 1978 to eighteen in 1985. Also, there were few hotels and residential centers for homeless families before 1982, but in 1983 there were more than fifty. Sixth, the content of service changed. Specialized shelters opened for subpopulations with different needs, such as pregnant women, women with infants, families, youth, the elderly, veterans, and substance abusers. Also, a new kind of shelter was created with facilities (such as private rooms for families, and refrigerators) that were intended for stays of several months. These were designed to be "transitional shelters," a form of accommodation intermediate between barracks-style shelters for single nights and permanent housing. Seventh, shelters in the 1980s could no longer turn people away when they were full, and the city government became legally obligated to provide a bed to every person who requested one.[4]

Ironically, the principal source of revenue for expanding emergency shelter for families was a federal grant hit by the Reagan retrenchment, Aid to Families with Dependent Children (AFDC).[5] Although the cuts curtailed a number of AFDC's benefits (such as day care for children and work expenses), its program of Emergency Assistance to Families (EAF) was not affected. New York State opted to use EAF for emergency shelter and extended the emergency period beyond the statutory allowance for federal reimbursement. For homeless individuals, also, New York took initiative in expanding use of federal funding sources, such as Veteran's Assistance, Social Security Disability Insurance, and the Supplemental Security Income program. New York's initiative to diversify shelter costs into federal funding streams indicated that the drive for expansion was state and local, and not top-down implementation of national policy.

Expansion of shelters came in response to a deterioration in living conditions that was visible to the city's general population. Homeless people were an everyday sight because of the magnitude of outdoor sleeping, its location in downtown and well-to-do areas, and the intrusiveness of begging. The problem spread over time. Single homeless men increased in the late 1970s, and then single women. After 1982, homeless families began to seek emergency shelter. The inequalities in living conditions were self-evident and represented deterioration below the historical threshold of popular acceptance. Thousands of beggars were able to subsist on donations from passers-by.

In summary, in the 1980s New York City government invested in a vast network

---

[4] New York City Human Resources Administration, *New York City Plan for Homeless Adults* (New York: Human Resources Administration, 1984); New York City Mayor's Office of Operations, *Mayor's Management Report* (New York: Citybooks, 1987).

[5] John L. Palmer and Isabel V. Sawhill, eds., *The Reagan Experiment* (Washington, D.C.: The Urban Institute, 1982).

of emergency shelters that were designed for short-term use. The shelter response was a minimal, emergency, protective function that mirrored the crisis definition of the problem. By the end of the decade, this system was embedded in the city's housing market, and temporary shelter for the homeless was institutionalized as a large new public social function. It became likely that only expansion of another public function, permanent housing for low-income renters, would diminish the scale of emergency shelter in the 1990s. The following sections test the series of direct political factors that hypothetically could have influenced expansion of public resources to shelter the homeless in New York City.

Bureaucratic Momentum

The push of bureaucratic momentum is said to impel a public organization to expand its domain. Internal forces are described as a "ghost within the machine," which generates new policy realms and new costs.[6] Bureaucrats are said to have self-interests like everyone else that propel them to ever expand their spheres of activity.[7] Bureaucratic factors can be linked to forces outside an agency through professional organizations, which are said to be driven by similar compulsions to dominate new terrain.[8]

Was bureaucratic empire-building a force in the New York City administration that impelled expansion of public shelters? City government did reject its prior practice of turning people away when emergency facilities were full, and its new policy offered shelter of some type to all persons upon request.[9] This policy reversal was, however, not self-initiated but came in response to litigation, which triggered higher institutional authority. Decisions to open new shelters were the mayor's, and hiring authority was controlled by the city's Office of Management and Budget, the deputy mayor, and the mayor, who were preoccupied with budget control. Decisions on geographic locations were mayoral. Opposition from neighborhoods was a well-recognized force that spawned the slogan "NIMBY," "Not in My Backyard!" Because political risk was high, mayoral control was critical to prevent, appease, and stonewall the opposition. Mayoral agencies were barraged by consumer demand and were preoccupied with the mammoth challenge of keeping up with the crisis in a responsive, not aggressive, fashion.

In sum, expansion of the shelter function was not automatic, and it was not self-propelled by a bureaucratic juggernaut. The mayor was not overwhelmed by the functional power of autonomous bureaucracies. City managers were fully cognizant of their obligations to provide a floor of social protection in the face of

[6] Richard Rose and Guy Peters, *Can Government Go Bankrupt?* (New York: Basic Books, 1978).

[7] Thomas E. Borcherding, *Budgets and Bureaucrats: The Source of Government Growth* (Durham, N.C.: Duke University Press, 1977).

[8] Samuel H. Beer, "Political Overload and Federalism," *Polity* 10 (Fall 1977): 5-17.

[9] Thomas J. Main argued that New York City's shelter policy itself contributed to the homeless family problem. See "The Homeless Families of New York," *Public Interest* 85 (Fall 1986): 3-?

emergency, but they did not seek out or exploit opportunities for bureaucratic aggrandizement and did not open shelters solely of their own volition.

Political Opportunity Structure

Opportunity for action by the U.S. national government has been associated with the opening of policy windows. Empirical examples include a change in administration that introduces a newly elected official with a fresh electoral mandate, a redistribution of congressional seats that shifts voting coalitions, a national mood shift, or a crisis or focusing event such as a natural disaster or major accident.[10] In New York City, however, none of the classic policy windows occurred. There was no new mayor who perceived his electoral mandate to be helping the poor. There was no new voting block in state or city legislatures. There was no natural disaster or accident, such as an earthquake or airplane crash. Nor was there any other major socioeconomic dislocation such as a war or mass migration. National social policy was retrenchment; and national, state, and local governments were preoccupied with cutback.

While the crisis was not a natural disaster or accident, the cumulative impact of the visibly homeless can be compared to an objective event to which the public reacts directly. The intrusive and prolonged image of homeless people was a focusing event, when a shared sense of crisis can lead to a widespread expectation that something be done, and people may tend to be receptive to remedial action by government. In this sense, the opportunity structure contributed to a potentially receptive environment that indirectly helped to make government action politically feasible. Mass temporary shelter was not, however, an old policy idea whose time had come; it developed as an "acute innovation"[11] that was desirable solely in crisis.

Political Culture

New York City has historically been called a "social welfare city" because of its "cosmopolitan liberalism," which supported government action to protect the less fortunate through redistribution of wealth and resources.[12] When the number of homeless people soared during 1978–1988, however, the mayor was not an exponent of liberal political culture. Mayor Edward Koch's inaugural speech in 1978

---

[10] John W. Kingdon, *Agendas, Alternatives, and Public Policies* (Boston: Little, Brown, 1984).

[11] Nelson Polsby, *Political Innovation in America* (New Haven: Yale University Press, 1984).

[12] Bernard R. Gifford, "New York City and Cosmopolitan Liberalism," *Political Science Quarterly* 93 (Winter 1978–79): 559–584. The present analysis understands political culture to be the discourse over central values concerning the legitimacy and appropriate roles of government. The argument is taken to be between egalitarian beliefs, which call for use of government to redistribute economic resources to the poor, and individualistic beliefs, which oppose redistribution by government (although public action may be supported for other purposes). The concept of political culture lacks a shared operational definition, but its appeal to scholars is recurrent, and its different meanings continue to

blamed the "monumental problems" that New York City faced on its history as a "lifeboat for the homeless." Koch's social policies were fiscally conservative and were supported by a majority of the voting population. The NIMBY opposition was sometimes spearheaded by local elected politicians, and it charged a political price for opening shelters. Nevertheless, cosmopolitan liberalism was not quashed in the 1980s. Egalitarian beliefs motivated the policy community that mobilized against the mayor and contributed to the size and strength of advocacy by social welfare, public law, and religious groups on behalf of the homeless.

New York City's political culture was not a unitary belief system. Expansion of the shelters resulted from conflict between opposing beliefs within the political culture. Egalitarian values supporting redistributive policy were advanced mainly by opponents to the mayor, while the mayor himself represented fiscal conservatism on social issues. Cosmopolitan liberalism within the political culture had, therefore, only an indirect influence that helped to shape the policy-making context to be partially receptive. Political culture was not a direct or immediate cause of shelter expansion, nor did it have a unitary or singular effect.

The Policy Regime

Regime theory calls attention to the dominant coalition of interests in a city and to the political leadership's connection to the economic and political environment. It treats a policy agenda as the product of struggle over the political arrangements in a city's governing coalition.[13] It thus connects policy choices to the interests of a coalition of actors who have substantial concerns. Public officials face cross-pressure from multiple imperatives that compel them to balance conflicting structural interests.[14] Current research on urban development argues that politics matters. Although emphasis lies on the economic and political context, it accords a central role to political choice and leadership. Clarence Stone notes: "The common good is something that doesn't just happen. It is something that must be brought into being, albeit imperfectly, by a set of political actors."[15]

How can the concept of a policy regime help to explain expansion of a social

---

provoke argument. See for example, Aaron Wildavsky, "Choosing Preferences by Constructing Institutions: A Cultural Theory of Preference Formation," *American Political Science Review* 81 (March 1987): 3–22; and David D. Laitin and Aaron Wildavsky, "Controversies: Political Culture and Political Preferences," *American Political Science Review* 82 (June 1988): 589–596; Gabriel Almond and Sidney Verba, eds., *The Civic Culture Revisited* (Boston: Little, Brown, 1980); John Kincaid, ed., *Political Culture, Public Policy, and the American States* (Philadelphia: Institute for the Study of Human Issues, 1982); Raymond Wolfinger and John Osgood Field, "Political Ethos and the Structure of City Government," *American Political Science Review* 60 (June 1966): 306–326.

[13] Stephen L. Elkin, *City and Regime in the American Republic* (Chicago: University of Chicago Press, 1987).

[14] Martin Shefter, *Political Crisis/Fiscal Crisis* (New York: Basic Books, 1985).

[15] Clarence N. Stone, "The Study of the Politics of Urban Development" in Stone and Heywood T. Sanders, eds., *The Politics of Urban Development* (Lawrence: University Press of Kansas, 1987), 10.

function in New York City? The empirical questions are to identify the coalition of interests that municipal leadership represents, to examine its links to the economic and political context, and to assess its impact on expansion of the shelter function. In New York City during 1978–1988, the dominant coalition was not a liberal one, and it had not incorporated minority groups.[16] Mayor Koch's voting block was not among the poor, the minorities, or the liberals, but among the white working-class and middle-class populations and the party machines in the outer boroughs. His constituency included real estate, developer, business, and financial interests that had promoted redevelopment since the late 1960s. Renovation and gentrification had displaced residents from flophouses and single-room-occupancy hotels; landlords had abandoned apartment buildings for more prosperous investments, leading to displacement of thousands of poor households. Koch's coalition thus tended to represent interests that favored economic redevelopment that had contributed to displacement and to underrepresent the poor and mostly minority people who had to seek emergency shelter.

The economic context of political leadership buttressed the preferences of the mayoral coalition for a conservative social policy. Because of the city's fiscal crisis and budget deficit, and the national cuts in intergovernmental grants in 1981, municipal priorities concentrated on cost control and reducing personnel positions. Competition for resources was high, and the city's budget process required that any new expenditure be justified on the basis of its potential to generate new revenues, its promise to save future costs, or its compliance with federal or state legislative, executive, or judicial orders.

Nevertheless, New York City was not Calcutta. A significant historical resource floor did exist, and policy response was not precluded. Several potential barriers that could have blocked revenue sources were weak in the 1980s. For example, there was no unusual inflation, nor a major taxpayers' revolt, nor an acute fiscal crisis, and economic recovery was rebuilding tax resources. The city achieved a balanced budget by 1981; short-term borrowing, net city debt, and debt service as a percent of total expenditures were by then below 1976–1977 levels.[17] Nevertheless, the municipal budget remained austere compared to its historical rates of increase, and in 1981 the Omnibus Budget Reconciliation Act cut millions of federal dollars. The mayor's ability to replace some, but far from all, of the federal cuts in social programs indicated that by 1981 there was some room for mayoral discretion to make modest increments for political needs.

Because the mayor's electoral coalition was fiscally conservative on social issues, he was under pressure to justify increased spending for shelters. He criticized the underfunding of affordable permanent housing by the state and national governments and took an entrepreneurial initiative to expand use of federal programs. Koch also blamed the homeless themselves for swelling shelter requests. He as-

[16] John Mollenkopf, "New York: The Great Anomaly," *PS* 19 (Summer 1986): 591–598.
[17] New York City, Office of the Comptroller, *Comparative Analysis of New York City's Financial and Economic Indicators, Fiscal Year 1982* (New York: Citybooks, 1983).

sailed religious organizations for the paucity of shelters, and his criticism motivated churches and synagogues to add more beds. Broadening private suppliers and accusations of shirking municipal obligations enabled the mayor to share the political liability for expanding shelter costs.[18] Mayoral policy on the homeless was reluctant; the first mayoral plan for family shelters predicted a decrease in use of family shelters, the course of least political risk.

In summary, growth of the shelter function did not result from voluntary action by the city's dominant coalition of interests. The mayor's electoral coalition remained fiscally conservative on redistributive policy, and it did not incorporate the interests of shelter beneficiaries who were largely poor and minority. 1978–1988 was a period of fiscal constraint and not relative abundance, and sheer wealth did not spur public social spending. Regime theory helps to explain the pattern of conflict and its connection to economic and political interests. This case does illustrate how politics matters. Expansion of this function was neither automatic nor neutral, but was conflictual and political.

OUTSIDE PULL FACTORS

Were there more proximate political factors in the environment of city government that directly affected functional expansion? This section assesses the effects of the political interest structure, the media agenda, and authoritative bargaining arenas.

Political Interest Structure

The structure of expressed political interests has been typed as subgovernments and as issue networks. The main threads of difference are the degree of cohesion and collusion among the participants; their degree of like-mindedness; the intensity of interest or commitment they feel; their ability to assert autonomy; their definitions of success; and their orientation toward achieving results. What was the structure of interests in New York City that might have exerted an outside pulling force on governmental decision makers that induced them to expand the shelter function?

First, subgovernments have been classically configured as iron triangles composed of interest groups, congressional committees, and federal administrators.[19] The label denotes their tight bonds, autonomy, shared interests that are deeply felt, and effectiveness in obtaining public benefits for their constituencies. Was there in New York City a structure of interests resembling an iron triangle on the homeless issue?

Provider interests can be strong forces for expanding public benefits, as when

---

[18] *New York Times*, 20 January 1983.
[19] Harold Seidman, *Politics, Position, and Power*, 2d ed. (New York: Oxford University Press, 1975).

defense industries lobby for military contracts. In New York City, however, profit-oriented providers of permanent housing were increasingly disinterested in welfare consumers. Owners of private apartment buildings and single-room-occupancy hotels were leaving the low-rent market, and developers aimed to attract higher-income tenants. Moreover public administrators did not form iron bonds with committees in the city's legislative bodies.

Also, the beneficiary population was a weak political force. The homeless were the poorest people in New York City and had no financial resources for political mobilization. The poor did not have an organizational base from which to press for their own needs. They tended to be inactive in electoral politics, and their support was not heavily courted by elected officials. The homeless also did not exert their force of numbers through organized protests or street demonstrations, which have been important to New York City's day care and senior citizen movements. About a third of homeless single persons were handicapped by major mental disabilities, and many suffered from substance abuse. Most heads of homeless families were young single women who had less than a twelfth grade education and less than a year of work experience, and they were preoccupied with caring for small children in unstable residences from which they had to move almost every other year. The main resource that the homeless possessed was moving their own bodies. By sleeping and begging in the streets and public places, their needs caught the public eye and activated the city's media and social welfare communities. In sum, there was no evidence of an iron triangle.

Second, was an issue network influential in pulling an expansion of public functions out of city government? Issue networks, in Hugh Heclo's definition, are loose associations of disinterested "journeymen" whose ties are for communication and ad hoc coordination.[20] In New York City, experts on the homeless issue did spring up in public bureaucracies, universities, and private nonprofit organizations, and their ties were open and informal. Many could be described as journeymen who were not personally identified with controversial opinions and were not independent political actors. Technicians contributed information on homelessness, such as studies of socioeconomic characteristics and shelter utilization; but they did not bring a direct or independent force for expansion to bear on government decision makers. Technicians in the public bureaucracy aided the top appointed officials who were their clients to manage the crisis according to mayoral policy.

If neither iron triangles nor issue networks of technicians impelled expansion, was there no pulling force from any political interest structure? This case suggests a hybrid type, in the middle of the continuum between iron triangles and issue networks, which can be called a "policy community."[21] A policy community

[20] Hugh Heclo, "Issue Networks and the Executive Establishment" in Anthony King, ed., *The New American Political System* (Washington, D.C.: American Enterprise Institute, 1978).

[21] Alice Sardell, *The U.S. Experiment in Social Medicine: The Community Health Center Program* (Pittsburgh: University of Pittsburgh Press, 1988), 206–208.

resembles an iron triangle in that its participants share a commitment to a particular policy direction. However, like an issue network, it has loose internal ties and does not exert autonomous power.

How can the activities of a policy community help to explain expansion of shelters for the homeless? The New York City environment was a likely breeding ground for a new policy community because of its high and conflictual level of political organization and its group activity that historically had mobilized on social issues.[22] Within this milieu, a new policy community sprang up to specialize on the issue of homelessness. It was an identifiable community of shared values, which consciously challenged the existing institutional structure. It consisted of people who were committed social advocates, not neutral technicians, and they were not based in the city bureaucracy. The internal structure of this policy community was loose and open, and contacts were ad hoc and informal. Many members knew each other, exchanged information, shared strategies, and at times coordinated particular actions.

The political impact of this policy community was diverse. The groups publicized the needs of the homeless before the city, state, and national executive and legislative branches. They evaluated the quality of public shelter services and monitored enforcement of governmental standards. They developed proposals for emergency and transitional shelters and advocated models for replication. Many groups were service providers who ran overnight shelters, drop-in centers, soup kitchens, and food pantries, and some tried to organize homeless people on their own behalf. They recruited thousands of volunteers who were an important resource base for donated labor and transmission of community education. The groups informed the public about the homeless and attracted attention particularly from religious organizations, student populations, and the media. Two channels of influence were most important, educating the media and triggering the authoritative apparatus of the state courts.

The policy community had a varied resource base. Many of the groups were nonprofit social welfare organizations whose board members included the social and economic elites of the city. Advocates more recent to the scene dubbed them a "charitable industrial complex." Some organizations, including religious federations, had succeeded in obtaining public and private support for human services for a century, and some had ties to business corporations. These groups were joined by prominent individuals from the professions, such as two co-chairs of a new watchdog group, the Emergency Alliance for Homeless Families and Children, who were former deans of two graduate schools of social work and former commissioners in past mayoral administrations.

Most striking were the many new groups without significant resources that sprang

---

[22] James W. Fossett, *Federal Aid to Big Cities* (Washington, D.C.: Brookings Institution, 1983); J. David Greenstone and Paul E. Peterson, *Race and Authority in Urban Politics* (New York: Russell Sage Foundation, 1973).

up in response to the homeless problem. Many were grassroots efforts that relied on volunteers to operate church basement shelters and soup kitchens. Some direct services received aid from the Federal Emergency Management Agency and later from New York State programs. A significant new organization was the Coalition for the Homeless, which was started by a young attorney then practicing at a well-known law firm and by individuals conducting advocacy research for the Community Service Society. The coalition formed initially on the problem of homeless single men in the late 1970s, but as the homeless grew to include single women, families, and children leaving foster care, their agenda widened also. The coalition developed ties with groups in other cities and helped to mobilize a national social movement on homelessness. The coalition started a newsletter in 1982, and a national conference of advocates for the homeless met in 1985.

The issue agenda of these groups had a high degree of specialization that reflected the diverse characteristics of the homeless population. Some groups focused only on the homeless, or only on homeless families, or only on hunger as a problem distinct from homelessness. People from the mental health and health fields might emphasize homeless single individuals among whom mental illness was significant, while those with a social service background might stress homeless families. More than fifty organizations became active on the specific problem of homeless families in only a three-year period. Initially, most social welfare and health-related groups entering the homeless issue were distant from groups that specialized in housing. Many groups with a homeless agenda wanted to alleviate the immediate crisis and concentrated on emergency shelters and feeding; and they initially lacked expertise on legislating, financing, and operating permanent housing for the poor. Their emergency emphasis paralleled the mayor's assignment of the new shelter system to a city agency that had long experience in social welfare but no jurisdictional authority over permanent housing.

Certain elected city officials were a significant part of the policy community. Main examples were City Council President Carol Bellamy, Comptroller Harrison Goldin, and Manhattan Borough President David Dinkins, all of whom were rivals of Koch within the Democratic Party for the mayoral position. The first mayoral plan for homeless families was produced at the request of the city's Board of Estimate, and it resulted from competition between the mayor and members of the board.[23] However, Bellamy went out of office in 1986, and Dinkins only came in then. Also, activist City Council members lacked an institutional base with strong committee resources and powers.

In sum, in this case the political interest structure was an issue network composed of congeries of organizations and individuals with homelessness on their agendas. Connections within the network were loose, and participants included committed advocates and disinterested journeymen providing information. Within the network, a nexus of organizations shared beliefs on desirable policy content.

---

[23] New York City Government, *A Comprehensive Plan for the Temporary and Permanent Needs of Homeless Families in New York City*, mimeographed, 1984.

This policy community was a direct and immediate force that helped to pull functional expansion out of city government.

This case suggests a modification in the theoretical concept of issue networks. The idea of an issue network can denote a dynamic collection of participants who may include, however, not only neutral journeymen but also a hub of organizations who share policy prescriptions and who compose a policy community that may have direct policy impact.

The Media Agenda

Two functions of the media can be direct political forces that might directly help to impel government to expand social policy. First, attention from the media can increase the salience of an issue in the public mind and thus can help to shape the agenda of governmental decision makers.[24] Second, particularly in the field of social policy, media attention can be crucial to the success of protest groups.[25]

First, media publicity on the homeless increased sharply in New York City from 1978 to 1988. Television ran news and human interest topics that visually depicted human suffering and poor shelter conditions. Often television reporters covered the same story several days in a row and drew prolonged attention; they also provoked responses from government. All the city's major newspapers increased their attention. Before 1978, homeless persons were not categorized in *The New York Times Index*, but were included under "vagrants and migrants," which had few entries. But as the numbers of homeless persons grew, *New York Times* coverage of homelessness increased from 4 items in 1978 to 8 in 1979, 12 in 1980, 60 in 1981, 85 in 1982, 72 in 1983, 159 in 1984, 235 in 1985, 290 in 1986, 370 in 1987, and 302 in 1988.[26]

New York Times editorials favored responding to the needs of the homeless by opening shelters and permanent housing. *Times* editors supported mayoral efforts in the face of opposition from elected politicians, private nonprofit organizations, unions, and NIMBY proponents. They considered public resources to be overwhelmed and called for cooperation from volunteers, private nonprofit agencies, and the business sector. Editorials supported city efforts to place homeless men in permanent jobs, to use public assistance monies to prevent eviction, and to decentralize to smaller shelters citywide. Their most critical voice urged the city government to open shelters more speedily, to empty the mass shelters and welfare hotels,

[24] Maxwell E. McCombs and Donald L. Shaw, "The Agenda Setting Function of the Press" in Doris A. Graber, ed., *Media Power in Politics* (Washington, D.C.: Congressional Quarterly Press, 1984); Elihu Katz and Tamas Szecsko, *Mass Media and Social Change* (Beverly Hills, Calif.: Sage Publications, 1981).

[25] Michael Lipsky, *Protest in City Politics* (Chicago: Rand McNally, 1970).

[26] See *New York Times Index*. Items included news and feature stories, editorials, op-ed articles, letters to the editor, and photographs of homeless individuals and families in New York City and elsewhere.

and to renovate permanent housing; the editors also prescribed federal and state actions to rebuild national subsidies for low-rent housing.

The effect of media coverage was, at a minimum, to cause the attention of public officials to focus on the homeless, among the welter of issues that competed for public recognition. To a large extent, the media agenda became the agenda of public officials. However, media contacts included press releases, personal communications, briefings, and meetings with city officials; and the city government influenced the media agenda. While *New York Times* coverage was urgent, it was sympathetic to the mayor's problems, including the scale of operations and his political opposition. To some extent, the *Times* could help the mayor to build the coalition he needed to expand shelters and permanent housing. Fundamentally, however, media coverage constituted a political liability for city officials. Media visibility increased the political cost of nonintervention. All coverage, sympathetic or confrontational, was implicitly a call for government action and set an expectation of results.

Second, media attention was an important political resource for the policy community active on the homeless issue. Their leadership considered the press a valuable ally and invested time and effort in courting its attention. Robert Hayes, who headed the Coalition for the Homeless, said that he was "educating the fifth generation of *New York Times* reporters."[27] The policy community used the media to communicate their policy recommendations to public officials. Hayes commented, "Our real purpose, though, is to be able to take this and get the *New York Times* to write about how wonderful it is that these 40 families are no longer in the Martinique Hotel, and Look, Governor Cuomo, if you—dope!—raise the welfare allowance by 50 bucks a month for these families, you could get a lot more families out of there! So there's a political edge as usual to this, too." In sum, media publicity offered the policy community a legitimate avenue of communication for educating their audience, including the general public, elected officials, and third parties.

Authoritative Bargaining Arenas

In two respects, the availability of an authoritative bargaining arena may be central to explaining growth of a local public function. First, use of bargaining arenas can facilitate policy change in the intergovernmental system by providing sites where actors can compete for political resources such as authority for programs, money, and jobs.[28] To be effective, bargaining arenas have to be authoritative institutions whose decisions to approve action and commit funds are binding on government policy. Jeffrey Pressman's examples of potentially effective arenas included political parties, interest groups, bureaucracies, the federal poverty programs, and the

---

[27] *Village Voice*, 28 July 1987, 21–37.
[28] Jeffrey L. Pressman, *Federal Programs and City Politics* (Berkeley: University of California Press, 1975), 14–15, 58, 72–78.

electoral process. However, another hypothesis can be posed that authoritative bargaining arenas may be just as important to expansion that springs from local policy communities, as Pressman showed they were to implementing national policy downward in the intergovernmental network.

Second, the policy community on the homeless was the weaker party in a conflict with the mayor over expansion of a new social function. While the policy community did have strengths of various sorts, it did not possess the authority to compel public resources for the purposes it advocated. Elmer Schattschneider predicts that in a contest the weaker party will broaden the scope of conflict to involve third parties that possess distinctive powers; the result of third party intervention will be a change in the bias in the status quo.[29]

This analysis conceives of a state judicial system as a potentially effective bargaining arena that can be activated by the weaker party in a dispute. How in New York City did the policy community on the homeless trigger the courts, and what was the impact of the state judiciary on expanding the shelter function?

In October 1979, the Coalition for the Homeless brought a class action law suit in the New York State court system. *Callahan v. Carey* became a seminal case for the decade of litigation that followed.[30] *Callahan* was brought on behalf of homeless men who ate meals at the city-operated Men's Shelter in Manhattan or who received vouchers that were redeemable in hotels or other shelters. The suit charged a critical shortage of beds, as well as conditions that were unhealthy and dangerous in the shelter that was available. Two months later, the court ordered a preliminary injunction. The court held that the New York State Constitution provided for the "aid, care, and support of the needy," and a consent decree was negotiated under the auspices of the court in August 1981. The decree set detailed standards for quality of public shelters and voucher hotels, including limits on capacity, the staff to resident ratio, the size of beds, and services such as laundry, mail, and telephones. The decree also contained a monitoring requirement, which had the city government send reports on shelter conditions to plaintiffs' attorneys.

When the number of homeless women increased sharply and the women's shelters overflowed, litigation recurred. The State court held in *Eldredge v. Koch* in December 1982, that the terms of the Callahan consent decree extended to homeless women on grounds of the equal protection clause.[31]

When numerous homeless families appeared in city shelters and emergency welfare offices, a third class action was filed in 1983 by the Legal Aid Society. The Appellate Division of New York State Supreme Court ruled in *McCain v. Koch* in May 1986 that all homeless families have the legal right to emergency shelter under the New York State Constitution and ordered the city to comply with state

---

[29] Elmer E. Schattschneider, *The Semi-Sovereign People* (Hinsdale, Ill.: Dryden Press, 1975).
[30] *Callahan v. Carey*, New York County Supreme Court, Index #42582/79.
[31] *Eldredge v. Koch*, 469 N.Y.S.2d 744 (A.D. 1 Dept. 1983).

regulations on safety and sanitation standards for the shelters.[32] The immediate effect was to bar the city government from letting welfare families spend the night sitting in chairs or lying on countertops at the welfare department's emergency offices.

Although the judiciary tended to support the plaintiffs' arguments, judges were aware of the impact that compliance with court orders would have on the public treasury. The courts were periodically sympathetic to the cost arguments raised by city attorneys. For example, the court was willing to lower the plumbing ratios, and it increased the number of residents per toilet from six to ten, and the number of residents per shower from ten to fifteen. This result, nevertheless, represented a compromise from the city's initial proposed relaxation of standards, which the court branded a "cruel and unacceptable hoax."

Judicial decisions were not, however, automatically self-executing. The plaintiffs remained active in monitoring implementation and triggering enforcement. They obtained orders requiring the city to provide more beds, adhere to standards, and reduce the population of certain shelters. In fact, the perspective of plaintiffs' attorneys was that litigation was not a very efficient avenue for social change. Hayes saw the litigation route as a "last resort," because lawsuits were "slow, god-awful, very ineffective, bull-in-china-shop kind of efforts."[33] Although litigation was their "central tool" and injunctions were their "main objective," Hayes thought litigation for economic rights was only the beginning of a "much longer race."

In summary, the *Callahan*, *Eldredge*, and *McCain* cases were the start of a litigation campaign brought in New York state courts on behalf of the homeless. These suits, as well as others, focused sequentially on homeless subpopulations and obtained a series of court actions over a ten-year period. Leadership of the policy community used the cases as rallying points for an educational campaign aimed at elected officials, the media, and the general public. Lawsuits, Hayes noted, had to stand up not only to judicial scrutiny but also to media scrutiny.

Litigation campaigns, composing a series of cases brought over a decade or more, have been found to be important in explaining expansion of social policy at the national level.[34] Activism of New York State courts on the homeless issue thus mirrored the expansion of judicial responsibility in social policy noted in federal courts over the last three decades.[35] Just as federal courts gradually engaged in general social problem solving, issued decisions with significant budgetary effect, and assumed supervisory responsibilities for the remedies they awarded, New York state courts acted similarly regarding the homeless.

[32] *McCain v. Koch*, 523 N.Y.S.2d 112 (A.D. 1 Dept. 1988).
[33] Robert Hayes, "Litigating on Behalf Of Shelter for the Poor," *Harvard Civil Rights-Civil Liberties Review* 22 (Winter 1987): 79–93.
[34] Jack Greenberg, "Litigation for Social Change: Methods, Limitations and Role in Democracy," *Record of the Association of the Bar of the City of New York* 29 (April 1974): 320–355.
[35] Donald L. Horowitz, *The Courts and Social Policy* (Washington, D.C.: Brookings Institution, 1977).

CONCLUSION

This analysis explored how human needs that are generated by inequalities in the mixed economy can become transformed by political conditions into political liabilities that can impel municipal leaders to expand social functions. The investigation tested the roles of multiple political factors in accounting for growth of a public social function in a single site. It assessed the case of expansion of the financing, regulation, and provision of emergency shelters for the homeless in New York City during 1978–1988.

Three major political forces — a policy community advocating on behalf of the homeless, the media agenda, and the state courts acting as authoritative bargaining arenas — were found to have a direct and immediate impact on the decisions by city officials to expand emergency shelters. Their joint effect magnified the political liability of perpetuating the status quo and engendered self-interest in the top elected officials to expand social policy. The case of the homeless in New York City portrayed a conflict model between the local elected executive and the policy community; and the government response can be understood as a result of the development of political liability, which made the cost of action outweigh the cost of inaction.

Growth of the shelter function resulted from confrontation by a new policy community, which was the weaker party in the dispute. The policy community represented the interests of the poor, minorities, and liberal reformers who generally were outside the dominant coalition represented by the top elected official. It therefore could not win policy change through cooptation or incorporation. Also, because shelters required a large magnitude of public funds and because of the retrenchment environment, the policy community had to trigger third parties that possessed resources that it did not. Policy expansion was compelled by a litigation campaign, which won judicial interpretation of the New York State Constitution, and standards for emergency shelters were monitored by the policy community and enforced by state courts over the period of a decade.

Two factors, the political opportunity structure and political culture, were found to have an indirect role. They helped to shape the environment in which political leaders made decisions and set outer limits on the political feasibility of public action. One factor, bureaucratic momentum, had a negligible role in initial expansion of the new function.

The results of this case suggest two models to explain expansion of subnational social functions. In short, an incorporation model could predict expansion when building an electoral coalition requires a mayor to satisfy significant constituencies who demand redistributive policies. Alternatively, a confrontation model would point out that if the dominant coalition excluded liberal reformers, minorities, and the poor, it could still be compelled to expand social functions by a combination of proximate political factors. The most important of these might be the activities of a policy community, the media agenda, and decisions by authoritative bargaining arenas, which together can transform inequalities in the mixed economy into political liabilities for the dominant political leadership.

Is this case a pluralist's dream, a success story of the "service-demanders" over the "money-providers?"[36] The case does demonstrate the ability of organized, educated groups with access to institutional resources to shift the local status quo to redistribute benefits to the poor. The more important point, however, is that temporary shelters persisted for a decade as the main response to homelessness in lieu of permanent housing. Expansion of the large new shelter function does not signal the permeability of political authority, but rather its sluggish response to major and enduring inequalities in living standards. The need for emergency shelters represented a bottoming out in the floor of social protection. Shelters offered only bedrock protection necessary for survival and were therefore well within the historically acceptable protective functions of the partial U.S. welfare state. The policy community had to seek that minimum because it was from their perspective the best policy they could initially win, given the existing economic and political structure. The courts authorized only shelters, because only emergency social protection was within the current interpreted parameters of New York state law. However, the policy community on the homeless, as well as other observers, have increasingly argued that successful long-term responses to homelessness must also include permanent housing, higher incomes, jobs, social services, day care for children, residential services for people with severe and chronic mental disabilities, and other aid from public and private sectors.[37]

[36] Wallace S. Sayre and Herbert Kaufman, *Governing New York City* (New York: Norton, 1965); 514.
[37] National Academy of Sciences, Committee on Health Care for Homeless People, *Homelessness, Health, and Human Needs* (Washington, D.C.: National Academy Press, 1988); Bruce C. Vladeck et al., *Supplementary Statement on Homelessness, Health, and Human Needs* (New York: United Hospital Fund, 1988).

The Dual Agenda of African American Organizations since the New Deal: Social Welfare Policies and Civil Rights

DONA COOPER HAMILTON
CHARLES V. HAMILTON

There are several extant discussions of public policy, race, and politics in professional journals, books, popular media, and on the political stump. These discussions involve debates about the "underclass," about the most appropriate approaches to dealing with long-standing problems of racial discrimination, as well as the impact of racial issues on the major political parties, especially the Democratic party. The Supreme Court nomination of Clarence Thomas focused more attention on a group of African American conservatives who have challenged what they call the outmoded policies of the traditional civil rights movement. One of the discussions, which this article joins, has centered on concerns about the most effective ways to deal with the persisting socioeconomic problems of a vast number of African Americans. Some argue that these economic problems should take precedence over specifically defined "civil rights, race-specific" issues, and the civil rights groups should opt for more "universal" policies, ones that deal not only with race, but with the class dimension. In this way, the argument goes, the political coalitional base will be broadened, and blacks will benefit along with many others similarly situated. This is referred to as the "hidden agenda" of race politics. Others have pointed out that the explicit

DONA COOPER HAMILTON is associate professor of social work at Lehman College, City University of New York. CHARLES V. HAMILTON is the Wallace S. Sayre Professor of Government at Columbia University. This article draws on their research for a larger study of social welfare policies of civil rights organizations covering six decades.

emphasis on race has over the last twenty years sent many former Democrats and supporters of civil rights into the Republican party ranks, thus diminishing the earlier coalition that brought to fruition the political achievements of the liberal and civil rights movements in the 1960s. The current admonition is that the civil rights forces need to focus much more on social welfare, less on civil rights. Unlike the conservative vs. liberal debate, this discussion is mainly one between left-of-center forces, ones who see themselves as progressive in both economic and racial matters. The suggestion is also made that the civil rights organizations have failed to recognize the central importance of socioeconomic structural consequences for poverty on not only blacks but other poor people as well. The charge is that the emphasis on civil rights per se has been too narrow, too race-focused, not only in the 1990s and 1960s, but even earlier. The argument is made that the social welfare agenda, one addressing the needs of *all* poor, black and white, has not received nearly the attention from civil rights groups that has been given the civil rights agenda. This emphasis, it is asserted, has been to the political and economic detriment of masses of black Americans. And the obvious conclusion is that this oversight needs to be remedied as liberals move into the 1990s and think about the kinds of politics necessary to mount viable political coalitions and fashion relevant policy demands.[1]

This article joins this particular discussion and examines the historical position taken by the major civil rights groups as far back as the New Deal. We focus on the two oldest and largest, the National Association for the Advancement of Colored People (NAACP) and the National Urban League (NUL). We contend that these civil rights groups have always understood the existence of *two* agendas: social welfare *and* civil rights, and they have attempted to deal with both. The struggle to achieve the goals of the civil rights agenda is well known. Much less is known about what those groups attempted to achieve regarding the social welfare agenda and how they responded to the political realities facing them over the decades. Indeed, many of the arguments made today about subordinating the race concern to the larger societal concern were made decades ago. Many of the warnings about political backlash made today were made decades before. In other words, harsh political realities faced in the 1990s are not new to the civil rights groups, who have always had to balance legitimate concerns for *both* agendas on a delicate scale of political calculation and pragmatic politics. Greater understanding of this history ought to improve discussion of the politics of race and social welfare today.

CONCERN ABOUT OTHER MATTERS

On 2 July 1939, Eleanor Roosevelt gave a speech before the 30th Annual Conference of the NAACP in Richmond, Virginia. She stated:

[1] William Julius Wilson, *The Truly Disadvantaged* (Chicago: University of Chicago Press, 1987); William Julius Wilson, "Race-Neutral Policies and the Democratic Coalition," *The American Prospect* 1 (Spring 1990): 74–81; Jim Sleeper, *The Closest of Strangers: Liberalism and the Politics of*

It is a great pleasure to me to be here today, but I think I should say at the start that while I think you have been considering subjects which are of primary importance to you as a group in this nation, I feel that I must talk to you as citizens of the United States on things which are not only of interest to you but which are of interest to every citizen in this country.[2]

Her point was that civil rights groups ought to be concerned with broader socioeconomic issues beyond the more narrow interests of their constituents in civil rights. In her speech she specifically mentioned education and health care, and she made reference to the "plight of *all* young people."

This was an often heard admonition to civil rights groups then. As far as we can tell, there were likely few, if any, in that audience that evening who disagreed with her. Certainly, the NAACP's leadership did not disagree. But the leaders must have had a sense of frustration, because they knew that they *had* been devoting a fair amount of attention over the decade precisely to such universal economic issues. Walter White, executive secretary of the NAACP, probably was turning over in his mind the correspondence two years earlier in 1937 between himself and Congressman Dow W. Harter (Ohio). Mr. White had received acknowledgment of a letter he had sent to several members of Congress. Harter's 25 October 1937 response read:

Dear Mr. White:

This will acknowledge receipt of your letter of October 21st. The Record will disclose that I have always been in favor of anti-lynching legislation. I am hopeful that a satisfactory bill may be passed at the coming session.

Very truly yours.

The next day, Walter White responded:

My dear Mr. Harter:

Thank you for your good letter of October 25. However, my letter to you of October 21 was not about the anti-lynching bill but regarding the passage of a nondiscriminatory wages and hours bill at the next session of Congress. I am not surprised that you assumed that my communication had reference to the anti-lynching bill since that has been the subject of our correspondence for so long a time. *But you can see from my letter of the 21st that after all I can write about other matters.*

Ever sincerely[3]

Race in New York (New York: Norton, 1990); Thomas B. Edsall and Mary D. Edsall, *Chain Reaction: The Impact of Race, Rights, and Taxes on American Politics* (New York: Norton, 1992); Theda Skocpol, "Sustainable Social Policy: Fighting Poverty Without Poverty Programs," *The American Prospect* 1 (Summer 1990): 58–70.

[2] Address by Eleanor Roosevelt before the National Association for the Advancement of Colored People (NAACP) Annual Conference, 2 July 1939, Richmond, Virginia, NAACP Papers, Manuscript Division, Library of Congress, Group 1, Box B-17.

[3] Correspondence between Congressman Dow W. Harter and Walter White, 25 October 1937, 26 October 1937, NAACP Papers, Group 1, C-256. (Emphasis added.)

There *has* been over the past sixty years a social welfare agenda that has attempted to do what Eleanor Roosevelt advocated and many current-day analysts suggest. We know, understandably, a lot about the civil rights agenda. We know about the struggle to overturn *de jure* segregation, but very little is known about the struggle to achieve viable social welfare goals. Even in the 1930s complaints and criticisms were heard from blacks and whites urging the civil rights groups to pay more attention to socioeconomic problems. No less a sensitive activist-scholar than Ralph Bunche severely charged:

> It is typical of Negro organizations that they concern themselves not with the broad social and political implications of such policies as government relief, housing, socialized medicine, unemployment and old-age insurance, wages and hours laws, etc., but only with the purely racial aspects of such policies. They are content to let the white citizen determine the expediency of major policies, and the form and direction they will assume, while they set themselves up as watch dogs over relatively petty issues, as whether the Negro will get his proper share of the benefits and whether the laws, once made, will be fairly administered. They thus demark for the Negro a residual function in the society.[4]

Research in the archives of these organizations reveals a quite different story, that the organizations, in fact, had a dual agenda.

We focus on the following questions: What did these civil rights groups say and do about such other matters as social security, the various New Deal programs, health care, and employment? To what extent did they have a dual agenda that attempted to address not only civil rights issues but the broader socioeconomic issues as well? And equally important: how has that dual agenda evolved over the last sixty years? That is, what were the reactions to the civil rights groups as they pursued the dual agenda, and how did these reactions affect subsequent strategy choices?

We identify three distinct stages in the evolution of the dual agenda. *The Consensual Stage, the years of the New Deal into post-World War II.* The organizations attempted to reconcile their social welfare policy agenda with their civil rights agenda. Sometimes they even agreed to subordinate the latter to the former, when the political realities of the time indicated that civil rights issues were not popular and would only hinder the possible achievement of liberal social policies.

The Conflictual Stage, the 1950s into the early 1960s. During the conversion to a peace-time economy and the heightened mobilization of the civil rights movement we find continued agreement with the basic principles of the liberal-progressive forces pushing for particular kinds of social welfare polices. But now we see a new development, no longer a willingness to subordinate the civil rights agenda to the social welfare agenda. This development precipitated an intense

[4] Ralph J. Bunche, "The Progress of Organizations Devoted to the Improvement of the Status of the American Negro," *The Journal of Negro Education* 8 (July 1939): 539–550.

debate within liberal circles, coming close at times to mutual questioning not only of strategy and tactics but of veracity.

The Complementary Stage, beginning with the mid-1960s. On the heels of victories over *de jure* segregation and discrimination and with the rising concern about issues of poverty, still another shift occurred. The organizations, as before, supported liberal social welfare policies (for example, full employment, expanded health care, increased governmental attention to the poor). But now they began to say that more was needed. Socioeconomic conditions had become so severe among some groups (especially blacks and Latinos) that more would be needed in the way of governmental assistance for these groups if the conditions were to be overcome. The legacy of decades of neglect, of failure to deal adequately earlier, now required more than mere attention to the problems of everyone. A vast left-out group had formed, and additional, targeted social policies would be needed. Thus, the dual agenda took on a complementary dimension, which spoke of something in addition, of filling out or completing. At the same time, the civil rights groups would continue to push for the end to discrimination and to overcome the effects of past discrimination.

Each stage, of course, was influenced by its own peculiar brand of national politics and the economic environment. But an important point to emphasize is that throughout this sixty-year period, there has always been, in political terms at least, a distinction between social welfare issues and civil rights issues. This distinction became blurred in the euphoria of the mid-1960s with the passage of both civil rights laws and antipoverty legislation when official and activist rhetoric began to equate racial conditions with poverty (almost exclusively economic conditions).

THE CONSENSUAL STAGE

The New Deal is the proper beginning for this discussion, because then this country launched its modern-day version of the American welfare-state. With the Social Security Act of 1935, the country established a two-tier social welfare system.

The first tier (social insurance) was contributory, funded from payroll taxes levied on employers and employees. Covering retirement pension and unemployment compensation, it has expanded over the years to include dependents, survivors, disability, and health insurance. This was indeed landmark legislation coming out of the crisis of the Great Depression. In many ways, it laid a sound foundation for the future economic protection of a working-class America. It was based in the labor market. One was able to participate in this new, important social insurance system *if* one had a job that was covered by its benefits.

The second tier (public assistance) was for those unable and generally not expected to work. This included dependent children (Aid to Dependent Children, later expanded to Aid to Families with Dependent Children) and the elderly poor who had not contributed to the social security fund. It has expanded to include disability and health care assistance. This category of assistance was means-tested, meaning that one had to prove that one was poor and in need. But it was also perceived to provide help on a temporary basis, because the able-bodied recipients were expected eventually to enter the labor market and become self-supporting. The elderly and to some extent the disabled, of course, were considered deserving of help for the remainder of their lives.

The NUL and the NAACP certainly agreed with the ideological premises of the legislation. They also agreed that government should develop mechanisms for social security and that the labor market should be the basis for receiving benefits in the first tier. But they did not support the bill, because it did not coincide with their social welfare agenda, that is, universal coverage under the first tier. The initial legislation did not cover agricultural and domestic workers, and this meant that initially a good two-thirds of the black labor force was not covered. Of 5.5 million black workers in the country, 2 million worked at that time in agriculture, and 1.5 million in domestic service. These occupations were left out, not, ostensibly because of their race but because of their unfortunate position in the labor market. Thus what was perceived by some as a universal program was not that at all.

Testifying before the Senate Finance Committee on 9 February 1935, Attorney Charles H. Houston of the NAACP stated:

> The NAACP regrets that it cannot support the Wagner Economic Security Bill (S. 1130). It approached the Bill with every inclination to support it, but the more it studied, the more holes appeared, until from a Negro's point of view it looks like a sieve with the holes just big enough for the majority of Negroes to fall through.[5]

He noted that provisions for old people (in the second tier) depended on the separate states adopting a program of assistance, and this was problematic in southern states where most elderly blacks lived. The NAACP thought it was likely that the black elderly would either be excluded from benefits or provided with very low levels of public assistance.

The NAACP favored a strictly federal old-age assistance program. The two tiers should be merged into one, under one national governmental program. Thus, the NAACP was not arguing for special treatment for blacks. The goal was to include blacks, to give them the same chance to be covered, to make it possible for them to contribute to the retirement funds, and therefore to be eligible for benefits. This meant, of course, being employed in occupations that were covered by the act. In this sense, the NAACP saw the social welfare agenda as consensual with the civil rights agenda. Both agendas sought no special treatment for blacks politically or economically. The appeal was economic, not race-specific.

---

[5] Testimony of Charles Hamilton Houston, U.S. Senate Finance Committee, 74th Congress, 1st sess. 9 February 1935, NAACP Papers, Group I, C-257.

Houston testified: "As to the agricultural worker, the situation is galling. First, throw him out of employment under the cotton reduction program, and then set up a program which excludes him from unemployment insurance! Frustration on top of frustration."[6]

The National Urban League was also critical of the proposed social security legislation. Its representative, T. Arnold Hill, testified in favor of the much more comprehensive and radical Lundeen Bill, which indexed benefits to the cost of living and were to be financed with inheritance and gift taxes. In addition, "it provided protection to all workers who refused to work as strike breakers or at less than the average local or trade union wage." Hill was of the opinion that the poorest groups should have "first call" on the benefits of the act.[7]

When the civil rights organizations sought help from liberal-progressive groups, they were sadly disappointed. In a 26 February 1935 memo to his NAACP colleagues, Roy Wilkins described a meeting he had with Abraham Epstein, executive secretary of the American Association for Old Age Security, a liberal organization strongly pushing for the Wagner Social Security Act. The memo revealed the rejection the civil rights groups faced in their attempt to form coalitions with their liberal friends. Wilkins wrote:

> Mr. Epstein, who has known of the work of the Association [NAACP] for many years and who is familiar with most of the problems of Negroes stated that colored people were in a tight place as far as this legislation was concerned, but he did not see that there was anything that could be done about it. *He said frankly that he was interested, first, in social insurance and that he did not see how we can solve the Negro problem through social insurance; in other words, there are realities existing with respect to Negroes and whites in this country which no program of social insurance can undertake to correct.* He suggested (1) that the Association not concern itself about the *contributory* old age assistance or the exclusion of farmers, domestics, and casuals from this contributory system. *The exclusion of these people means that they will not be required to contribute toward an old age pension fund and will not, therefore, draw any benefits from it.* The chief reason for such exclusion is the difficulty of collecting and administering these contributions. (2) That the exclusion of farmers, domestics, and casuals from the contributory old age assistance does not exclude them from the *non-contributory* old age pensions, to which they are entitled regardless of contributions to the Fund.[8]

But this was precisely what the NUL and the NAACP did *not* want. The Urban League's motto was "Jobs, not alms." There was serious concern that people left out of the first-tier social insurance system would be precariously on the margins of the economy and would run the risk of becoming perennial dependents and wards of the state. The civil rights groups foresaw the long-term danger in this,

---

[6] Ibid.

[7] T. Arnold Hill, "A Statement of Opinion on H.R. 2822," 8 February 1935, National Urban League (NUL) Papers, National Urban League Library, New York, NY.

[8] Memo from Roy Wilkins to the Board of Directors, NAACP, 26 February 1935, NAACP Papers, Group 1, C-257. (Emphasis added.)

so much so that they were decidely less interested in public assistance legislation. A 22 October 1947 NAACP memo on the need to amend the Social Security Act noted:

> The relief rolls are no substitute. Relief is a dole which robs a person of self-respect and initiative. Unemployment compensation is more like an insurance against hard times, and as insurance may be accepted with self-respect and self-assurance.[9]

As the civil rights groups saw mattters, the dual agenda was really but one. Their concern for social welfare went hand in hand with their concern for civil rights. They advocated a social welfare agenda that extended first-tier coverage to lower paying jobs. (This was an effective response to some critics, then and later, who criticized the two organizations for being inattentive to the lower, working class and more concerned with helping middle class, white collar blacks.) And they advocated a civil rights agenda that would make jobs in the first tier available on a nondiscriminatory basis.

To the two civil rights groups, these were consensual goals. They consistently supported the more progressive measures, such as the comprehensive Wagner-Murray-Dingell Social Security Bill in 1943–1944. They certainly favored national government efforts in the areas of more federal aid to education, health care, and public housing. And they were consistently and actively on the side of organized labor in fighting the anti-union Taft-Hartley Law.

In pursuing this consensual approach the organizations even agreed at times to subordinate the civil rights agenda to the social policy agenda. This was the case with their support for the Wagner-Murray-Dingell Bill. Although the NAACP endorsed the bill, it questioned the lack of "safeguards for minority groups." NAACP officials had discussed this with Senator Robert Wagner, who had no objection to amending the bill to include an antidiscriminatory clause. But in anticipation of a "spirited fight over the Bill," the NAACP decided to give the bill its "unqualified support even though it [did] not contain anti-discriminatory clauses." The legislation was too important to jeopardize, and including such a clause might "endanger the measure."[10] The same position was evident in the NAACP's support in 1945 for the proposed Full Employment Bill. The question arose: should the NAACP insist that the bill contain a provision against racial discrimination in hiring, a practice which was quite prevalent? For political reasons, the organization opted to go along with its liberal allies who counseled not to raise the civil rights issue. In a 1945 memo, Leslie Perry, the NAACP's Washington lobbyist, wrote to Walter White:

> I had a long talk on Friday, July 6, with Bertram Gross, a member of Senator Murray's staff who helped draft the Full Employment Bill. He stated that Senator Murray greatly

---

[9] Memo from Charles Hamilton Houston to Walter White, 22 October 1937, "Memorandum on Discrimination under the Federal Social Security Act," NAACP Papers, Group 1, C-406.

[10] Letter from Leslie Perry to Roy Wilkins, 11 February 1944, NAACP Files, NAACP Papers, Group II, A-521.

appreciated the resolution of the [NAACP] Board endorsing the Full Employment Bill. We discussed at some length the rationale of the bill. Gross called particular attention to the fact that the preamble states that it is the right of "all Americans" to be gainfully employed. *In those circumstances, he felt that no particular reference to racial groups as say, "without discrimination on account of race" was necessary. I heartily agree with him inasmuch as the bill will probably have tough going at best. If we put in it any provision which can be construed as a little FEPC [Fair Employment Practices Committee] its chances of enactment will be greatly lessened.* Frankly, in my judgment any such provision in the enactment clause would be completely meaningless in so far as it confers any positive benefits on minority races. I think that the establishment of a national budget with respect to total employment would be an important and far reaching step and that the bill, therefore, merits our all-out support.[11]

And the NAACP did support the bill, although the final version fell far short of obtaining full employment guarantees.[12] This was an effort on the part of the civil rights groups to accommodate the two agendas, even though accommodation might mean at times subordination of civil rights to social welfare policy.

The two organizations wrestled with the problem of how to reconcile the two agendas. In congressional testimony in 1946 in support of a national health bill (S.1606), the health policy adviser to the NAACP, Montague Cobb, stated:

This Association [NAACP] is most acutely aware of the need for such legislation in respect to that segment of the population which it primarily represents (i.e., Negroes). It cannot be overemphasized, however, that health is not a racial problem, that the health conditions of Negroes are largely a reflection of their socio-economic circumstances, and that poor health in any segment of the population is a hazard to the nation as a whole.[13]

Cobb proceeded: ". . . The NAACP has a natural and vital interest in any measures which make for the improvement of the *general* health, particularly that of the economically poorly circumstanced." In his testimony, he constantly linked the health needs "of Negroes as well as of millions of whites in poor economic circumstances."[14]

Even though health care facilities in the local and state agencies would remain segregated, the NAACP, while expressing strong opposition and "concern" about that situation, opted not to push the issue, but to ask for fair, equitable treatment. In other words, it was prepared to support the liberal social policy, even though this meant maintaining the "separate but equal" racial practice. The same issue was faced on the subject of federal support for education in 1945. A proposed

[11] Memo to Walter White from Leslie Perry, 10 July 1945, NAACP Papers, Group II, A-111. (Emphasis added.)

[12] Stephen Kemp Bailey, *Congress Makes a Law, The Story Behind the Employment Act of 1946* (New York: Columbia University Press, 1950).

[13] Statement, "Support of National Health Bill, S. 1606, on Behalf of the National Association for the Advancement of Colored People," *Journal of the National Medical Association* 38 (July 1946): 133–137.

[14] Ibid., 134. (Emphasis added.)

measure, S. 181, Educational Finance Act of 1945, clearly would not deal with the problem of segregated schools. Nonetheless, the NAACP felt compelled to support the bill. Testifying before a Senate committee, Leslie Perry stated:

> While this legislation will not wipe out existing differentials obtaining in State expenditures for Negro and white schools, current estimates of the funds Negro schools will receive under it indicate that in practically every one of these States per capita expenditures for Negro pupils and teachers will increase by more than 100 percent. . . .

> As much as we deplore the discriminatory action of many States . . . I want to make it clear that we do not regard this legislation as a proper vehicle or means of correcting this type of inequality.[15]

No one misunderstood the political bind the civil rights groups were in; they had to make hard strategic decisions given the political realities facing them. In fact, Perry testified that the organization would continue its fight through the courts challenging the segregated school systems. The organization was reconciling the two agendas by dealing with them in separate political decision-making arenas.

THE CONFLICTURAL STAGE

The benefits from social welfare, however, did not keep pace with the changes in the private sector economy and with the negative consequences of continued segregation and discrimination in the society. Structural economic developments — automation, urban renewal, factories moving out of the inner cities, suburban growth, continued racial segregation and discrimination — combined to limit participation of black Americans in the mainstream economy. In 1949 the NAACP began to pursue a strategy that put the liberals' social welfare agenda in open conflict with the civil rights agenda. The organization even drafted amendments to liberal social legislation that called for no federal funds to be allocated to any local district or state that would use such funds in a racially segregated or discriminatory manner. The vehicle for this was the controversial Powell Amendment, named after its congressional sponsor, Representative Adam Clayton Powell, Jr. from Harlem in New York. The catalyst, in fact, for this major shift in strategy was President Harry Truman's Committee on Civil Rights. The committee's 1947 Report, *To Secure These Rights*, went far beyond anything to date that spoke to forceful implementation of civil rights by the national government. Composed of a panel of independent-minded private citizens, the committee recommended:

---

[15] Testimony of Leslie Perry, administrative assistant, Washington Bureau of the NAACP before the Senate Education and Labor Committee on S. 181, Educational Finance Act of 1945, 31 January 1945, NAACP Papers, Group II, A-663.

The conditioning by Congress of all federal grants-in-aid and other forms of federal assistance to public or private agencies for any purpose on the absence of discrimination and segregation based on race, color, creed, or national origin.[16]

Charles H. Houston of the NAACP urged the committee not to issue such a recommendation. In testimony before the committee, he felt that such action very likely would result in rejecting the aid funds ". . . and you would fail to give aid to people who need it most."[17]

But after the report's strong stand, the NAACP pursued the strategy in collaboration with Powell.[18] Clearly, the position of such a prestigious presidential committee would carry enormous weight with public opinion, or so it was hoped. At any rate, the main civil rights group could hardly be caught lagging in this matter. Its role was to lead, not follow. Perhaps this was the shift in political climate they could seize to make a major new thrust in the struggle for civil rights.

The point was that the organization decided not to continue the subordination strategy, and to argue that unless the civil rights agenda was included, then the social welfare agenda should not be enacted. Evidence was mounting even then that a rising tide did not necessarily lift all boats. Even with economic growth and universal programs, some people could and would be left behind.

The civil rights groups still favored the basic socioeconomic goals of the liberal agenda, but they were no longer sanguine that subordination of the civil rights agenda would yield the ultimate benefits sought. This strategy of denying funds to segregated facilities created an intense debate within liberal civil rights circles. Even some NAACP board members objected, as did Walter Reuther of the United Auto Workers, Eleanor Roosevelt, and liberal senators and representatives such as Paul Douglas of Illinois and Stewart Udall of Arizona. They argued that to continue to insist on the Powell Amendment would mean the defeat of otherwise very good and badly needed progressive social legislation. Not enough votes could be obtained in Congress, and this would give the southerners and conservatives cause to rejoice. Such a strategy, they concluded, would get neither the social legislation nor the civil rights protections.[19]

Congressman Udall pleaded in a letter to Clarence Mitchell of the NAACP's Washington Bureau and a staunch proponent of the Powell Amendment not to mix civil rights with aid to education:

Of course, there is room for honest disagreement on this whole question. Perhaps our main differences arise from the fact that by habit we are schooled in the art of the

---

[16] *To Secure These Rights, The Report of the President's Committee on Civil Rights* (New York: Simon & Schuster, 1947), 166.

[17] William E. Juhnke, "President Truman's Committee on Civil Rights: The Interaction of Politics, Protest, and Presidential Advisory Commission," *Presidential Studies Quarterly* 14 (Summer 1989): 593–610, cited at 601.

[18] See Charles V. Hamilton, *Adam Clayton Powell, Jr., The Political Biography of an American Dilemma* (New York: Atheneum, 1991), esp. chap. 10.

[19] Ibid., 224.

possible, while *principle* is the central thing in your work — and rightly so. Sometimes in our desire to get half-a-loaf, our principles hang on the brink (and sometimes go over), but generally speaking we have found that a modest program is better than none.[20]

Senator Paul Douglas stated in a letter to the NAACP:

I have joined in sponsoring 11 specific civil rights bills, and I will fight for them. But I wonder if our best chance for such gains is not in narrowing the issue so that our real supporters may all stand up and be counted on a single, clear civil rights issue, rather than being divided by a combination proposal which some proponents of all welfare legislation, joined with opponents of civil rights, will help to defeat.[21]

These were arguments the civil rights organizations had heard before and understood. But their political patience had run out. They had seen too often that otherwise good social legislation did not necessarily lead to sufficient advancement for blacks. And all the while some blacks were falling farther and farther behind. Roy Wilkins expressed the impatience and wariness in a letter to a group of liberals in New York who wanted the NAACP to back off:

Our Association is committed to federal aid to education, but with assurances in the legislation that funds will not be used to further segregation. It would seem that the friends of federal aid might well expend some of their persuasive powers on those who want to have their cake (segregation) and eat it, too (federal aid).[22]

The NAACP officials were keenly aware of the clash between the two agendas. Clarence Mitchell broached the issue directly when he stated that the NAACP "supported the great programs that improve the lot of the common man." But there were other equally important concerns, namely, civil rights. Mitchell's biographer quotes Mitchell as saying:

But blacks also wanted "an FEPC law to guarantee that we can get jobs in those plants where the minimum wage is a dollar or more. Blacks wanted to walk in the front door of hospitals that receive Federal grants instead of having to sneak in through the back door and ride up on the freight elevator to the wards or clinics. . . . We want enough civil rights bills passed to make it possible for us to enjoy the great benefits of social welfare laws without the threat of being shot down or bombed just because we also want to vote and enjoy the full rights of American citizenship in Atlanta, Georgia, as well as Atlantic City, New Jersey."[23]

[20] Letter from Stewart Udall to Clarence Mitchell, 1 July 1955, NAACP Washington Bureau Papers, Box 71, Manuscript Division, Library of Congress.

[21] Letter from Senator Paul Douglas to Clarence Mitchell, 11 March 1955, NAACP Washington Bureau Papers, Box 71, Manuscript Division, Library of Congress.

[22] Letter from Roy Wilkins to Frederick F. Greenman, New York State Committee for the White House Conference on Education, 15 November 1955, NAACP Washington Bureau Papers, Box 71, Manuscript Division, Library of Congress.

[23] Cited in Denton L. Watson, *Lion In the Lobby, Clarence Mitchell, Jr.'s Struggle for the Passage of Civil Rights Laws* (New York: William Morrow, 1990), 333.

This overtly conflicting stage of the dual agenda effectively ended with the passage of Title VI of the Civil Rights Law of 1964. That provision prohibited the use of federal funds in segregated facilities, exactly what the NAACP and the Powell Amendment sought. Now, for all official purposes racial segregation and discrimination were ended. De jure segregation was no longer sanctioned in those areas under the purview of federal protection. But this did not address an array of issues left in its wake. There was still discrimination in the private housing market; there were still problems of discrimination in voting regulations and laws; there were still educational systems that were segregated and not rapidly implementing the school desegregation decision of a decade before. Above all, there remained a class of citizens on the economic fringes of society. They were never effectively brought into the first-tier social insurance system; and when they were, they came in at the lower rungs of the labor market. Years of refusal to deal with a viable social welfare agenda advocated by the civil rights groups left a legacy as the society moved into the late-1960s and beyond.

The victories of the civil rights agenda — Supreme Court decisions, Civil Rights Act of 1964, Voting Rights Act of 1965, executive decrees of the early 1960s, Housing Law of 1968 — set the stage for more concentrated attention to the social problems still persisting.

The Complementary Stage

Thus far we have emphasized the basic purposes and content of some of the social welfare policies of the civil rights groups. In the consensual stage the goal was to be included, to make the various New Deal programs truly universal, not restricted by race or other economic conditions. While the political realities made this goal unattainable, the groups persisted. At times, in the face of certain political realities, they reluctantly agreed to subordinate their civil rights agenda to the social welfare agenda in the hope that even within a racially segregated society there would be benefits of a substantial nature to blacks.

In the conflictual stage, the deliberate purpose was to challenge the political realities of the time, to put the two agendas into direct conflict. This was the experiential recognition that while the political realities were essentially the same as before, there was another reality: that unless the civil rights agenda was dealt with, blacks would likely end up permanently behind and, in fact, not be accorded sufficient benefits from the new and expanding social welfare policies. Structural socioeconomic changes were occurring that led to the conclusion that economic growth could occur for many and still leave others outside the orbit of a steadily advancing prosperity.

In each of the two stages, the civil rights groups understood that blacks shared common needs with other disadvantaged groups in the society. They never denied this relationship, but they also wanted the other recognition that race per se was also a factor that had to be dealt with. It was, indeed, during the conflictual stage that the mounting civil rights movement began to achieve its greatest victories in the courts and Congress over segregation and discrimination. Ironically, these victories created tension among some civil rights allies. The argument was made that it was not necessary to put the two agendas into conflict inasmuch as racial equality was being achieved. In time, it was hoped, separate civil rights laws would settle the racial issue. Thus, liberal social welfare policies should be pursued on their own merits, unhampered by appeals to race-specific remedies.

This argument was not entirely persuasive among some civil rights advocates. In April 1963, Clarence Mitchell testified before a House subcommittee about the discriminatory practices in administering the Manpower Development and Training Act:

> In its report on vocational training and apprenticeship, the Civil Rights Commission pointed out that there was a wide difference between the types of training offered at so-called Negro vocational schools and the training offered at schools predominantly white.
>
> Electronics, tool and die design, and machine shop training are vital areas for today's job training. These are made available to white young people, but even in many of the school systems that are supposed to be desegregated, the colored children are still jammed into such things as shoe repairing, dry cleaning, and auto mechanics. Very often even these courses use inferior equipment and those who take them come out unsuited for employment. . . . It is just amazing to see the difference between the type of training that is given in one school and in the other.[24]

The National Urban League was also sensitive to certain proposed aspects of the New Frontier's Vocational Education Act of 1963. Otis E. Finley testified that the NUL was wary of a provision that based allocation of funds on a needs-assessment by the states: "The experience of the Urban League indicates that this basis of need has always posed a problem with Negro youth." Suggesting that the basis for receiving educational funds should be a national needs test, he stated:

> . . . I would suggest that any consideration of the adoption of the Vocational Education Act would take a long hard look at this requirement of allotting funds on the basis of needs as determined by States and sections. . . . Expand vocational and technical training programs consistent with employment possibilities and *national* needs.
>
> The present needs of vocational education require massive financial support. Unless immediate steps are taken to provide these funds, the cost to the Nation will be even greater. *We face a clear alternative of providing our children with the best in education and training or paying for increased welfare costs, higher crime rates, and human demoralization. Either way money will be spent.*
>
> The Urban League believes that the problems confronting education today transcend State and local concerns, and thus now become an urgent national concern.[25]

---

[24] Testimony of Clarence Mitchell before the House General Subcommittee on Education and Labor, 26 April 1963, Hearings, 88th Congress, 1st sess., 604–605.

[25] Testimony of Otis E. Finley, assistant director in charge of Education and Youth Incentive,

Without question, there was a new, more liberal political environment in Washington and throughout most of the country in the 1960s. But the civil rights groups were aware that with the increase in social welfare legislation, there still had to be attention paid to the problems of continuing racial discrimination.

What developed in the early 1960s was the view that special efforts had to be made to help those, especially blacks, who had been left out for so long. Whitney M. Young, Jr. of the NUL proposed a domestic Marshall plan. Essentially a proposal to provide compensatory assistance on a massive scale, the NUL was going on record in favor of preferential treatment. In a speech at the National Conference of Churches in New York City on 30 January 1965, he told the audience:

> I say that for a century Negroes have borne a disproportionate burden of unemployment, and now it is of disaster proportions, and that emergency aid is needed. Not tomorrow, but now. Not when "full employment" is achieved, for there is no evidence that we will have full employment in the foreseeable future unless extraordinary emergency action is taken — but now.

> That is why the Urban League has called for special effort in employment, as well as in education, housing, health, and welfare. These are the crucial areas of concern in making equality a meaningful reality for Negroes. . . . A special effort in the area of employment for Negroes must be made.[26]

Years of failure to reconcile the two agendas during the consensual and conflictual stages had created a class of people with these special needs. This new complementary stage of the dual agenda would emphasize support as before for the universal social welfare programs, and it would also call for additional help for the most needy, especially blacks.

There was also a new dimension to the civil rights struggle at that point. In addition to the two older organizations, other organizations and leaders were emerging: Martin Luther King, Jr. and the Southern Christian Leadership Conference [SCLC]; James Farmer and the Congress of Racial Equality [CORE], (although founded in the early 1940s, its ranks now were growing with the Freedom Rides of 1961); the Student Nonviolent Coordinating Committee [SNCC]; Bayard Rustin (by no means new on the scene, but given greater prominence from his role as coordinator of the 1963 March on Washington) and in

---

National Urban League, before the House General Subcommittee on Education and Labor, 88th Congress. 1st sess., 9 April 1963, 529–534. (Emphasis added.)

[26] Remarks by Whitney M. Young, Jr. before the State of the Race Conference held at the National Council of Churches, 475 Riverside Drive, New York City, 30 January 1965, A. Philip Randolph Papers, Library of Congress. Several histories of this period have linked Young's thoughts to the speech by President Lyndon B. Johnson at Howard University on 4 June 1965. In that commencement address, Johnson talked of the "next, more profound stage of the battle for civil rights," namely, providing special efforts for those denied for so many years. ". . . equal opportunity is essential, but not enough." See Lee Rainwater and William L. Yancey, eds., *The Moynihan Report and the Politics of Controversy* (Cambridge, MA: M.I.T. Press. 1967).

the late 1960s, George Wiley and the National Welfare Rights Organization [NWRO]. There were also numerous local protest and community activist groups around the country of varying sizes and duration, many developed out of the antipoverty programs of the Great Society.

In 1966, a major proposal, the Freedom Budget, was made by the A. Philip Randolph Institute under the direction of the venerable labor leader, A. Philip Randolph, and Bayard Rustin, calling for a $180 billion ten-year commitment to deal with the country's major socioeconomic problems. Drawn up by liberal black and white economists and policy analysts, the document was signed by many civil rights, liberal, labor, and religious leaders. This was distinctly not a racially-specific proposal, but everyone recognized the benefits to blacks if it were taken seriously. A central feature was the creation of jobs and the attainment of full employment. It was clearly an attempt to combine the class and race components of what had become a complex set of interrelated problems. But its price tag, apparently, was too high.

At one Senate subcommittee hearing, a witness suggested "that a careful reading of volumes like the Freedom Budget would be of very great value in terms of thinking on the part of our legislators toward really the eradication of poverty."[27] Senator Joseph Clark (D-PA) was blunt and candid in his response:

> . . . I have had a look at the [Freedom] budget and I think in the best of all possible worlds, it would be a wonderful thing but as a matter of pragmatic politics, it seems to me utterly unrealistic. . . . and I don't think our constituents are anywhere near ready for that budget.[28]

The Poor People's Campaign, initially under King's leadership before his assassination, and the Wiley-led welfare rights movement gave further indication of the move toward greater attention to economic needs of poor people. Both movements were deliberately aimed at crossing racial lines and carving out a social welfare agenda of a decidely liberal-progressive orientation. At his death in 1973, George Wiley was beginning to form a new organization, the Movement for Economic Justice, that would attempt to address in a comprehensive way the economic needs of a "majority" of Americans, namely those concerned about equitable redistribution of income, adequate jobs, and tax reform.

When the Nixon administration introduced the Family Assistance Plan [FAP], calling for a form of negative income tax and a guaranteed annual income, along with a "workfare" provision, most civil rights groups followed the lead of George Wiley of the NWRO and opposed the plan. Essentially, in their view, the amount to be received per poor family was too low. The new head of the National Urban League, Vernon E. Jordan, Jr., was clear in his deference to Wiley on this issue:

[27] Testimony by Arthur C. Logan, chairman, Antipoverty Committee, United Neighborhood Houses, New York City, before U.S. Senate Subcommittee on Employment, Manpower, and Poverty, Hearings held in New York City, 8 May 1967, 90th Congress. 1st sess.
[28] Ibid.

George did the best organizing job of anybody after the sixties had reached their peak. When it came to welfare legislation, I was very impressed with his detailed knowledge. He could quote from page four of the bill and he knew what section A meant, and that was very important. He commanded support.[29]

Throughout the 1970s one of the main items on the social welfare agenda of the various civil rights groups was full employment. The specific legislative proposal was the Humphrey-Hawkins Full Employment Bill, which was the catalyst for the creation of an umbrella organization, the Full Employment Action Council, a coalition of civil rights, labor, business, religious, academic, and liberal interest groups. Appropriately, it was cochaired by Murray H. Finley, president of the Amalgamated Clothing Workers of America, AFL-CIO, and Coretta Scott King, president of the Martin Luther King, Jr. Center for Nonviolent Social Change. Again, as with the Freedom Budget, the full employment bill was by no means a race-specific proposal. As its proponents viewed it, it addressed the needs of all persons "willing and able to work." The 1974 annual conference of the National Urban League devoted its four-day meeting to the theme: "Full Employment as a National Goal." The initial bill introduced by Congressman Augustus Hawkins (D-CA) and one of the featured speakers at the NUL conference, was race neutral, but it called for a commitment of expenditures the decision makers were not prepared to make. In 1978, a relatively weak Full Employment and Balanced Growth Act was passed.

Given the new civil rights laws against discrimination and segregation, some civil rights groups thought that the passage of a strong Full Employment Bill in the 1970s would have been a fitting (albeit, not final) achievement of their dual agenda. There would still need to be diligent enforcement of laws against racial discrimination. There would be no need to subordinate concern for civil rights to that for social welfare, as was often the case in the consenual stage. As a result of the end to de jure segregation, there would be no need to place the two agendas in conflict with each other.

CONCLUSION

Unlike earlier years, in the 1980s and 1990s there were no legal institutional barriers separating the two agendas. Passage of viable social welfare legislation would have to be done without restrictions based on race. The civil rights groups had always wanted that, and they were consistently in the ranks of the liberal-progressive forces. As the history recounted in this article indicates, except during the approximately fifteen-year period of the conflictual stage, the civil rights groups have been willing allies for a progressive alliance. When the legal barriers based on race that precipitated the disagreement in the 1950s over the Powell

---

[29] Quoted in Nick Kotz and Mary Lynn Kotz, *A Passion for Equality, George Wiley and the Movement* (New York: Norton, 1977), 276.

amendment were removed, the path for viable potential coalitions opened. But more often than not, sufficient allies were not available. The country moved to the right; the civil rights groups stayed left of center on social welfare issues.

In the late 1970s and into the 1980s, as the conservative mood accelerated, civil rights groups began to suspect that even the gains made in civil rights might be jeopardized. Thus, on the civil rights agenda, there came to be policy remedies such as affirmative action, goals, timetables, quotas, minority set-asides, and the like. These remedies are properly seen as part of the civil rights agenda. They are race-specific (and, of course, gender-specific in some cases). They aim to address needs created in the minds of the proponents by past and present discrimination. The important point, however, is that this civil rights agenda is not necessarily at odds with a liberal social welfare agenda.

The political coalitions conceivably available for pursuing a liberal social welfare agenda might well not be available for achievement of a race/gender-specific agenda. This is not unusual. As the three-stage evolutionary account reveals, over the last sixty years there have always been political problems between those supporting the respective agendas. There have always been political realities complicating the relationship between the two agendas. Civil rights groups struggling to achieve the goals of both agendas have known this all too well. In the 1990s, critics on the left and right raise questions long recognized by the civil rights groups. It was the civil rights groups that warned of a growing dependent class, not the conservative right. It was the civil rights groups that decades before called for real race-neutral social welfare policies. The current discussion over universal versus race-specific policies is not new. Neither is the concern for what is politically feasible or realistic. What is also clear is that past capitulation to conservative forces, leading to failure to enact truly universal programs, has created even more social and racial problems to be resolved. The civil rights leadership has not been unmindful of this fact. Rather than presenting new insights, present-day liberal and conservative policy analysts are finally beginning to acknowledge the truths understood and articulated all along by the civil rights groups as they dealt with both aspects of their dual agenda.

The Government's Role in Building the Women's Movement

GEORGIA DUERST-LAHTI

Many aspects of the women's movement's resurgence have been ably considered. These include its political history,[1] social forces that gave rise to the movement,[2] and insights of key women involved in advancing women's status.[3] Other works comprehensively recount issues involved in the movement,[4] or cover the development of particular governmental policies.[5] However, one aspect remains largely unexplored: the role played by federal and state governmental bodies as organizational entities in helping to build the current women's movement.[6] Gov-

[1] Judith Hole and Ellen Levine, *Rebirth Of Feminism* (New York: Quadrangle Books, 1971); Jo Freeman, *The Politics of Women's Liberation* (New York: David McKay Co, 1976); Sara Evans, *Personal Politics* (New York: Vintage Books, 1979), among others.

[2] Ethel Klein, *Gender Politics* (Cambridge: Harvard University Press, 1986); and Evans, *Personal Politics*.

[3] Irene Tinker, *Women In Washington: Advocates For Public Policy* (London: Sage, 1983); Betty Friedan, *"It Changed My Life": Writings on the Women's Movement* (New York: W.W. Norton, 1985); Judith Paterson, *Be Somebody: A Biography of Marguerite Rawalt* (Austin, Tex.: Eakin Press, 1986).

[4] Barbara Deckard, *The Women's Movement: Political, Socioeconomic, and Psychological Issues* (New York: Harper & Row, 1975).

[5] Cynthia E. Harrison, "A 'New Frontier' for Women: The Public Policy of the Kennedy Administration," *The Journal of American History* 67 (December 1980); and Patricia G. Zelman, *Women, Work, and National Policy: The Kennedy-Johnson Years* (Ann Arbor, Mich.: UMI Research Press, 1982). Also see Harrison, *On Account of Sex: The Politics of Women's Issues, 1945–1968* (Berkeley: University of California Press, 1988).

[6] Some work touches this area. For example, see Debra W. Stewart, *The Women's Movement in Community Politics in the United States: The Role of Local Commissions on the Status of Women* (New York: Pergamon Press, 1980) and "Institutionalizing of Female Participation at the Local Level,"

GEORGIA DUERST-LAHTI is associate dean of the college and associate professor of government at Beloit College. Her research interests focus on gender and power in American politics.

155

ernmental bodies have the capacity to assist interests generally, and in this case women's interests specifically, in ways governmental outsiders found difficult, if not impossible.

This article attempts to demonstrate that governmental entities concerned with women were critical to national mobilization — an aspect essential to any political movement in the United States — in ways which have not been recognized. Informed by interest-group and bureaucratic politics in a federal system, the analysis is based upon the observation that governmental bodies have at their disposal especially significant resources: access to and knowledge of governmental data collection and information, public funding, full-time expert personnel, established relationships with political decision makers, and perhaps most critically, their "legitimate" nature. They also operate through the existing federal organizational structure of federal regions and state governments. The analysis traces from 1963 to 1969 how government officials consciously and actively used public resources to establish a legitimate agenda for action and then mobilized nationwide support by creating a communication infrastructure to disseminate that agenda — most importantly through State Commissions on the Status of Women. To a lesser degree, it demonstrates collaborative efforts with women's organizations outside government.

The governmental bodies considered at the federal level are the U.S. Department of Labor Women's Bureau (established in 1920), the President's Commission on the Status of Women (PCSW-1962), Citizens' Advisory Council on the Status of Women (CAC-1963), the Interdepartmental Committee on the Status of Women (IC-1963), and the Task Force on Women's Rights and Responsibilities (TFWRR-1969). At the state level, the State Commissions on the Status of Women (established from 1962–1967) are considered. Governmental documents, reports, and brochures comprise the major data of this analysis. These data are buttressed with supporting evidence from archival holdings and interviews with key individuals.[7]

Background

The government's involvement in the resurgence of the women's movement may have been overlooked or underestimated for several reasons. First, the social-movement approach employed in earlier studies led scholars to focus on extragovernmental aspects. Second, many major contributions have come from

Women and Politics 1 (Spring 1980): 37–64; Rina Rosenberg, "Representing Women at the State and Local Levels: Commission on the Status of Women" in Ellen Boneparth, ed., *Women, Power and Policy* (New York: Pergamon Press, 1982); Leila S. Rupp and Verta Taylor, *Survival in the Doldrums: The American Women's Rights Movement, 1945 to the 1960s* (New York: Oxford University Press, 1987), 166–174; and Harrison, *On Account*, 159–165.

[7] All interviews were conducted by the author in 1985 and were tape recorded. Those with Kathryn Clarenbach on 21 May and 25 June, and with Esther Peterson on 29 June were in person. Those with Catherine East on 11 June and 16 July, Mary Hilton on 16 July, and Virginia Allan on 1 August were by telephone. Citations below will refer only to the names of the respondents.

historians who tend to avoid social theory in treatments of subjects. Finally, the orientations of feminist scholars come into play. The suffrage coalition disintegrated into two camps with differing orientations — one militant and radical feminist centered around Alice Paul and the National Women's Party, the other liberal and reformist comprising the Women's Bureau coalition.[8] The former maintained a feminist label, while the latter was generally seen as antifeminist. In the 1960s these camps were labeled "women's liberation" and "women's rights" respectively.[9] Contemporary feminist scholars have tended to identify with and see the women's liberation branch as the movement's heart and vanguard. Hence, they were likely to dismiss or underestimate "conservative" efforts of governmental bodies largely concerned with women's rights. Most attention paid to the latter branch tended to concentrate on important contributions of women working in government and not on the role played by government per se.

Yet, the Women's Bureau, along with the several federal advisory bodies and the State Commissions on the Status of Women that joined it in the 1960s, were integrally involved with the reformist branch of the resurgence. The Women's Bureau nurtured a coalition of groups concerned with the plight of working women and favoring protectionist legislation, and in the process it kept a spark of activism alive.[10] According to activists Virginia Allan and Kathryn Clarenbach in interviews, Women's Bureau reports kept a flame burning in "traditional" women's organizations like the Young Women's Christian Association, the National Federation of Business and Professional Women's Clubs (BPW), and the American Association of University Women during the decades between suffrage and the resurgence. Early in the resurgence, the federal government, through bodies concerned with women, was the only game in town that marshalled and directed its resources towards the broad based concerns of women.[11] But the involvement of the governmental bodies has been interpreted differently.

[8] See Harrison, "A 'New Frontier'"; and Judith Sealander, *As Minority Becomes Majority* (Westport, Conn.: Greenwood Press, 1983), esp. 28–36, for an elaboration of the Women's Bureau coalition. Labels attached to the various branches by scholars are many and relationships are complex. Generally speaking, the former branch, "radical individualism" feminism, promoted the Equal Rights Amendment through militant action. The other, "familial" or "relational" activism (which became feminism) was based upon social reform working through the political system and defended protectionist labor legislation. The former recognized sex differences but saw them as irrelevant for women's civil and political rights. The latter sought to preserve sex differences. See Joan Hoff-Wilson, ed, *Rights of Passage: The Past and Future of the ERA* (Bloomington: Indiana University Press, 1986), 4–5, based upon work done by Karen Offen. See also Kathryn Kish Sklar, "Why Were Most Politically Active Women Opposed to the ERA in the 1920s," in Hoff-Wilson, *Rights of Passage*, 25–38.

[9] Hole and Levine, *Rebirth of Feminism*, divide orientations into "women's rights" and "women's liberation" branches of the movement. Freeman employs an "older and younger" conceptual framework and emphasizes the complementary nature of two branches.

[10] BPW was unique among members of the Women's Bureau coalition in endorsing the ERA in 1937. See Sealander, *As Minority Becomes Majority*, 76, on the BPW.

[11] Interview with Kathryn F. Clarenbach, who headed the Wisconsin State Commission on the Status of Women, served as president of the Interstate Association On the Status of Women in 1970 to 1972,

Jo Freeman can be credited with the best overall account of the politics behind the formation of the current women's movement.[12] Perhaps because she stresses developments at the end rather than the beginning of the time period investigated, she overlooks or downplays the critical role played by governmental bodies in creating the initial infrastructure that sustained the larger movement. While she mentions government entities, her analysis neglects to detail the critical nature of their contributions. For example, Freeman credits the activity of federal and state bodies with laying the groundwork for the future movement by bringing the right women together, unearthing evidence of unequal status, and creating a climate of expectation for action. She also recognizes that because the involved women corresponded and met annually at federally-sponsored conferences for state commissions, they were in a position to share and reinforce their growing awareness of women's concerns. They also "created an embryonic communications network among people with similar concerns."[13]

Unfortunately, Freeman does not carry the line of reasoning further, even though she deems a preexisting, cooptable communications network or infrastructure essential to the origins of a movement.[14] Clues to this apparent oversight are found in her view of the Women's Bureau as a "*latent* resource for the spread of feminism, once groups developed that could make use of its material"[15] and in her conclusion that "a *symbiotic* relationship [exists] between feminists within our governmental institutions [and] feminists operating in the private sphere. . . ."[16] In the former case Freeman casts the Women's Bureau in the role of a passive actor and ignores other governmental bodies concerned with women. In the latter, symbiosis is predicated upon a social movement of feminists that is already present. Like other scholars, she does not adequately consider the resources used to sustain the movement initially and contribute to the rise of feminists in nongovernmental arenas.

Prior research on the origins of the current women's movement has also largely ignored the legitimizing function governmental bodies played with the issues of concern to feminists for the nonfeminist majority — in other words, the mobilization potential. First, numerous political sociology studies point to high levels of

---

and was a founder of the NOW, among other involvements. The breadth of the constituency and number of concerns remain key to this claim. Clarenbach was definitely part of the Women's Bureau coalition so, like other "reformist" women, she saw it as essential. However, the National Women's Party's (NWP) strategy of moving for equal rights on national and international fronts arguably incorporated more women's concerns through fewer fronts.

[12] Freeman, *Politics of Women's Liberation.*
[13] Ibid., 52–53.
[14] Ibid., 48.
[15] Ibid., 52, n.23. (Emphasis added.)
[16] Ibid., 230. (Emphasis in original.)

citizen trust in government during the time period being considered.[17] By extension, if citizens generally trusted government, they were likely to trust information generated by it. Second, the government is often the only source with the capacity to gather data on the entire gamut of national concerns. This has implications for the context into which a particular concern is placed. For example, the Soviet lead in the space race stimulated the publication of *Womanpower* (1957), which bemoaned the underutilization of women's abilities in the context of national security.[18] Finally, information or recommendations generated by private groups with vested interests are more suspect than those produced by government. Government, constrained by a need to balance concerns of competing interests, is generally perceived by citizens as more likely to present reliable information. While the degree to which these explanations operate may vary, citizens who accept government's legitimacy are also likely to accept the authoritativeness of its reports. Government outsiders have no such an advantage.

Of course the actions of individual women and traditional organizations already studied by others were indeed vital. Nevertheless at least two facets of governmental entities require attention for a complete understanding of the movement's resurgence: the availability and active use of public resources to build a communication infrastructure, which hastened the development of the movement; and the ability to establish a legitimate public agenda for action on women's concerns. While the role of the government in the movement should not be inflated, it should be recognized for its unique and essential contributions.

Government As Stimulus for Interest Organization

Women's interests are far from alone in using governmental resources to create outside organized efforts. Within the agricultural arena, the largest and most important association had a

> close relation to government from its beginnings . . . in the form of Federal funds and encouragement for the formation of farm bureaus. . . . With the aid of officials of the United States Department of Agriculture, the American Farm Bureau was launched in 1919–20.[19]

This type of relationship between government and interests has accelerated in the past two decades with the explosion of interest-group activity and the development of issue networks. One of the most notable consequences of the growth of issue networks — bureau and agency administrators, members of Congress and their

[17] For example, see Paul R. Abramson, *Political Attitudes In America* (San Francisco: W.H. Freeman, 1983), esp. 230.

[18] National Manpower Council, *Womanpower: A Statement by the National Manpower Council with Chapters by the Council Staff* (New York: Columbia University Press, 1957). Clarenbach in interview states that *Womanpower* served as an important precursor for the PCSW.

[19] See David B. Truman, *The Governmental Process* (New York: Alfred A. Knopf, 1971/1951), esp. 87–93.

staffs, and affected interest groups—has been the rise of "second generation interest groups."[20]

The birth and maturation of most new groups depend upon prior governmental policies or programs that bureaucrats are charged to carry out. Then, within an already established broad policy area, bureaucrats become advocates for additional activities. Examples of these dynamics include welfare and environmental interest areas, among others.[21] It is within this context that members of governmental bodies concerned with women applied governmental resources to create the infrastructure upon which the women's movement grew.

Governmental bodies then find it in their interest to engineer, if possible, or at least encourage the development of a strong outside constituency. From 1963 to 1969, governmental bodies concerned with women did just that as officials proactively applied resources to establish women's concerns on the public agenda and to foster and control a mobilized outside constituency.

ESTABLISHING A LEGITIMATE WOMEN'S AGENDA

While governmental bodies are by definition authoritative, activities deemed appropriate or legitimate for each vary according to each body's stated purpose. Therefore, in order to understand the ways in which governmental involvement contributed to perceptions of a legitimate women's agenda, one must also understand the importance of the structures and processes of the governmental organizations concerned with women.

Although the Women's Bureau had been generating authoritative reports for over forty years by 1961, no movement had developed. Certainly, a society increasingly aware of "a general sense of disenchantment with the idyllic image of female fulfillment in domestic life" was a necessary ingredient.[22] Lacking this, the government was unlikely to act. Even so, its bureaucratic structure constrained Women's Bureau activity.[23] The critical difference within governmental structures can be traced to the development of advisory bodies.[24] Once these were added to the for-

---

[20] Advisory Commission on Intergovernmental Relations, *The Federal Role In the Federal System: The Dynamics of Growth*, Report A-86 (Washington D.C.: U.S. Government Printing Office, June 1981), 16.

[21] Ibid., 11–19.

[22] Gayle Graham Yates, *What Women Want: The Ideas of the Movement* (Cambridge, Mass.: Harvard University Press, 1975), 3, cites the 1959 publication of Eleanor Flexner's history of American feminism, *Century of Struggle* (Cambridge, Mass.: Harvard University Press, 1959); Mable Newcomer, *Century of Higher Education for Women* (New York: Harper, 1959) documents the decline of women's involvement in academic life; and Robert W. Smuts, *Women and Work in America* (New York: Columbia University Press, 1959) shows little change for women working outside the home as examples of this growing awareness.

[23] See Sealander, *As Minority Becomes Majority*, 8, for a cogent discussion of this problem from 1920 to 1963.

[24] Sealander, *As Minority Becomes Majority*, 5, notes examples of previous advisory bodies but underestimates the ability of the Women's Bureau to engineer outcomes due to its control of resources.

mula in a time of growing social consciousness, governmental dynamics concerning women took on an entirely different cast.

Synergy: The Best-of-Both-Structures

Different types of organizational structures are endowed with different kinds of resources. For that reason, creating advisory bodies able to complement the capacity of the Women's Bureau proved an essential ingredient for establishing and disseminating a legitimate women's agenda. Women activists in the federal government had created a situation in which beneficial resources inherent in each structure could be used.

Statutory bodies, such as the Women's Bureau, have many structural advantages. Bodies created by legislatures are likely to continue once established in the bureaucracy; they usually have sufficient budgets to undertake larger and longer term projects; and they have offices that afford resources such as staff expertise, clerical support, telephone, and copying. Of greater importance in establishing a nationwide communication network, the Women's Bureau was stably located and easily found over an extended period of time. However, a bureau is "neutral," at least technically, and constrained to advocacy within its legal mandate. Recommendations for action beyond its mandate are not legitimate.

Alternatively, appointive structures are usually advisory bodies; the President's Commission On the Status of Women, the Citizen's Advisory Council on the Status of Women, the Task Force on Women's Rights and Responsibilities, and State Commissions are examples. Their purpose differs from the neutral bureaucratic unit. They are generally short-lived and mandated to investigate a specific area in order to make recommendations. This mandate enables considerable freedom both in defining their own objectives or agendas and in critically evaluating public policy. Most important, appointed advisory bodies control the legitimate agenda, a fundamental power in the policy process. However, these bodies usually lack fiscal resources, technical expertise, and long-term connections.

While the strength of one structure is the weakness of the other, by working together synergy can result. Synergistic dynamics from combining the expertise, stability, and budget of statutory bodies with the agenda control and policy-generating capacity of appointed advisory bodies are evident on many fronts among the federal entities concerned with women.

The Initial Agenda and a Climate for Action

Esther Peterson, director of the Women's Bureau, was cognizant of the bureau's limits. She persuaded President John F. Kennedy to appoint individuals to the PCSW from the "power structure."[25] By breaking the tradition of partisan ap-

---

[25] Information in this paragraph is from the interview with Esther Peterson. The impetus for creating the PCSW has been placed squarely with Peterson, who was then the director of the Women's Bureau. See Zelman, *Women, Work, and National Policy*, esp. chap. 2.

pointments, both believed a program of action with the potential to achieve results would develop. With the prominence of persons on the PCSW whose careers were not primarily identified with working women's concerns, "[t]here is no question that the members . . . , as a group, were able to tap resources and gain attention more easily than the Women's Bureau."[26] Peterson also secured sufficient funding for the PCSW to publish and distribute 200,000 copies of its report, *American Women*, and assured continued attention to the PCSW agenda through the immediate creation of the Interdepartmental Committee on the Status of Women and the CAC, which were also linked to the Women's Bureau.

The governmental capacity to produce and widely distribute well-researched reports with recommendations was an important contribution in two ways: it established an agenda carrying expectations for public action and raised feminist consciousness among professionally employed women holding positions within "the establishment."[27] These women were able to muster their personal and positional resources to foster mainstream acceptance of the women's movement and to cajole other women into pushing for governmental activity. While Betty Friedan's *The Feminine Mystique* was critical in raising consciousness among women, including those in traditional roles, it did not provide an organized agenda for action.[28]

According to Mary Hilton, deputy director of the Women's Bureau from 1964 to 1981, *American Women* set the agenda for both women activists inside and outside government.

> [It] wasn't any great original thought on the part of the Commission. These certainly were issues that were in the air and that other women's organizations had been working on. What the Commission did, and it was an invaluable service, was to codify those issues and clarify them. My own view is that the Women's Bureau and then the PCSW powered the women's movement.[29]

Though not original in issues addressed, no other single work on women contained the breadth of isssue, clarity of statement, or was so widely distributed at that time.

Although the PCSW's recommendations were intentionally presented in a very acceptable (if not conservative) manner, as advisory bodies the PCSW (and the CAC and TFWRR, which followed) had the latitude to bring new and controversial subjects into the realm of public discourse.

> One of the least measurable and most far-reaching results of the Roosevelt (Kennedy's) Commission was to make discussion of women's "role" and "status" respectable. Almost

---

[26] Sealander, *As Minority Becomes Majority*, 144.

[27] See, for example, Catherine East's conversion to a pro-ERA position during PCSW meeting discussions, in Paterson, *Be Somebody*, 136.

[28] Clarenbach, Peterson, East, and Hilton all refer to Friedan's contribution to the movement in their interviews.

[29] Interview with author.

83,000 copies of the report, *American Women*, were distributed in the first year and its recommendations were quoted and summarized in women's organizations' publications.[30]

A broad range of women's issues entered the realm of legitimate public debate for the first time since suffrage.

Furthermore, the government's ability to attract and pay women of stature like Dr. Mary I. Bunting, president of Radcliffe College, and Mary R. Callahan, member of the executive board of the International Union of Electrical, Radio, and Machine Workers, to participate in making recommendations was a critical factor in mobilizing mainstream support by giving the reports credence with potential feminists. In Allan's view, because of the regard for individuals on the commissions by members of outside organizations, "Women who belonged to organizations paid attention. We tried to help to implement those recommendations [because] . . . they listened to the so-called constituency."[31]

The CAC was especially granted latitude to expand the agenda because its inside counterpart, the Interdepartmental Committee on the Status of Women, lacked authority to control its recommendations. The CAC was also mandated to serve as a liaison with private organizations. Both provisions were unususal for citizen advisory bodies and both enabled it to expand the agenda and constituency for women's concerns through annual and in-depth subcommittee reports. Along with the changed social climate, these provisions help explain the mobilization that followed from these advisory bodies, and not from the earlier bodies that Judith Sealander discusses.[32]

Critical to successful action, government funds were used to disseminate these informative reports to interested parties such as professional women, establishment women's organization leaders, state legislators, and libraries. Between 1964 and 1969, the CAC maintained a mailing list of about 10,000 who received all reports. In total, about 20,000 of each CAC report were distributed nationally at no charge, with many copies disseminated at traditional women's groups' meetings throughout the country.[33]

The 1969 report of the TFWRR, *A Matter of Simple Justice*, also made far-reaching recommendations. In it, a governmental body recommended passage of the Equal Rights Amendment and reaffirmed prior CAC positions on no-fault divorce, relaxed abortion laws, and others. Because of these controversial recommendations, the director of the Women's Bureau, Elizabeth Koontz, needed to

[30] Catherine East, *American Woman: 1963, 1983, 2003* (Washington, D.C.: National Federation of Business and Professional Women's Clubs, Inc., 1983), 10.

[31] Interview with author.

[32] Sealander, *As Minority Becomes Majority.*

[33] East's interview for mailing list information. Allan mentions distributing 300 copies of *American Women* at a conference in Michigan in 1963. At a 1969 Leadership Conference in Wisconsin, the Women's Bureau supplied 100 copies each of fifteen different women's publications. Clarenbach papers, Wisconsin Memorial Library Archives, Madison, Box 6, File 2.

convince the White House to release the report publicly.[34] While the National Organization For Women (NOW) and other outside groups had by then taken such stands, with this report the government provided legitimacy.

This best-of-both-structures arrangement enabled a synergistic approach to women's issues at the federal level. Advisory bodies could broaden the agenda and spark debate on policy-related matters. Simultaneously, the Women's Bureau applied data collection resources and longstanding expertise for background information, thereby making the reports unquestionably legitimate. Ironically, the perception that the Women's Bureau was antifeminist under Peterson and Mary Keyserling probably contributed to the legitimacy in a time when mere discussion of the status of women was controversial. The efforts of the PCSW and later advisory bodies broke public sod that lay fallow for decades, addressing some issues that had never been tilled by a governmental agency. By doing so, the government set the broad public agenda of women's concerns for several years.[35]

But accommodating structures and a legitimate agenda were only the beginning. Individuals within the federal bodies concerned with women also made conscious efforts to establish the necessary infrastructure for a larger women's movement by mobilizing a constituency around the agenda they helped develop.

ACTIVISM: DETERMINED USE OF GOVERNMENTAL RESOURCES

In an era of issue networks, second-generation interest groups constitute an essential ingredient if government officials are to be successful advocates for additional activity. First, civil servants in the network are expected to remain neutral and are therefore limited in their ability to lobby for a cause. Second, various interests compete for the attention of elected officials and for public funds. If the Women's Bureau and the advisory bodies were to obtain funding for increased levels of activity, a mobilized constituency was needed to lobby Congress and the White House. For these reasons, feminists within the government would quite rationally and consciously attempt to transform themselves into a movement. They needed a mobilized constituency throughout the country to be successful. The development of State Commissions on the Status of Women became critical in creating the mobilized constituency, which in turn became a nationwide infrastructure for the women's movement.

The availability of simple but essential office resources was indispensable in the creation and maintenance of the fledgling communication network. Federal bodies facilitated an interstate communication network by using WATS line telephone privileges, maintaining and dispersing mailing lists, copying pertinent materials,

[34] Both East and Allan cite the efforts of Koontz as critical for the report's release. It was widely disseminated at the conference for the fiftieth anniversary of the Women's Bureau.

[35] Peterson, East, Hilton, Allan and Clarenbach all agreed emphatically on this point. While they all were insiders and can be expected to hold this view, East and Clarenbach played critical roles in outsiders efforts also.

and providing postage for meeting notices. Many of these resources were applied on an informal basis and Catherine East — through her centralized position as executive secretary for the CAC — was at the hub of the newly emerging network from 1964 onward. Kathryn Clarenbach recounts the utility of East's "midnight phone calls" for keeping abreast of activities at the federal level and in other states.[36] Virginia Allan describes the value of East's work more poignantly: "Catherine East was the Thomas Paine of the women's movement. She used her xerox machine like he used his printing press."[37] Using such organizational resources, the small staff of the CAC gathered information from across the states and distributed both federal and state advances in thinking throughout the country.

The national government's regional organization structure also proved useful in establishing the movement's infrastructure.[38] While regions differed in activities and effectiveness, regional Women's Bureau offices were directed to serve as hubs by utilizing their administrative resources. Marguerite Gilmore from the Chicago office was especially active. She went so far as to design a number of pamphlets to aid State Commissions.[39]

The role of the Women's Bureau in establishing the infrastructure was formal as well. In 1965 the Women's Bureau's stated functions and services were to "provide informed, active leadership; serve as a clearinghouse for the exchange of ideas and information by sharing its data and findings on a wide scale; and serve as a reference resource which includes giving assistance to State Commissions as they organize."[40] These stated purposes belie Freeman's view that the Women's Bureau served as a "latent resource" that waited for groups to develop.

Neither the Women's Bureau nor the CAC appeared to behave as passive helpmates waiting to provide latent assistance to developing groups. While the Women's Bureau did not support feminism per se prior to 1969, its technical and advisory assistance to state and local level activities (as well as outside constituencies) fostered the development of women's rights groups and the larger movement mainly by working through state governments. Furthermore, the pattern of involvement suggests members of governmental entities were quite deliberate in their attempts to create (and in some cases, control) the development of State Commissions.

Deliberately Creating A Network: Proactivity

To ascertain if individuals in the federal bodies consciously intended to create a national commmunication network or infrastructure necessary to sustain a movement, in interviews I posed related questions to Esther Peterson, director of the

[36] Interview with author.
[37] Interview with author.
[38] According to Hilton, Peterson charged the regional offices of the Women's Bureau with the task of helping to establish State Commissions in 1963 and that mandate continued under Keyserling.
[39] East, Hilton, and Clarenbach all state this in interviews.
[40] U.S. Department of Labor, *Women's Bureau*, Brochure.

Women's Bureau from 1960 to 1964; Mary Hilton, deputy director of the Women's Bureau from 1964–1981; Catherine East, executive secretary for the CAC from 1963 to 1975; and Virginia Allan, program chair (1962) and president of the National Federation of Business and Professional Women's Clubs (BPW) in 1963, member of the CAC from 1968 to 1971 and chair of the TFWRR in 1969–1970. Their responses are revealing.

Peterson reports that she was not particularly conscious of creating an ongoing network. For her, the move to establish State Commissions was a practice in "the art of the possible," a pragmatic strategy to take the action program of the PCSW report to the source of the difficulty — state laws. "Quite naturally we moved to the states. . . . I think unconsciously we thought that the whole women's movement would come out of this. But we really had to go after those [state] laws. . . . We had to be practical."[41] Although this practical strategy was consistent with the anti-ERA approach, the move to the states involved the BPW, one of the few traditional women's organizations to support ERA.[42] This perhaps indicates that Peterson was indeed more concerned with action than with blocking ERA. Allan was critical as they "moved to the states" and recounts her intention at the time.

> I was appointed to the Governor's Commission in the state of Michigan [in 1962, the first in the nation]. What we were doing in Michigan impressed me greatly. At the same time, I was the first vice-president in charge of programs for the national BPW. It occurred to me that it would be wonderful if we had State Commissions across the country. . . . I got an appointment with Peterson and she thought it was a great idea. . . . We [BPW] said we were willing to push the idea. She said that was great but she wanted all possible organizations to get involved. That's what BPW did. We gave the major push but encouraged other organizations to go along with them.[43]

Allan describes an attempt to involve a wide range of organizations. In other words, Allan sought to create State Commissions across the country and consciously used the existing national structure of the BPW to do so.[44]

East's comments reveal that she was quite aware of the role she played as information conduit mentioned by Clarenbach and Allan above. Furthermore, when asked to characterize the relationship between the Women's Bureau and outside women's organizations, she responded:

> I think it was proactive. The regional directors of the Women's Bureau . . . were very active in getting the State Commissions set up. They worked closely with the BPW . . .

---

[41] The Women's Bureau, U.S. Department of Labor, *Milestones: The Women's Bureau Celebrates 65 Years of Women's Labor History* (Washington, D.C.: U.S. Government Printing Office, 1985). Quote from author's interview with Peterson.

[42] Jo Freeman reminds me, in personal correspondence.

[43] Interview with author.

[44] One cannot overstate the importance of BPW for establishing State Commissions in all the states. Paterson argues, "Without Rawalt and a few others (like Allan) there would have been no bridge between suffrage and the women's movement of the 1960s," *Be Somebody*, xviii. Jo Freeman, in personal correspondence, argues that "there would not have been state commissions without BPW."

in getting staff services. . . . They were very supportive . . . and it became even more so when Libby Koontz became director of the Women's Bureau. It was always a very open and active support.[45]

In a caveat East adds that one reason Women's Bureau directors prior to Koontz provided support was to control the direction of the emerging movement.

Mary Hilton reports overt intentions on the part of the Women's Bureau to foster a nationwide communication network.

> That was always one of our ambitions. But the Bureau had a very small staff. . . . Although we tried informally, I don't think we were ever able to establish any formal communication between the State Commissions. But lots happened informally. . . . People knew each other from the conferences and the conferences were really important for developing the network.[46]

The conferences were carefully orchestrated to serve as a vehicle for reproducing the federal approach and agenda within the states and to put women together in such a way that a network was likely to emerge.

These key women report at least some awareness that a national network would follow from efforts by federal bodies to establish State Commissions. Most state those intentions explicitly. Furthermore, all saw the federal bodies consciously playing an active role in laying the foundation for what eventually became the women's movement. While all agreed that governmental efforts alone would have been insufficient, governmental services remained critical in creating and sustaining the embryonic infrastructure.

FEDERAL ACTION, STATE REACTION

Most accounts of State Commissions credit them with little short-term success in implementing recommendations for action on the women's agenda. As Freeman indicates, however, they were useful for raising consciousness and bringing women across the country together to discuss specific issues — those raised in *American Women*.[47] By examining the rise and fall of State Commissions, one can detail their catalyst function for the nascent women's movement.

The extent of federal influence on the direction taken by State Commissions is evident on a number of counts. Federal advisory bodies recommended that states form commissions and then served as models to states. Women's Bureau representatives used the prestige of their federal affiliation to aid state women in obtaining gubernatorial action and then applied federal resources to maintain State Commissions initially. Perhaps most important, dynamics surrounding a series of federally sponsored conferences for the states illustrate the overall pattern of federal action and state reaction from 1963 to 1969. The pattern demonstrates strong fed-

---

[45] Interview with author.
[46] Interview with author.
[47] Freeman, *Politics of Women's Liberation*, esp. 52–53.

eral influence on the internal structure and perceived purposes of state commissions — a course of action that helped launch the mainstream women's movement.

Creating State-level Interest and Structures

Before the PCSW had filed its report on 11 October 1963, President Kennedy urged
a nationwide effort to create a Commission on the Status of Women in every state.
The BPW, under the leadership of Virginia Allen, spearheaded the effort, with
the support and direction of the Women's Bureau under Esther Peterson.[48]

The Women's Bureau plied its resources in a number of ways. As early as February
1963, Peterson raised the question of establishing a State Commission patterned
after the PCSW in Wisconsin before a group of fifty statewide women leaders.[49]
She took every opportunity to travel to states and plant the seed across the country.
In 1964 the Women's Bureau sponsored a series of regional meetings to disseminate
ideas and stimulate discussion.[50] Regional Women's Bureau staff worked closely
with state women to establish State Commissions, even accompanying them to
meetings with governors to broach the subject. Upon request, representatives from
the Women's Bureau met with newly-formed commissions to advise on organizational procedures, help plan and participate in programs, supply background information and special studies, advise on the formulation of proposed legislation,
and assist with conferences and other commission meetings.[51] Inasmuch as forming
a governmental advisory body was novel to most of these women, let alone formulating legislation, the advice of the Women's Bureau was indispensible. Other
than the National Woman's Party (NWP), no outside mainstream feminist groups
were as yet in existence.[52]

On a more concrete level, most states were reticent to fund their commissions,
which proved to be a particular problem. For example, in 1965 one governor
responded to a commission member's concern over the lack of a budget that it
"shouldn't be any particular problem to finance the activities through one of the
companies with whom some of the gals are associated."[53] So the Women's Bureau

[48] East, *American Woman*, 10, as well as Allen and Peterson interviews; and Zelman, *Women, Work*.

[49] "On Wisconsin Women: Chronology of Recent Highlights of Wisconsin's Women's Movement
(1962-77)," prepared for Wisconsin International Women's Year Meeting, 3–5 June 1977, Madison.
From Kathryn Clarenbach's personal papers. Next sentence from her interview.

[50] Zelman, *Women, Work*, 74. Three of the four regional meetings she cites occurred within
the Chicago region.

[51] U.S. Department of Labor, *Women's Bureau*, brochure, 1965.

[52] However, the NWP focused mainly on efforts to pass the ERA and was not successful in renewing
its membership. Hole and Levine, *Rebirth of Feminism*, 78–79. It also maintained an elite posture,
generally lacking concern for issues affecting working-class or poor women in contrast to the Women's
Bureau coalition. Leila J. Rupp, "The Women's Community in the National Woman's Party, 1945–1960s,"
Signs 10 (Summer 1985): 715–739, esp. 719.

[53] Letter to Nancy K. Knaak from Governor Warren P. Knowles, 29 October 1965. Clarenbach papers,
Box 6, File 8.

assistance with mailings and conference materials made simple operation in pursuit of State Commission mandates possible.

Lack of interest on the part of the governors led them to establish commissions to appease a handful of interested women. Mostly, according to Clarenbach, governors "couldn't have cared less what they did or didn't do."[54] Few state officials apparently saw harm in letting female activists meet under state auspices. But because state officials were generally indifferent to the efforts of state women and provided little support, the role of the Women's Bureau took on additional meaning.

Undoubtedly some states would have formed a commission without federal support. Michigan, for example, established its commission in August 1962. However, many probably would not have come into existence without the considerable federal urging and support.[55] Even with it, one state formed its commission as late as 1967. One can also predict that the State Commissions would have been slow to develop sophistication without assistance from federal women's entities. Nevertheless, governmental bodies dealing with the status of women were established across the country and women's concerns achieved a measure of legitimacy at the state level.

Solidifying the Infrastructure: National Conferences

As part of their mandate, the IC and CAC were to assist State Commissions by sponsoring (with Women's Bureau technical and other support) national conferences for State Commissions. They did so with national conferences held in Washington D.C. in 1964, 1965, 1966, and 1968, and regional conferences in 1967. Prior to 1968 the conferences were planned and fully orchestrated by key individuals from the federal entities.[56] Implications for the nationwide feminist infrastructure are found in the conferences' agendas and through the expansion of types of women attending.[57]

The 1964 First National Conference of Governors' Commissions on the Status of Women program was devoted entirely to organizing State Commissions based upon the federal model. While states were under no obligation to mimic the federal approach, the conference's message encouraged it. Twenty-four State Commissions represented by seventy-three delegates and eight states considering estab-

---

[54] Interview with author.

[55] *Progress Report on the Status of Women: October 11, 1963 through October 10, 1964*, First Annual Report of the Interdepartmental Committee and Citizens' Advisory Council On the Status of Women (Washington, D.C.: U.S. Government Printing Office), 20.

[56] Indicated in the conferences' Programs and confirmed in interviews.

[57] Paterson, *Be Somebody*, 152, quotes a letter about the 1964 conference from Rawalt to Alice McRae in which she notes the importance of these conferences for the revival of feminism. "Out of favor since suffrage, the word 'feminist' was slipping back into the language. In speaking of the new state commissions Virginia Allan, then national president of BPW, used the word favorably and in its broadest meaning."

lishing commissions participated. The conference program lists fifty-four observers from twenty states, a large contingent from Washington, D.C., and representatives from Puerto Rico and Canada.[58]

The 1965 conference evidenced the increasing stature of State Commissions and an ability of the federal-level entities to command more attention. Of the forty-four State Commissions in existence at the time, forty-three sent representatives, as did the remaining six states that as yet had no State Commissions. President Lyndon B. Johnson headed the day-long parade of Washington dignitaries who addressed the 446 people in attendance—a marked change in both the list of speakers and the number of state women present. Symbolically, this suggests increased prestige for State Commissions. Pragmatically, it implies that women as a constituency were beginning to be recognized—especially mainstream women, perhaps bolstered in order to counter the growing number of those making more radical demands.

The Information Exchange program was designed by planners to give their preferred substance and form to the burgeoning communications network. Eleven morning workshops presented information from *American Women* (plus Title VII) that delegates "needed to know." By default and concern, these were topics for State Commissions to consider. The six afternoon sessions covered the nuts and bolts of a successful State Commission.[59]

By 1966 the idea of governmental commissions on the status of women had a toehold across all levels of government. Conference planners had dropped the "Governors'" from the title in order to include city and territorial representatives. The meeting also attracted a large contingent of observers. For the first time, the conference did not concentrate on organizing state commissions. Instead it focused on a greatly expanded issue agenda covered in twenty-eight panel discussions. The agenda was becoming more sophisticated as women's consciousness inside and outside government increased. While many State Commissions faced expiring mandates, the conference presented the message that even more issues than before required attention. Of greater importance to the larger women's movement, for the last time governmental-sponsored activity served as the only game in town. The National Organization for Women was born at this conference.

Pressed by expiring State Commissions mandates, a conference format that prohibited participants from passing resolutions, and understanding of the need for an outside constituency, Catherine East and the "Washington underground" decided an autonomous group was needed.[60] East had been encouraging women with national organizational experience such as Marguerite Rawalt, former president of BPW, to start an action-oriented women's organization.[61] Eventually, East and

[58] Conference data from Hole and Levine, *Rebirth of Feminism*, 402; "Program of the 1964 Conference," Clarenbach papers, Box 6, File 5.

[59] *Report of the Second National Conference of Governors' Commission on the Status of Women* (Washington, D.C.: U.S. GPO, 1965), 43-61.

[60] See Friedan, *"It Changed My Life,"* 76-83.

[61] See Paterson, *Be Somebody*, 157-168 for Rawalt's perspective.

others cajoled a reluctant Betty Friedan into working on the idea, secured her conference invitation, and provided her with the names of key women from state commissions, including Kathryn Clarenbach. Friedan then invited a carefully selected group of women attending the conference to a meeting in her hotel room. East also attended. After Clarenbach learned Keyserling, the director of the Women's Bureau, would not allow the conference to take action and pass a resolution, Clarenbach changed her position and supported the formation of NOW, much to the dismay of Keyserling.[62] In an ironic turn of events, a conference called by federal entities for state representatives served as the vehicle to end governmental dominance of the infant women's movement — an end largely precipitated by women long active in government.

The year of 1967 was a tenuous time for State Commissions. A majority of states did not provide travelling or general operating expenses.[63] In addition, some of the most active people's efforts were drained off into NOW. Recognizing these limitations, the federal governmental bodies sponsored and supported conferences within each of the federal regional divisions and the Women's Bureau regional offices easily served as a resource.

The regional conferences served several purposes. First, the cost of attending decreased so that greater numbers of women came to participate and the base of the audience with a raised consciousness expanded.[64] Second, conferences fostered regional communication networks, because like-minded women in the same proximity — many of whom could not attend national conferences — got to know one another. Third, because the agenda of these conferences dealt with national not regional concerns, a crossfertilization of ideas and identification of tactics appropriate for a geographical area occurred.[65] This arguably increased the saliency of agenda items for participants and the effectiveness of their efforts. In effect, regional conferences expanded the mobilized constituency for the Women's Bureau, CAC, State Commissions, and the newly emerging women's issues organizations outside of government.

A transition period began in 1968. Commissions were disintegrating as state officials withdrew authorization and support and federal efforts proved inadequate to maintain their needs.[66] State governments could no longer be indifferent to a few harmless female activists. Women were establishing autonomous pressure groups and mobilized, mainstream women were no longer dependent solely on governmental direction. Conditions had changed and roles began to shift. A power transfer was underway.

[62] According to East's interviews. Clarenbach's interviews support this version of her actions and Keyserling's reaction.

[63] *Third Annual Report of the IC and CAC*, 80.

[64] Clarenbach in interviews states that the expanded number of women with a raised consciousness was a critical outcome of the regional conferences.

[65] Hilton interview.

[66] Clarenbach papers, Box 6, File 5; letter from Clarenbach to members of 1968 planning committee discusses this disintegration.

172 | GEORGIA DUERST-LAHTI

The skill and mobilization levels of State Commission members had increased, and momentum swung away from Washington. Seven State Commission members participated in conference planning thereby ending the federal monopoly over the program. However, the federal government, still superior in issue development and resources, continued to fund the conference, including provision of expenses for the state representatives to participate in a planning meeting.[67]

Nonetheless, the product of those resources began to change in a reflection of the growing sophistication of women inside and outside of government. With the goal "that the exchange of ideas this conference made possible will serve as a spur to action throughout the country,"[68] the conference program included how-to's of implementation and leadership. Further, the program encouraged state women to support CAC recommendations drawn mainly from several task forces commissioned to develop indepth reports. Included in the program were action-oriented sessions on equal employment opportunities, childcare services, and women in leadership. Recommendations of the CAC included legal abortion, repeal of a number of protective labor laws, and maternity benefits. But while the issue agenda was still introduced to state representatives by spokespersons on the federal advisory bodies, many of key advisory body members also belonged to NOW. As a result, "[d]espite the difference in tone . . . their [the CAC Task Force reports] women's agenda mirrored NOW's Bill of Rights and the aims of the moderate women's movement in general."[69] In short, governmental bodies no longer fully controlled the agenda.

The 1968 conference also encouraged further development of an infrastructure in two ways. First, an afternoon session devoted to "outlining an Action Program for Day Care" was organized according to geographic regions. Consistent with their charge, Women's Bureau staff members served as recorders for each regional session. This arrangement fostered relationships much as the regional conferences had. Second, one session was devoted to strategies for involving all types of groups in commission structures and activities. It was a short course on mobilizing a women's constituency.

By June 1968 the pattern of federal action and state reaction was no longer clear. Federal efforts had succeeded in establishing the foundation of a nationwide infrastructure for a women's movement, even if that was not the original intent and if some individuals feared the loss of control. All fifty states claimed some form of State Commission providing at least a symbol of a legitimate public forum for debate about women's concerns. And through individual state commission members, who constituted walking coalitions with overlapping membership in

[67] Ibid., copy of "Travelers authorization" for the planning meeting paid out of the Woman's Bureau account.
[68] *1968: Time for Action*, highlights of the Fourth National Conference of Commissions on the Status of Women, Washington D.C., 20–22 June 1968, iii.
[69] Paterson, *Be Somebody*, 189.

public and private women's organizations, the public debate began to take on a decidedly different, more feminist tone.

With the 1969 appointment of Elizabeth Koontz as director of the Women's Bureau, feminists gained an ally inside the most stable governmental unit devoted to women's concerns. Among other changes, the bureau reversed its longstanding opposition to the Equal Rights Amendment (ERA). Koontz actively used the director's status and cordial relations with key congresswomen like Martha Griffiths to promote its passage in Congress. The rise of women's issues organizations outside of government and the increasing sophistication of issues tackled by State Commissions blurred the direction in which agenda issues flowed, even though the federal entities maintained the upper hand in structural resources. The Women's Bureau and CAC now served more as a supporter of state and outside efforts than as the sole agenda setter and facilitator of the network's development.

Probably the best example of changes underway was the shift in the federal relationship with the State Commissions. In lieu of the regular national conference for commissions, Koontz proposed a meeting of governor-appointed state representatives to discuss the possibility of the State Commissions forming their own private organization. This federal proposal was accepted, and throughout 1969 the Women's Bureau paid costs for the organizing committee of the newly forming Interstate Association of Commissions on the Status of Women (IACSW).

The IACSW held its first annual meeting in conjunction with the Women's Bureau's fiftieth anniversary celebration. While no direct, on-going federal funding ever existed for the IACSW, the Women's Bureau contributed money by acting as a sponsor for their annual meetings, providing materials, and serving in advisory and technical roles for conferences and individual State Commissions. The Bureau also continued to act as the communications hub by maintaining up-to-date mailing lists and generally keeping track of developments in State Commissions.[70] They continued this last function through the Reagan administration.

CONCLUSION

To project how the movement might have proceeded without these mundane but essential organizational services can be no more than speculation. With the changed social context, women were likely to have mobilized anyway. However, without the active application of governmental resources to the needs of the movement's infrastructure, the movement's resources, pattern of national mobilization, and issue construction undoubtedly would have been quite different. Much like the radical wing of the movement, the organizational structure probably would have remained localized for a longer time; and gaining legitimacy for women's concerns would quite probably have proved much more difficult. In short, govern-

[70] Interview with Hannah Rosenthal, executive director of Wisconsin Women's Council, 20 May 1985.

mental activity promoted nationalization of the women's movement — the root of any movement — and hastened its development.

One must remember the timing of the governmental activity. In the early 1960s, by and large a women's agenda and feminist consciousness existed only among women long active in government. The federal government, through the Women's Bureau and commissions/councils, initiated action as advocates for women. During the critical early stages of the women's movement, governmental entities provided a base in government for policy change, access for a sympathetic hearing, and insiders to influence decision makers. By working with and through state governments and outside organizations, these activists used governmental resources to initiate a nationwide constituency knowledgeable in legitimate facts of women's status in America. And they created mobilized second-generation interest groups required by modern bureaucratic politics. In the process, they created a foundation upon which the women's movement could build; they also helped make concerns about women's status legitimate for mainstream America.*

* This paper is the product of the Dynamics of Divorce Law Reform project under the direction of Herbert Jacob supported by National Science Foundation Grant No. SES-8319321 and research funds from the Hawkins Chair in the Political Science Department at the University of Wisconsin. Thanks go to Herbert Jacob and Virginia Sapiro whose comments on drafts of this paper improved it immeasurably, and to Jo Freeman for additional insights.

Where Have All the Consumers Gone?

LOREE BYKERK
ARDITH MANEY

Despite a promising start, organized consumer activity at the national level was largely neglected as a research topic by political scientists in the 1980s.[1] Recent accounts of public interest group activity mention consumers only in passing and focus instead on governmental reform organizations like Common Cause or environmental organizations.[2] Whether or not the generalizations drawn based on those parts of the public interest community apply to consumer organizations has not been thoroughly explored. The general inattention and the charges of failure made by some accounts would lead an observer to conclude that organized consumer activity has disappeared or become entirely ineffective.[3] At the

---

[1] Mark V. Nadel, *The Politics of Consumer Protection* (Indianapolis: Bobbs-Merrill, 1971); David Vogel and Mark Nadel, "Who Is a Consumer: An Analysis of the Politics of Consumer Conflict," *American Politics Quarterly* 5 (January 1977): 27–56.

[2] Andrew McFarland, *Common Cause* (Chatham, NJ: Chatham House, 1984); Michael W. McCann, *Taking Reform Seriously: Perspectives on Public Interest Liberalism* (Ithaca, NY: Cornell University Press, 1986).

[3] Michael Pertschuk, *Revolt Against Regulation: The Rise and Pause of the Consumer Movement* (Berkeley: University of California Press, 1982); McCann, *Taking Reform Seriously*, 209–257.

LOREE BYKERK is associate professor of political science at the University of Nebraska at Omaha. She has published articles on interest group politics and insurance issues. ARDITH MANEY is associate professor of political science at Iowa State University. During Spring 1993 she was a Fulbright Lecturer in political science at the University of West Bohemia in Pilsen, Czech Republic. She has published articles on consumer interests and food policy.

same time, there are several general trends which seem to heighten the potential role that might be played by organized consumer voices.

Recent studies of interest groups detect an explosive growth in the number of groups and their activities in Washington.[4] There is general agreement that business interests in particular have mobilized new resources and are more active on the Washington scene.[5] By adapting innovations first developed by public interest groups, business interests have become more influential than before. The 1980s were dominated by business complaints about the costs of government regulation and by efforts to deregulate. Under the rubric of industrial policy and public/private partnerships, corporatist-like relationships have developed that involve a range of explicit government help for business.[6] Ought one to expect a responding upsurge on the part of consumer interests or at least scan the horizon for it?

This general expectation that there will be an organized consumer response parallels the pluralist argument for countervailing power recently revived by prominent political scientists.[7] Their explanations of the complex relationships between government and business argue that cycles of countervailing influences are visible in the long run.

Finally, economists and other observers have raised an audible outcry over the consumption-wild economy of the United States.[8] The acute, widely-shared concerns over the deficit, the debt, the trade imbalance, and the future of the United States in the world economy appear to offer organized consumer groups ample opportunity to wield influence on behalf of the shopper's role in macropolitical issues.

It is the tension between the two sets of messages that leads us to ask expectantly: Where have all the consumers gone? Are advocates for the consumer interest still alive and well in Washington after a decade that observers have generally characterized as sympathetic to the policy agenda of business?

[4] Jeffrey M. Berry, *The Interest Group Society* (Boston: Little, Brown, 1984), 16–45; Kay Lehman Schlozman and John T. Tierney, "More of the Same: Washington Pressure Group Activity in a Decade of Change," *Journal of Politics* 45 (May 1983): 351–377; Robert H. Salisbury, "Interest Representation: The Dominance of Institutions," *American Political Science Review* 78 (March 1984): 64–75.

[5] David Vogel, "The Power of Business in America: A Reappraisal," *British Journal of Political Science* 13 (January 1983): 19–43; Graham Wilson, "American Business and Politics" in Allan J. Cigler and Burdett A. Loomis, eds., *Interest Group Politics*, 2nd ed. (Washington, DC: Congressional Quarterly Press, 1986), 221–235.

[6] Mark Petracca, "The Reagan Revolution and the Role of Federal Advisory Committees" (Paper presented at the annual meeting of the Midwest Political Science Association, Chicago, 1988); Richard A. Harris, "Politicized Management: The Changing Face of Business in American Politics" in Richard A. Harris and Sidney M. Milkis, eds., *Remaking American Politics* (Boulder, CO: Westview Press, 1989), 261–286.

[7] Andrew McFarland, "Interest Groups and Theories of Power in America," *British Journal of Political Science* 17 (April 1987): 129–147; Jeffrey M. Berry, "The Post-Reagan Research Agenda for Business-Government Relations" (Roundtable presentation at the annual meeting of the Midwest Political Science Association, Chicago, 1988).

[8] Peter G. Peterson, "The Morning After," *The Atlantic Monthly* 260 (October 1987): 43–69.

The Nature of the Inquiry

Earlier studies began by defining the universe of people who might under some conditions be organized to pursue the consumer interest before a wide range of national government decision makers.[9] A different approach is taken here; we capture a distinct arena of consumer policy under consideration by government decision makers and then investigate which groups contest for favorable public policy outcomes.

To make the task manageable we chose a time period, roughly 1970–1985, and an arena where we could trace interactions among the various protagonists— congressional committee and subcommittee hearings. Representation by groups and individuals takes a variety of forms on Capitol Hill, many of which have been studied intensively by political scientists. Making political action committee (PAC) contributions, launching letter-writing campaigns, and seeking direct access to members of Congress and their staffs are all well-known examples.[10]

One measure of group activity insufficiently studied is group appearances when committees hold public hearings. There are a number of reasons to believe that this measure of activity deserves more attention. Research into committee activity was useful in pinpointing the decentralization of power and the rise of a generation of policy entrepreneurs, two trends that took place in Congress during the 1970s.[11] More recently, data on committee hearings has been used to show changing workload characteristics of Congress in the 1980s.[12]

Members of Congress hold committee hearings to advance legislation, educate the media and their colleagues about policy problems, investigate and oversee the work of executive branch agencies, and for other reasons.[13] Holding a hearing is a complicated undertaking for legislators; it requires the commitment of staff and other resources, which are then unavailable for other purposes.

Analyzing hearing participation captures as complete a picture of interest group activity as is possible. Kay Lehman Schlozman and John T. Tierney's Washington Representatives Survey shows that virtually all organizations seeking to exercise influence in Washington present testimony at congressional hearings. That study

[9] Nadel, *Politics of Consumer Protection*, 155–204; Vogel and Nadel, "Who Is a Consumer," 27–30; Joan Lucco, "The Voice of Consumer Groups in White House Policymaking from Kennedy to Reagan" (Paper presented at the annual meeting of the Midwest Political Science Association, Chicago, 1987), 3–4.

[10] Kay Lehman Schlozman and John T. Tierney, *Organized Interests and American Democracy* (New York: Harper & Row, 1986), 148–169.

[11] Roger H. Davidson, "Subcommittee Government: New Channels for Policymaking" in Thomas E. Mann and Norman E. Ornstein, eds., *The New Congress* (Washington, DC: American Enterprise Institute, 1981), 99–133; David E. Price, "Policymaking in Congressional Committees: The Impact of 'Environmental' Factors," *American Political Science Review* 72 (June 1978): 548–74.

[12] Roger H. Davidson and Carol Hardy, *Indicators of House of Representatives Workload and Activity*, Congressional Research Service Report for Congress, 87–4295, 8 June 1987.

[13] William J. Keefe and Morris S. Ogul, *The American Legislative Process*, 7th ed. (Englewood Cliffs, NJ: Prentice-Hall, 1989), 181–188.

showed that presenting testimony led the list of twenty-seven techniques for exercising influence.[14] Also, this activity is on the record and accessible for research, while other common techniques of influence such as contacting officials directly or making informal social contacts are not so accessible.

Finally, undertaking to testify before a congressional committee or subcommittee represents an important commitment of time and resources on the part of the interest group. Thus, evaluation of their involvement in hearings ought to yield important information about interest groups and the policy agendas they are pursuing.

GONE TO CONGRESS EVERY ONE?

Earlier literature on consumer group activity focused on just a handful of organizations. Later we will present detailed information about groups claiming to represent the consumer's interest that have been active before congressional committees during the period under study here. But first we provide an overview of consumer group activity by using two key organizations identified from earlier studies of consumer interest groups — the Consumer Federation of America (CFA), Consumers Union (CU), and one individual activist, Ralph Nader. For each of the three we cite data in connection with all House and Senate hearings from 1969 to 1985 as indexed by Congressional Information Service (CIS) for 1970–1986.[15] Overall activity totals show that these consumer groups participated as witnesses in 349 Senate hearings and 307 House hearings. Figure 1 reveals an activity peak in the mid-1970s, particularly 1975, with lower levels of activity thereafter. Overall, activity in the Carter and Reagan years is at about the same level as it was in the early 1970s. Figure 1 also suggests a trend of activity shifting more toward the House than the Senate. These consumer activitists directed more attention to House hearings in every year except two. The same general trend of focusing toward the House also holds for the three sets of activists taken separately.

It is also possible to make comparisons between and among these three sets of activists. CFA was cited in the CIS Index in conjunction with 208 hearings during the entire period; CU was mentioned 182 times, and Nader on 166 occasions. But we are, of course, comparing the activities of two organizations to those of one individual!

Figure 2 shows that hearing activity by both CFA and CU peaked in the mid-1970s and has continued at a substantial level. However, Ralph Nader's appearances decreased dramatically. Attention to Nader's charismatic presence and then his relative absence has contributed to the impression that consumer influence has disappeared in Washington. Nevertheless, his record is impressive for both his volume of activity over more than two decades and his success in developing spin-off organizations designed to pursue the consumer interest.

---

[14] Schlozman and Tierney, *Organized Interests*, 150.

[15] The information on hearing participation is from *CIS Indexes and Abstracts*, published annually since 1970.

Figure 1

HOUSE AND SENATE COMMITTEE APPEARANCES BY CONSUMER GROUPS 1970–86

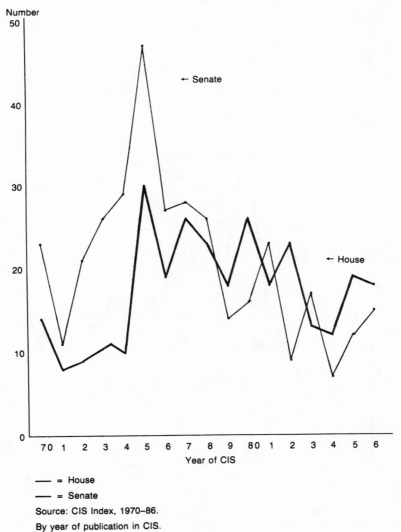

——— = House
——— = Senate
Source: CIS Index, 1970–86.
By year of publication in CIS.

While Nader clearly has devoted less of his personal attention to appearing before Congress in recent years, what could be called Ralph Nader, Inc. has taken
up some of the slack. The yearly CIS Indexes published from 1970 to 1986 cite
various organizations with which Ralph Nader is affiliated. Congressional hearing

Figure 2

CONGRESSIONAL COMMITTEE APPEARANCES BY CONSUMER GROUPS 1970–86

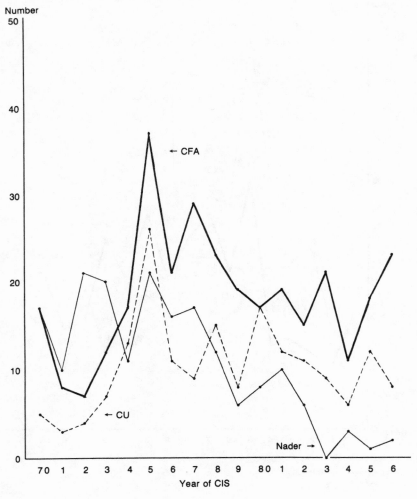

Source: CIS Index, 1970–86.
By year of publication in CIS.

activity for Nader and the most prominent of his affiliated organizations was extensive during this period. Those organizations cited in just the 1986 CIS Index were the Aviation Consumer Action Project, Public Citizen's Congress Watch, Public Citizen Inc., Public Citizen's Health Research Group, Public Citizen's Litigation Group, and the Public Interest Research Group. When the total of the Nader groups' hearing activity is compared with that of the other two consumer organizations during 1986, the results are as follows in Table 1.

In summary, evidence confirms that three of the best known sets of activists and organizations discussed in the earlier literature about consumer policy remain alive and active on Capital Hill. Their activity has shifted more to the House than the Senate, Ralph Nader has been replaced by Nader, Inc., and overall hearing activity has declined from a 1975 peak but continues to be significant.

CONGRESSIONAL CONTEXT OF CONSUMER PROTECTION ACTIVITY

In order to discover the extent of consumer policy in Congress and ascertain what other organizations are active on these issues, we focus on a definition. Consumer protection policy involves issues of availability, affordability, safety, and efficacy of goods and services to the final user. Hearing activity indexed under the CIS consumer protection topic descriptor, we believe, represents the core of consumer protection hearing activity in Congress. (See Appendix.)

The consumer protection hearings indexed by CIS show that the House outdistanced the Senate in hearings during the period under study here. Some 436 hearings were held by House committees and 404 by their Senate counterparts. The data as displayed in Figure 3 reinforces the earlier finding of a rise in activism by the House beginning in the mid-1970s. The House overtook the Senate in total number of hearings years before Ronald Reagan's election ushered in a more conservative Senate in 1980.

Has anything concrete resulted from this hearing activity? A partial answer lies in a related data set, the totals that CIS kept for legislative enactments. During the period from 1970–1986, CIS indexed forty-five public laws under the same consumer protection descriptor. Figure 3 shows that legislation involving consumers continued to be enacted during this period. Congressional consumer protection activity reached a peak in the mid-1970s, declined somewhat thereafter, and later stabilized.

TABLE 1

Hearing Activity

	House	Senate
Consumer Federation of America	18	12
Consumers Union	6	2
Ralph Nader, Inc.	21	20

Figure 3

CONSUMER PROTECTION HEARINGS AND BILLS PASSED 1970–86

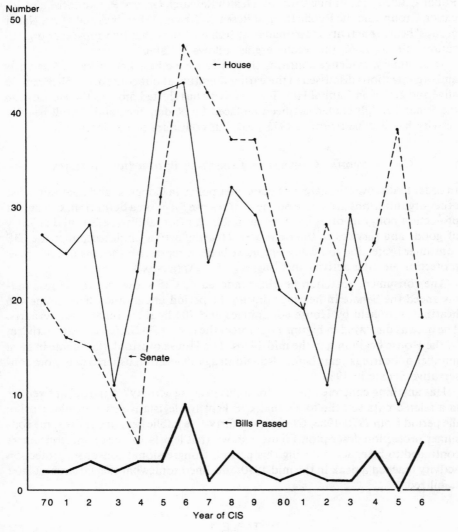

--- = House

—— = Senate

—— = Bills passed

Source: CIS Index, 1970–86.

By year of publication in CIS.

What has happened since Reagan's first term in office remains problematical, because the indicators begin to swing back and forth during the period of intense partisan and ideological conflict that characterized the mid-1980s. Why congressional committees take on particular issues such as consumer protection at some times rather than others has not been adequately addressed. But part of the explanation may depend on the role that organized interest groups play.

MORE DETAIL ABOUT MORE GROUPS

Analysis of the organizations testifying at House consumer protection hearings from 1977 through 1987 yields additional information about where all the consumers have gone. Although the literature on this period would lead one to expect that consumer groups have gone away or into hiding, in fact a significant number of consumer organizations appeared to provide testimony. Those groups whose representatives appeared more than ten times are included in Table 2.

Consumer Federation of America and Consumers Union are clearly the workhorses among consumer organizations; each appeared substantially more often than any other organized consumer voice. Public Citizen's Congress Watch is by itself a significant contributor, and if all the other members of Nader, Inc. are added, (the others appear in subsequent tables) the total brings the Nader family up to the status of a peak voice for consumers.

Senior citizens organized in the American Association of Retired Persons (AARP), now formally merged with the National Retired Teachers Association, represents a notable share of the consumer presence and one which the population curve is likely to augment in the future. Other organizations representing the elderly or retired appear on consumer issues as well, but none approaches the AARP in frequency of providing testimony. Although there is evidence that organized labor has fallen on hard times recently, this data shows the AFL-CIO to be a frequent player in the consumer protection arena as the peak voice for workers as consumers.

On the producer side, the most frequent participant is the American Bankers Association. The high profile of this organization on consumer protection issues confirms journalistic evidence that credit, lending practices, and regulation of financial services were often on the agenda in the period under study here. The Amer-

TABLE 2

*Organizations Appearing More Than 10 Times
with Number of Appearances*

Consumers Union	33
Consumer Federation of America	32
American Bankers Association	23
American Association of Retired Persons/National Retired Teachers Association	19
AFL-CIO	15
Public Citizen's Congress Watch	11

TABLE 3

Organizations Appearing 5–10 Times by Type
and Number of Appearances

	Appearances
Consumer organizations	
National Consumers League	10
Public Interest Research Group	9
National Consumer Law Center	6
Aviation Consumer Action Project	5
Consumer Energy Council of America	5
National Peoples Action	5
Total appearances	40
State and local agencies and their associations	
National Association of State Regulatory Utility Commissioners	10
National Association of Attorneys General	9
National Association of Insurance Commissioners	9
American Public Power Association	6
Total appearances	34
Producers	
American Medical Association	10
Chamber of Commerce of the U.S.	9
National Association of Home Builders	9
National Association of Realtors	9
U.S. League of Savings Associations	9
American Dental Association	8
Small Business Legislative Council	7
American Insurance Association	6
Edison Electric Institute	6
American Bar Association	6
Air Transport Association	5
American Council of Life Insurance	5
American Society of Travel Agents	5
Blue Cross/Blue Shield	5
Consumer Bankers Association	5
Independent Bankers Association of America	5
Insurance Institute for Highway Safety	5
National Association of Manufacturers	5
National Automobile Dealers Association	5
Total appearances	124

ican Bankers Association's twenty-three appearances are more than twice that of any other organization representing producers.

Those organizations that appear less often but roughly once or twice per Congress, that is five to ten times overall, are displayed in Table 3. It includes other components of the extended Nader family of organizations, as well as the National Consumers League, a long-standing, if lower-profile group representing consumer concerns.

Another substantial voice on consumer protection issues is brought to you by the federal system. Associations of state government officials representing utility regulators, insurance commissioners, and attorneys general often come before Congress on consumer protection issues. Their presence indicates that many consumer protection issues are a lively topic at the state and local level as well as at the national level of government.

Notable by their absence among these organizations are the environmental and government reform groups. The literature has led us to see environmentalists as the muscle, if not the heart, of the public interest movement.[16] Some observers have argued that this segment of the public interest movement has replaced labor as keeper of the liberal vision for America.[17] Although environmental groups may have gained strength by contrast with most of the public interest community during this decade, this data does not show that strength extended in support of consumer issues. Not a single environmental group appears among these most frequent testifiers in spite of the fact that energy consumption issues were on the agenda. This is not to claim that environmental groups are not active during this period in the congressional forum, but that they attend to topics other than consumer protection as defined in this data set.

In Table 3, one can see organizations representing professionals such as doctors, dentists, and lawyers providing testimony. Also visible are the housing block of builders, realtors, and lenders, and the insurance block. Of some curiosity is the relatively low profile here of the business peak associations — the Chamber of Commerce and the National Association of Manufacturers — by comparison to the various trade associations and professional organizations.

While Table 2 depicted a dominance of consumer groups, Table 3 reflects a relationship of these groups to producers that is more typical of the whole data set. Here the consumer groups are seriously outnumbered — six consumer organizations provided testimony forty times while nineteen producer groups provided testimony on 124 occasions.

Table 4 includes summary data on organizations that testified four or fewer times in this period before the House. Here it becomes necessary to categorize separately core consumer organizations and other critics of producers. These other critics are usually allied with the consumer groups and one may even argue that they often act as groups of special-focus consumers, particularly in the case of the elderly. However, because the CIS abstracts do not always give adequate information on which to judge alliances among groups, the relationship is evaluated conservatively for categorization purposes. Labor is treated separately because of the possible competition between consumers and producers for its allegiance. State and local officials have separate and potentially independent stakes in the outcome of consumer issues before Congress and also are treated separately.

---

[16] McCann, *Taking Reform Seriously*, 87–90, 244–257; David Vogel, *Fluctuating Fortunes: The Political Power of Business in America* (New York: Basic Books, 1989), 104, 260–270, 299.
[17] Vogel, *Fluctuating Fortunes*, 293.

TABLE 4

Organizations Appearing 1–4 Times

	Number of Groups	Number of Appearances
Consumer organizations	82	116
Other critics		
Elderly groups	4	7
Environmental groups	10	19
Government reform groups	3	4
Health groups	14	22
Miscellaneous groups	11	18
Total	42	70
Labor	24	33
State and local agencies and their associations	88	106
Producers	437	580
Miscellaneous	6	6

In Table 4 one sees a large number of core consumer organizations carrying the load on consumer protection issues. Joining them are a wider array of the other public interest groups one might have expected to see making more frequent appearances.

The core consumer organizations included in this level of activity are exemplified by the Center for Auto Safety, Bankcard Holders of America, and the National Insurance Consumer Organization. These organizations are more specialized in their focus and thus less likely to provide testimony as often as the Consumer Federation of America or Consumers Union. Also included are state and local consumer groups who only bring their concerns to national policy makers on occasion.

Among the advocacy groups for the elderly noted here is the National Council of Senior Citizens. The Natural Resources Defense Council, Environmental Action Foundation, Environmental Defense Fund, Friends of the Earth, and the Sierra Club appear in the environmental category. Their support here approximates the level predicted by the general wisdom. The American Civil Liberties Union is among the government reform organizations and it makes two appearances. The American Cancer Society, American Heart Association, American Lung Association, Arthritis Foundation, and the National Womens Health Network appear to advocate as health groups. Public Citizen Health Research Group is included here but is categorized as a core consumer group because of its affiliation with the larger Nader network.

Labor is represented here by individual unions such as the International Ladies Garment Workers Union, International Brotherhood of Teamsters, and United Steelworkers of America as well as by state groups such as the Minnesota AFL-CIO. At this point the CIS data offer an example of the role of organized labor

of Machinists and the International Union of Steelworkers appeared along with auto industry parts suppliers at hearings on automobile bumpers standards. The labor representatives expressed concern over potential job losses as well as concern with the safety impact of the standards.

Prominent again are associations of state and local officials whose responsibilities include some aspects of consumer protection. These include the U.S. Conference of Mayors, the National League of Cities, and the National Association of Consumer Agency Administrators. At this level of activity one also sees representatives of individual jurisdictions bringing testimony to the House; these include the New York State Consumer Protection Board, the Minnesota Office of Consumer Services, and the New York City Department of Consumer Affairs.

Outstanding among the 437 producers are trade and professional associations in banking, insurance, and health care. Joining them are small trade associations such as the Peanut Butter Manufacturers and Nut Salters Association and the Wine Grapegrowers of America and many individual banks, insurance companies, pharmaceuticals manufacturers and retailers, general merchandise retailers, investment firms, grocery manufacturers, and funeral directors. These examples merely suggest the wide array of issues on which organized consumer interests may be challenged.

Are the consumer groups outnumbered? Yes, the producer organizations are there in greater numbers. Even if all the nonproducer interests ally together, they are still seriously outnumbered. However, one may also note that Ralph Nader personally appears more often on consumer protection issues than does the Bank of America, Ford, or General Motors.

A final look at the data in aggregated form shown in Table 5 allows one to draw an overall impression of who appeared to present testimony on consumer protec-

TABLE 5

All Organizations, Number and Percentage of Appearances

	Number of Groups	% of Groups	Number of Appearances	% of Appearances
Producers	457	64.0	727	58.5
Consumer groups	91	12.7	232	18.7
State and local agencies and their associations	92	12.9	140	11.3
Labor	25	3.5	48	3.9
Other critics				
Elderly groups	5	.7	26	2.1
Health groups	14	2.0	22	1.8
Environmental groups	10	1.4	19	1.5
Government reform groups	3	.4	4	.3
Miscellaneous groups	11	1.5	18	1.4
Sub-totals	43	6.0	95	7.1
Miscellaneous	6	.8	6	.5
Totals	714	99.9	1,242	100.0

tion issues during this period. The strongest message is that producer organizations dominate the array of groups appearing in the hearings, which is consistent with other research findings on the rise of business presence in Washington.

The dominance of the core consumer groups compared to other critics of producer interests is clear. They are the ones who carry the load on these issues. Among their probable allies, labor is most visible. Although environmental and government reform groups have come to be treated as the vanguard of the public interest movement and its main survivors against the conservative tide in Washington, that is not what is seen here. If one looks at the percentage of appearances, the health groups and the elderly are the most important sources of consumer interest testimony after that provided by labor. Finally, in comparing the percentages of total groups and the percentages of total appearances, it is clear that the core consumer organizations are the ones most likely to be spread thin in trying to cover all of the House hearings on consumer protection during these years.

The large share of participation claimed by state and local government officials on consumer protection issues before the federal government was not predicted by the literature on consumer policy or interest group activism in the Washington community. State and local government officials assume substantial shares of both the group and appearance totals. Where their considerable weight is thrown on consumer protection issues — as expert witnesses, as claimants for regulatory authority, or for other purposes — is a critical variable.

FINDINGS AND FURTHER QUESTIONS

The research discussed here leads to several conclusions about the continuing policy agendas pursued by organized consumer interests and other critics of producers in America. Beyond that, questions are raised about the traditional contours of consumer policy and further research is suggested into the role that Congress may play as a countervailing influence to producer interests.

The congressional hearing activity examined here highlights the key role played by the Consumer Federation of America, Consumers Union, and the family of Nader organizations we have termed Ralph Nader, Inc. All have remained active before Congress throughout the period under study here. That their activism peaked in the mid-1970s is consistent with evidence of a reaction against government in the Carter years.[18] The principal consumer groups responded by digging in and demonstrating considerable staying power since then. That all three have continued to be significant participants on consumer protection issues before the U.S. Congress is evidence that consumer policy has become institutionalized on the margins of the national agenda, rather than disappearing from the agenda.

Organized consumer interests have become more active on the House than the Senate side of Capitol Hill in the past decade. This shift of attention is consistent

[18] Seymour Martin Lipset and William Schneider, *The Confidence Gap: Business, Labor, and Government in the Public Mind*, rev. ed. (Baltimore: Johns Hopkins University Press, 1987), 13–29.

with evidence from the literature on congressional decision making, which points to House subcommittees catching up with their Senate counterparts as attractive forums for policy activists by the late 1970s. The trend was reinforced when Senate leadership changed hands with the arrival of a Republican majority in 1981.

Activities of the core consumer groups are supplemented by a second category of more specialized consumer groups that also take their cases to Congress on a regular basis. They include groups such as the Consumer Energy Council of America, Bankcard Holders of America, and the National Insurance Consumer Organization. Each of these focuses on the cost, availability, safety, or efficacy of goods or services from a specific industry or economic sector.

These two types of consumer organizations carry most of the load on consumer protection issues, but they have allies as well. Organizations for senior citizens, particularly the AARP, and labor, including the AFL-CIO as well as individual unions, argue the case for their members as consumers. It is reasonable during periods of inflation and recession when their members' buying power is threatened that consumer issues would be important for organizations claiming to speak for low and moderate-income segments of society. By contrast, the roles of environmental groups and government reform groups were much smaller than the literature would lead one to hypothesize.

This study also suggests that more attention be devoted to the complex role of organizations active on health issues. A health block was identified as participating in consumer protection policy before Congress. However, deciding who speaks for producers and who for consumers in this field is a complicated task. Whether organizations fighting heart disease, cancer, and the like should be considered as representing the interests of consumers of health care is an open question.

Representatives of state and local government officials played a more prominent role than we had expected. The National Association of Regulatory Utility Commissioners, the National Association of Attorneys General, and others appear frequently before Congress on consumer protection issues. More research could profitably be directed toward understanding the roles of these and other state government regulatory officials on consumer issues.

Although consumer activists have survived on the national scene, they continue to face a daunting array of producer representatives. From the bankers to the undertakers, the producer voices outnumbered consumers by wide margins. However, this is not to imply that producers always form a unified opposition to consumer interests. Further research needs to be directed toward understanding the complexity of producer interests and the conditions under which producers ally with as well as compete with some consumers.

This research also suggests new questions about why subcommittees hold hearings on consumer policy issues and what the interest groups who attend hope to gain from their participation. There is surprisingly little on these subjects in either the interest group or Congress literature. We see committee hearings as a window on Congress's role in the policy process and plan to explore the varying stakes that participants have in them.

Consumer protection policy can also be a useful vantage point from which to assess business power. The results of this research suggest that greater attention be given to the role of Congress in theories of interest group power. We hypothesize that consumer advocates have concentrated their energies on Congress (and the House in particular) in response to the strong alliance that developed between the president, executive branch officials, and producers during the past decade, a period when regulatory relief has been the watchword in Washington. Such a strategy would be in keeping with the operation of what Andrew McFarland has called "countervailing power."[19]

Finally, it is important to call attention to the wide-ranging nature of the subjects included in the consumer protection hearings. Among these issues are many of the major domestic policy issues that have been before Congress during the past decade, such as air transportation deregulation, government ethics and reform, financial services regulation, taxation, and trade policy. They shared the agenda with concerns about particular products or services (for example, food additives, tire safety, variable rate mortgages, etc.) that reflect the image consumer policy has had in the past. How these new issues relate to traditional definitions of consumer policy and what this activity says about consumers' stake in complex public policy issues is a topic we intend to take up in future research.*

APPENDIX

In comparing the two ways of estimating consumer group presence (appearances of Nader, Inc., Consumer Federation of America, and Consumers Union and appearances at hearing indexed as consumer protection) we noted a curious discrepancy in the number of hearing appearances. University reference librarians and other information specialists with whom we consulted attested to the high quality of the CIS data base, and we generally agree. However, we decided to explore further. We focused on just one year, the 1986 CIS Index, to compare the two approaches in more detail. In the 1986 CIS Index, the peak groups made a total of 72 appearances while consumer protection was cited as an issue in 33 hearings. Cross-checking hearing titles reveals that only 10 of the hearings indexed as consumer protection feature testimony by one or more of the peak groups. This indicates that none of the peak groups appears at most (23 of 33) of the consumer protection hearings. However, if one is willing to credit what the groups think is important to the topic of consumer protection—a sort of additive definition—this also means that there were an additional 62 hearings (at which one of the peak groups appeared but which were not indexed under the consumer protection descriptor) which may be regarded as part of the topic. It is also notable that the groups tend not to appear at the same hearings, either because they are

---

[19] McFarland, "Interest Groups and Theories of Power," 141–146.

* The authors wish to acknowledge research support from the Adeline and Ralph Dorfman Fund for Political Science, the Graduate College of Iowa State University, and The Brookings Institution.

spread so thin or because they specialize with different issues. Of the 72 group appearances, only 8 feature more than one group at the same hearing.

It is our sense that the consumer protection descriptor catches the core of the subject. However, including the additional hearings at which the peak organizations testify along with the consumer protection descriptor may capture a wider sense of the consumer agenda.

Public Opinion and the Welfare State: The United States in Comparative Perspective

ROBERT Y. SHAPIRO
JOHN T. YOUNG

To what extent do citizens of the United States and other countries prefer particular social welfare policies? How have these opinions changed over the last twenty years? What have been the effects of these preferences on government policies? This article reviews some of the empirical English language literature that has directly or indirectly considered these matters by examining national-level survey data.[1] Although we initially expected an investigation of this research to be a mammoth undertaking, we found that the literature was not very extensive.

---

[1] We have undoubtedly omitted relevant works that are not available in English. We have also limited our review to studies using survey data. Opinion processes might also be studied without survey data through other historical methods, including content analysis of the media, which influence mass and elite opinions. Lawrence R. Jacobs, and Robert Y. Shapiro, "Public Opinion and the New Social History: Some Lessons for the Study of Public Opinion and Democratic Politics," *Social Science History* 13 (forthcoming, 1989); Peter Golding and Sue Middleton, *Images of Welfare: Press and Public Attitudes to Poverty* (Oxford, England: Martin Robertson, 1982); Benjamin I. Page, Robert Y. Shapiro, and Glenn R. Dempsey, "What Moves Public Opinion," *American Political Science Review* (APSR) 81 (March 1987): 23–43.

ROBERT Y. SHAPIRO is associate professor of political science at Columbia University. He has written many articles and contributions to books about public opinion and the policy-making process. JOHN T. YOUNG is a doctoral student in political science at Columbia University. He is currently doing research on political campaigns, elections, the media, and the presidency.

PUBLIC OPINION TOWARD SOCIAL WELFARE POLICY

Although there has been much debate about the growth of social welfare programs in the bonafide welfare states and elsewhere, and there has been considerable interest in public opinion, there have been few analyses of survey data concerned with the full range of social welfare issues.[2] For the United States, several reports have examined public preferences toward the government's role in providing for public welfare, medical care, Social Security, income assistance to the poor, and employment.[3] The general conclusion of these analyses has been that despite some criticism and qualifications and despite—or perhaps because of—the retrenchment efforts of the Reagan administration, the American public has accepted and even expected an active government role as the last economic resort.[4] Although there are clear differences between the United States and other welfare states, the research and evidence for other countries lead to the same conclusion.

The public opinion data show that support for social welfare policies in the United States has generally remained solid and stable from the 1970s to the early 1980s,

[2] An exception is Michael E. Schiltz, *Public Attitudes toward Social Security 1935-1965* (Washington D.C.: U.S. Government Printing Office, 1970).

[3] Hazel Erskine, "The Polls: Government Role in Welfare," *Public Opinion Quarterly* 39 (Summer 1975): 257-274; Natalie Jaffe, "Appendix B: Attitudes Toward Public Welfare Programs and Recipients in the United States. A Review of Public Opinion Surveys, 1935-1976" in Lester Salamon, ed., *Welfare: The Elusive Consensus* (New York: Praeger, 1978); Fay Lomax Cook, *Who Should be Helped?* (Beverly Hills, Calif.: Sage Publications, Inc., 1979) and "Public Opinion and Social Welfare Policy: What We Know and Need to Know," unpublished paper, Northwestern University, 1985; Robert Y. Shapiro and John T. Young, "The Polls: Medical Care in the United States," *Public Opinion Quarterly* 50 (Fall 1986): 418-428; Robert Y. Shapiro and Tom W. Smith, "The Polls: Social Security," *Public Opinion Quarterly* 49 (Winter 1985): 561-572; Robert Y. Shapiro, Kelly D. Patterson, Judith Russell, and John T. Young, "The Polls: Public Assistance," *Public Opinion Quarterly* 51 (Spring 1987): 120-130; Doris Yokelson, *Public Attitudes toward Poverty and the Characteristics of the Poor and Near Poor*, vol. III, Doris Yokelson, ed., *Collected Papers on Poverty Issues* (Croton-on-Hudson, N.Y.: Hudson Institute, 1975); Connie De Boer, "The Polls: Attitudes Toward Unemployment," *Public Opinion Quarterly* 47 (Fall 1983): 432-441; Robert Y. Shapiro, Kelly D. Patterson, Judith Russell, John T. Young, "The Polls—A Report: Employment and Social Welfare," *Public Opinion Quarterly* 51 (Summer 1987): 268-281. For other references, see Shapiro and Young, "Public Opinion Toward Social Welfare Policies: The United States in Comparative Perspective" in Samual Long, ed., *Research in Micropolitics*, vol. 3, *Public Opinion* (Greenwich, Conn.: JAI Press, 1989).

[4] Hazel Erskine, "The Polls: The Role of Government in Welfare"; Carll Everett Ladd, Jr. and Seymour Martin Lipset, "Public Opinion and Public Policy" in Peter Duignan and Alvin Rabushka, eds., *The United States in the 1980s* (Stanford, Calif.: Hoover Institution, Stanford University, 1980), 49-84; Cook, *Who Should be Helped?*; Robert Y. Shapiro and Kelly D. Patterson "The Dynamics of Public Opinion toward Social Welfare Policy," paper presented at the annual meeting of the American Political Science Association, Washington, D.C., 1986; Richard M. Coughlin, *Ideology, Public Opinion, and Welfare Policy* (Berkeley, Calif.: Institute of International Studies, 1980); Everett Carll Ladd, "Public Attitudes toward Policy and Governance: Searching for the Sources and Meaning of the 'Reagan Revolution'" in Lester Salamon and Michael Lund, eds., *The Reagan Presidency and the Governing of America* (Washington, D.C.: Urban Institute Press, 1984); James R. Kluegel, "Macroeconomic Problems, Beliefs about the Poor and Attitudes toward Welfare Spending," *Social Problems* 34 (February 1987): 82-99.

FIGURE 1
High and Stable Support
For Spending on Education and Welfare

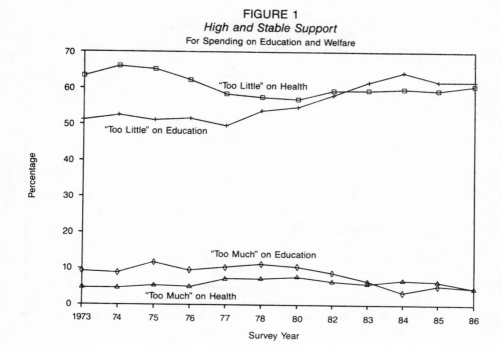

Source: NORC/GSS ("Don't Know" excluded, N > 1400 unless noted).
Question: "We are faced with many problems in this country, none of which can be solved easily or inexpensively. I'm going to name some of these problems, and for each one I'd like you to tell me whether you think we're spending too much money on it, too little money, or about the right amount of money. . . . Are we spending too much, too little, or about the right about on . . . Improving and protecting the nation's health . . . Improving the nation's educaton system?" Survey dates: 3/72, 3/73, 3/74, 3/75, 3/76, 3/77, 3/78, 3/80, 3/82, 3/83, 3/84 (N = 465 for health, N = 475 for education), 3/85 (N = 727 for health, N = 724 for education), and 3/86 (N = 702 for health, N = 705 for education). These data for the United States were taken from the NORC General Social Survey. See James A. Davis and Tom W. Smith, *General Social Surveys, 1972–1986: Cumulative Codebook*. (Chicago: NORC, 1986).

despite some sizeable increases in opposition mainly to income maintenance and related "welfare" activities. Coinciding with the rhetoric and policies of the Reagan administration and especially with the recession, public support for maintaining and expanding government assistance rebounded since the early 1980s, and Americans rejected further cuts in social welfare programs. Examples of this high and stable support for social welfare policies in the United States and the liberal rebound are shown in Figures 1 and 2.

The same overall stability can be found in other affluent western democracies, but there have also been some clear shifts in preferences as great or greater than those in the United States. Conservative shifts or welfare backlashes have occurred

FIGURE 2
Liberal Rebound in Opinion
Toward Welfare Spending

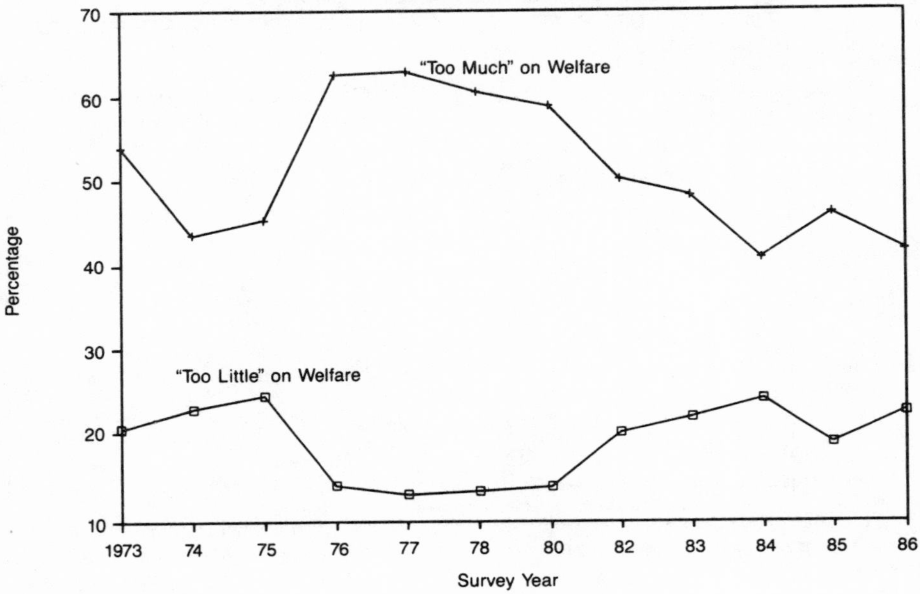

Source: NORC/GSS ("Don't Know" excluded, N > 1400 unless noted).
Question: "We are faced with many problems in this country, none of which can be solved easily or inexpensively. I'm going to name some of these problems, and for each one I'd like you to tell me whether you think we're spending too much money on it, too little money, or about the right amount of money. . . . Are we spending too much, too little, or about the right amount on . . . welfare?" Survey dates: 3/72, 3/73, 3/74, 3/75, 3/76, 3/77, 3/78, 3/80, 3/82, 3/83, 3/84 (N = 471), 3/85 (N = 719), and 3/86 (N = 700). These data for the United States were taken from the NORC General Social Survey. See James A. Davis and Tom W. Smith, *General Social Surveys, 1972–1986: Cumulative Codebook*. (Chicago: NORC, 1986).

in a number of countries in recent years. This has coincided with deteriorations in economic growth, increases in inflation, and changes in employment and perceived tax burden. The shift to the right occurred in Great Britain more dramatically than in the United States and contributed to Margaret Thatcher's ascendancy. But similar to the liberal rebound occurring later during the Reagan administration, public opinion reversed itself substantially after Thatcher became prime minister, rejecting further retrenchment of the welfare state.[5] Despite the political leader-

---

[5] See Thomas Ferguson and Joel Rogers, *Right Turn* (New York: Hill and Wang, 1986); David R. Gergen and Anthony King, "Following the Leaders: How Ronald Reagan and Margaret Thatcher have Changed Public Opinion," *Public Opinion* 8 (June/July 1985): 16–19, 55–58; Joel Krieger, *Reagan, Thatcher and the Politics of Decline* (New York: Oxford University Press, 1986); Carll Everett Ladd,

ships' rhetoric of cuts, there has continued to be popular support for major cash transfers, education, and health services financed by taxation; other direct services were perceived to be less central.[6] Ivor Crewe and Donald Searing observed that while British opinion may have continued to move to the right on social welfare issues in 1979, opinion rebounded afterward and clearly supported the view that spending on welfare state programs should be extended even if this required a tax increase. By 1983 the entire electorate, including Conservative Party identifiers, moved to the left of its 1974 position concerning whether welfare spending had gone too far.[7] Moreover, despite clear divisions on some issues, there is a broad consensus or "collectivism" toward the positive role of the welfare state in society: support for welfare state programs such as the National Health Services and efforts to end poverty and to redistribute wealth drew large measures of support even during the conservative British shift in the late 1970s.[8]

The expansion of the welfare state elsewhere was also challenged, and cuts were proposed as a result of reactions to increases in taxes, including visible direct taxes versus programmatic taxes.[9] Douglas Hibbs and Henrik Madsen evaluated arguments about the visibility of taxation and the consequences of welfare services versus direct transfers in Denmark, Sweden, Great Britain, the Netherlands, and West Germany. They concluded that the backlash was more fundamentally a reaction to the perception of government inefficiency and an objection to particular forms of taxation, rather than a revolt against social security or equality.[10]

The public backlash did not last long nor occur to the same degree in all Euro-

---

"Converging Currents in British and American Politics," *Public Opinion* (June/July 1983): 4–6, 55–60; David Butler and Donald Stokes, *Political Change in Britain: The Evolution of Electoral Choice*, 2nd ed. (New York: St. Martin's Press, 1974); Ralph Harris and Arthur Seldon, *Over-Ruled on Welfare* (London: Institute of Economic Affairs, 1979); Peter Taylor-Gooby, *Public Opinion, Ideology, and State Welfare* (Boston: Routledge & Kegan Paul, 1985); Bo Sarlvik and Ivor Crewe, *Decade of Dealignment: The Conservative Victory of 1979 and Electoral Trends in the 1970s* (Cambridge, England: Cambridge University Press, 1983); Richard Parry, "United Kingdom" in Peter Flora, ed., *Growth to Limits: The Western European Welfare States since World War II*, vol. 2, *Germany, United Kingdom, Ireland, Italy* (New York: Walter de Gruyter, 1986), 155–240; Ivor Crewe and Donald Searing, "Thatcherism: Its Origins, Electoral Impact and Implications for Downs's Theory of Party Strategy," no. 37 *Essex Papers in Politics and Government* (Department of Government, University of Essex, 1986).

[6] Parry, "United Kingdom."

[7] Crewe and Searing, "Thatcherism."

[8] Nick Bosanquet, "Interim Report: Public Spending and the Welfare State" in Roger Jowell, Sharon Witherspoon, and Lindsay Brook, eds., *British Social Attitudes: The 1986 Report* (Brookfield, Vermont: Gower Publishing Company, 1986), 127–139; Taylor-Gooby, *Public Opinion, Ideology, and State Welfare.*

[9] Harold L. Wilensky, *The Welfare State and Equality: Structure and Ideological Roots of Public Expenditures* (Berkeley: University of California Press, 1975); Wilensky, *The 'New Corporatism,' Centralization and the Welfare State* (Beverly Hills, Calif.: Sage Publications, 1976).

[10] Douglas A. Hibbs, Jr. and Henrik Jess Madsen, "Public Reaction to the Growth of Taxation and Government Expenditure," *World Politics* 33 (April 1981): 413–435; see also Richard Eichenberg, *Society and Security in Western Europe*, unpublished ms., Tufts University, 1987, concerning the defense-social welfare trade-off.

pean countries, and it did not necessarily produce changes in expenditures and policy. In the Scandinavian countries, for example, leftist opinion did not deteriorate in the 1970s.[11] In Norway support for social welfare policies (that is, expansion of cradle-to-grave social security) diminished from 1965 to 1973 and returned to a high level by 1977.[12] In Sweden no overall change in very high and stable support appears to have occurred in the 1960s and 1970s concerning payment for welfare state programs. In fact, from 1967 to 1978 there apparently was a sizable increase in support for state responsibility for ensuring everyone a good standard of living. This contrasts sharply with the rightward shift occurring elsewhere during the same period. But resistance to state intervention and other signs of backlash did occur in Sweden by the early 1980s.[13]

In Denmark, while there was demand in 1972 for lower government expenditures, there was resistance to cuts in welfare spending.[14] Although there were important cuts during the two years after the 1973 elections, the antispending and antitax issues became less salient for voters during the following elections.[15] Real disposable income decreased steadily after 1976, and the welfare backlash in Denmark was a short-lived phenomenon: public opinion had changed considerably by 1979, reestablishing by the mid-1980s the consensus registered in the 1960s.[16]

West Germans were much more willing to cut back social services and social transfers in 1983 than in 1978 or 1979. Under conditions of fiscal strain, reductions in services were more popular than an increase in the tax burden. At the same time, however, there was no measurable decline in commitment to the welfare state and to state responsibility as opposed to individual responsibility for social welfare.[17]

Similarly, a noticeable decline in public support for expansion in certain social

[11] Diane Sainsbury, "Scandinavian Party Politics Reexamined: Social Democracy in Decline?" *West European Politics* 7 (October 1984): 67–102.

[12] Henry Valen and Willy Martinussen, "Electoral Trends and Foreign Politics in Norway: The 1973 Storting Election and the EEC Issue" in Karl H. Cerny, ed., *Scandinavia at the Polls* (Washington, D.C.: American Enterprise Institute, 1977), 39–71.

[13] Sven Olson, "Sweden" in Peter Flora, ed., *Growth to Limits: The Western European Welfare States Since World War II*, vol. 1, *Sweden, Norway, Finland, Denmark* (New York: Walter de Gruyter, 1986), 1–116; Hans Zetterberg, "Maturing of the Swedish Welfare State," *Public Opinion* (October/November 1979): 42–47; but see Bo Sarlvik, "Recent Electoral Trends in Sweden" in Cerny, ed., *Scandinavia at the Polls*, 73–129.

[14] Sainsbury, "Scandinavian Party Politics Reexamined"; see also Ole Borre, "Recent Trends in Danish Voting Behavior" in Cerny, ed., *Scandinavia at the Polls*, 3–37.

[15] Lars Norby Johansen, "Denmark" in Peter Flora, ed., *Growth to Limits:* vol. 1; Jorgen Goul Andersen, "Electoral Trends in Denmark in the 1980s," *Scandinavian Political Studies* 9 (June 1986): 157–174.

[16] Johansen, "Denmark"; Andersen, "Electoral Trends."

[17] See Jens Alber, "The West German Welfare State in Transition," paper presented at the meeting of the International Study Group of Trends in the Welfare State, University of Massachusetts, Boston, 22–26 September 1986; and "Germany" in Peter Flora, ed., *Growth to Limits:* vol. 2, 1–154; see also Eichenberg, *Society and Security in Western Europe*.

welfare areas occurred in Finland from 1975 to 1980, but this was probably not a threat to the provision of a welfare system that had become very firmly entrenched and had overwhelming public support. A similar phenomenon occurred in the Yugoslavian republic of Slovenia, in which there was a steady increase in support for retrenchment over the entire 1968-1983 period.[18]

Thus we find substantial similarity in patterns of changes in public preferences across countries — changes at the margin, independent of the levels of support for social welfare policies. Although we have not seen the most recent data, in some cases, the conservative shift in certain preferences occurred later and has not yet reversed itself. But the German case, for example, does not differ much from modest opinion movements elsewhere: some conservative shifts in preferences subsequently reversed themselves substantially, and preferences that did not rebound still showed extremely high levels of support for social welfare programs. It can be argued there and elsewhere that there is substantial support for the modern welfare state, and various marginal shifts in preferences represent essentially its consolidation rather than movement toward dismantling its components.[19]

Important social cleavages can be found in variations in support for the welfare state. The largest and most persistent demographic differences in preferences in the United States are still those associated with race and economic status. There is no unequivocal evidence that these political cleavages have changed substantially since the first national surveys of the 1930s and 1940s. Of course, the focal points of public debate about social welfare issues have changed as have government policies themselves, which is why socioeconomic differences in such preferences *appear* to have diminished.[20] Differences in preferences due to party identification are among the largest as well, but they vary depending upon whether or not Democratic and Republican leaders take more clearly distinctive positions

[18] See Matti Alestalo and Hannu Uusitalo, "Finland" in Flora, ed., *Growth to Limits:* vol. 1, 197-292; Peter Jambrek, "Socialism Without Welfare? Preliminary Analysis of Popular and Elite Preferences about Public Spending in Yugoslav Communes" in Terry Nichols Clark, ed., *Research in Urban Policy,* vol. 2, part A (Greenwich, Conn.: JAI Press, 1986), 219-226.

[19] Alber, "The West German Welfare State" and "Germany"; see Olson, "Sweden"; Albert Hirschman describes this as "growing pains" in "The Welfare State in Trouble: Systemic Crisis or Growing Pains?" *American Economic Review* 70 (May 1980): 113-116.

[20] Shapiro and Patterson, "The Dynamics of Public Opinion"; David Knoke, "Stratification and the Dimensions of American Political Orientations," *American Journal of Political Science* (AJPS) 23 (November 1979): 772-791; David Colby and David Baker, "Socioeconomic and Psychological Determinants of Welfare Policy Attitudes: Path Models," *Journal of Social Science Research* 1 (Summer 1978): 345-356; A. Wade Smith, "Social Class and Racial Cleavages on Major Social Indicators," *Research in Race and Ethnic Relations* 4 (1985): 33-65; Avery Guest, "Class Consciousness and American Political Attitudes," *Social Forces* 52 (June 1974): 496-510; Jon P Alston and K. Imogene Dean, "Sociological Factors Associated with Attitudes Toward Welfare Recipients and the Causes of Poverty," *Social Service Review* 46 (March 1972); Joe R. Feagan, *Subordinating the Poor: Welfare and American Beliefs* (Englewood Cliffs, N.J.: Prentice-Hall, 1975); Ladd and Lipset, "Public Opinion and Public Policy."

on the economic and social issues that divide the parties.[21] In general, however, as public opinion has shifted on social welfare issues there have been parallel changes in opinion for different demographic subgroups.[22]

Very noteworthy demographic differences in preferences are associated with age. Contrary to media reports and popular beliefs, new cohorts of young adults in the United States tend to be the most supportive of virtually all social welfare policies. They are not more liberal than other recent cohorts as they enter adulthood, nor are they more conservative, even though they have been likely to call themselves Republicans and supporters of President Ronald Reagan. Their liberal positions on social and economic issues may simply reflect what have become typical aging (life cycle) differences, so that new cohorts differ little from their immediate predecessors; or they may be more liberal or accepting of the American welfare state, since they have been socialized in it and have come to expect certain functions of government.[23]

Such age differences can be found in a number of European countries, leading us to stress similarities rather than differences. While Ronald Inglehart and others have described generational differences in issue salience and what they have referred to as "post-materialist" values, the broad collectivist support for British welfare state programs may in part be due to the views of a generation that came to adulthood during a period when welfare provision was hardly debated.[24] Younger cohorts, however, are not more liberal on all issues across all nations. Support for the antitax, antispending Progress Party in Norway came largely from younger voters in 1973, and this might portend a generational schism on welfare in the future. But, whereas young Norwegian voters tended toward the Progress Party in 1973 and toward other conservative parties later in the 1970s, the left-of-center Swedish and Danish parties have had much greater success in attracting the loyalties of new cohorts.[25]

---

[21] For a discussion of such party cleavage issues, see Benjamin I. Page, *Choices and Echoes in Presidential Election* (Chicago: University of Chicago Press, 1978).

[22] But there are interesting and important exceptions attributable to processes involving partisanship and the influence of the party in the White House; see Shapiro and Patterson, "The Dynamics of Public Opinion."

[23] Herbert McClosky and John Zaller, *The American Ethos: Public Attitudes toward Capitalism and Democracy* (Cambridge, Mass.: Harvard University Press, 1984); James R. Kluegel and Eliot R. Smith, *Beliefs about Inequality: Americans' Views About What is and What Ought to be* (Hawthorne, N.Y.: Aldine de Gruyter, 1986); Richard F. Hamilton and James D. Wright, *The State of the Masses* (New York: Aldine, 1986); Shapiro and Patterson "The Dynamics of Public Opinion"; Michael Delli Carpini and Lee Sigelman, "Do Yuppies Matter? Competing Explanations of their Political Distinctiveness," *Public Opinion Quarterly* 50 (Winter 1986): 502–518.

[24] Ronald Inglehart, *The Silent Revolution: Changing Values and Political Styles Among Western Publics* (Princeton, N.J.: Princeton University Press, 1977); and Paul R. Abramson and Ronald Inglehart, "Generational Replacement and Value Change in Six West European Societies," *AJPS* 30 (March 1986): 1–25; Eichenberg, *Society and Security in Western Europe*; Bosanquet, "Public Spending and the Welfare State"; Wilensky, *The Welfare State and Equality*; Coughlin, *Ideology*.

[25] Sainsbury, "Scandinavian Party Politics Reexamined."

Notwithstanding the above observation about Great Britain, the youngest British cohort has not been the most supportive of all welfare state programs. In 1984, 18–34 year olds were somewhat less supportive of extra spending on the National Health Service, young males markedly so; but they were more supportive of spending on benefits for the unemployed, help for industry, and education than were older citizens. Retirement pensions drew far less support among younger males and females than they did among the oldest cohort, although the young cohort was as supportive or more supportive of increasing social spending and taxes than their elders. There was greater support among the young for spending on poverty and for aid to families with children.[26]

Part of the differences in preferences among Americans can be attributed to self-interest: mainly those general differences associated with economic status and race, and particular cases such as the high levels of support among urban residents for aid to cities or the alarm among retirees or near retirees when Social Security or Medicare benefits are threatened. Self-interest, however, is often difficult to disentangle from group interests, or group consciousness, or concerns about the well-being of the nation as a whole. Age and other differences in preferences can only rather remotely be connected to self-interest, particularly the more liberal positions of young adults and women. These preferences are complex, and many people no doubt are motivated by a collective interest or by symbolic concerns. Although the influence of personal self-interest is consistent with some of the evidence, it alone is an inadequate explanation for the generally parallel subgroup trends in preferences and for all the variations in attitudes toward particular social welfare policies.[27]

Such questions about personal versus collective concerns have not been studied much crossnationally.[28] The less than expected role of self-interest in influencing preferences has been found in Europe as well, although the fact that the benefits provided are more substantial there than in the United States raises the stakes for more people. On the other hand, the importance of partisanship and ideology

[26] Nick Bosanquet, "Social Policy and the Welfare State" in Roger Jowell and Colin Airey, eds., *British Social Attitudes: The 1984 Report*. (Brookfield, Vt: Gower Publishing Company, 1984), 75–104; Gordon Heald and Robert J. Wybrow, *The Gallup Survey of Britain* (Dover, N.H.; Croom Helm, 1986). For related findings on support for medical care and pensions in Italy and Canada, see Maurizio Ferrera, "Italy" in Peter Flora, ed., *Growth to Limits:* vol. 2, 385–482; and Mildred A. Schwartz, *Public Opinion and Canadian Identity* (Berkeley: University of California Press, 1967).

[27] For example, Donald R. Kinder and Roderick D. Kiewiet, "Economic Discontent and Political Behavior: The Role of Personal Grievances and Collective Economic Judgments in Congressional Voting," *AJPS* 23 (August 1979): 495–527; David O. Sears, Ricard R. Lau, Tom R. Tyler, and Harris M. Allen Jr., "Self-interest vs. Symbolic Politics in Policy Attitudes and Presidential Voting," *APSR* 74 (September 1980): 670–684; Robert Y. Shapiro and Harpreet Mahajan, "Gender Differences in Policy Preferences: A Summary of Trends from the 1960s to the 1980s," *Public Opinion Quarterly* 50 (Spring 1986): 42–61.

[28] James E. Alt, *The Politics of Economic Decline* (Cambridge: England: Cambridge University Press, 1979).

in these countries may extend political debate beyond personal or family gains. The fact that the comparative public opinion and politics literature stresses ideology, partisanship, voting, and the relationship among them indicates that self-interest is of less concern than ideological, symbolic, or other more collective considerations.[29] This comparative research prefers to examine states' policies largely in terms of political party support and a single general left-right ideological continuum, and not to compare similar kinds of social policy issues across nations.

Much of what we observed about public preferences in the United States — their patterns of change and sources — applies to other countries as well. The differences between the United States and other welfare states are not as consistently different as might be expected by the staunchest advocates of America's exceptionalism. When we look at overall support for the current welfare state policies and at marginal changes in support and their causes during the last twenty years, there are many similarities and shared experiences.

There are congruities in various program-specific preferences in the United States and European welfare states. Striking differences emerge, however, when underlying ideology is considered, which is most obviously reflected in the timing of the establishment of welfare state policies.[30] The similarities in preferences also extend to the ranking in importance of sets of benefits and forms of assistance. Support for social security and old-age assistance, medical care, and perhaps education is the highest in virtually all countries for which public opinion data have been examined. Ranked next, but less consistently, are government efforts to provide for employment. This is followed by income assistance, in cases in which the beneficiaries are likely to be deemed deserving although not necessarily poor.[31] This includes family allowances and in-kind assistance, such as housing and U.S.

[29] For example, see Ian Budge, "Strategies, Issues, and Votes: British General Elections, 1950–1979," *Comparative Political Studies* 15 (July 1982): 171–196; Karl H. Cerny, ed., *Scandinavia at the Polls* (Washington, D.C.: American Enterprise Institute, 1977); Harold D. Clarke and Gary Zuk, "The Politics of Party Popularity: Canada 1971–1979," *Comparative Politics* (April 1987): 299–315; Harold D. Clarke and Marianne C. Steward, "Partisan Inconsisitency and Partisan Change in Federal States: The Case of Canada," *AJPS* 31 (May 1987): 383–407; Hilde T. Himmelweit, Patrick Humphreys, Marianne Jaeger, and Michael Katz, *How Voters Decide: A Longitudinal Study of Political Attitudes and Voting Extending over Fifteen Years* (New York: Academic Press, 1981); Peter McDonough, Antonio Lopez Pina, and Samuel H. Barnes, "The Spanish Public in Political Transition," *British Journal of Political Science* 11 (January 1981): 49–79; McDonough, Barnes, and Pina, "Economic Policy and Public Opinion in Spain," *AJPS* 30 (May 1986): 446–479; Howard R. Penniman, ed., *France at the Polls* (Washington, D.C.: American Enterprise Institute, 1975); Penniman, *The French National Assembly Elections of 1978* (Washington, D.C.: American Enterprise Institute, 1980); G. Bingham Powell Jr., "Comparative Voting Behavior: Cleavages, Partisanship, and Accountability" in Samuel Long, ed., *Research in Micropolitics*, vol. II (Greenwich, Conn.: JAI Press, 1987): 233–264.
[30] Coughlin, *Ideology*; Wilensky, *The Welfare State and Equality*; King, "Ideas, Institutions, and the Policies of Governments: A Comparative Analysis: Parts I and II, Part III," *British Journal of Political Science* 3 (July-August 1973): 291–313, 409–423.
[31] Cook, *Who Should be Helped?*

food stamps. Of course, there is less support when survey question wordings suggest that there might be some abuse of the assistance or that the benefits provide disincentives to employment. Although there may be some differences across nations in the intensity of opinions and salience of certain issues, and in the question of whether particular policies should be thought of as social welfare issues, there are also similarities in preferences toward spending more or less relative to existing levels. Americans, for example, are no more opposed to their current burden than Europeans.[32] Thus there is much evidence indicating a convergence across nations.

But when we examine closely the specific levels of support based upon the most recent data and evaluate ideologies or underlying philosophies, especially those having to do with principles of collectivism and individualism, (or egalitarianism versus individualism), there are striking differences.[33] The attitudes and policy preferences of citizens in the United States and a number of European welfare states correspond to the differences in the historical development and contemporary policies of these states.[34] These differences go beyond differences in ideological support for actions by which governments explicitly promote equality. Americans are less positive than Europeans, even on social welfare matters that have very high levels of support in the United States — retirement benefits, health care, jobs, and housing. The United States is consistently at the bottom in its support for different kinds of social welfare benefits.[35]

The comparative evidence, however, need not minimize the continual incremental extension of U.S. social welfare policy. But the differences are large and they do strengthen the case for the ideological distinctiveness of the United States. An important additional piece of evidence is that there is one major social welfare issue

[32] See Tom W. Smith, "The Polls: The Welfare State in Crossnational Perspective," *Public Opinion Quarterly* 51 (Fall 1987): 404–421.

[33] See Coughlin, *Ideology*; McClosky and Zaller, *The American Ethos*; Sidney Verba and Gary Orren, *Equality in America: The View from the Top* (Cambridge, Mass.: Harvard University Press, 1985); Sidney Verba, Steven Kelman, Gary R. Orren, Ichiro Miyake, Joji Watanuki, Ikuo Kabashima, and G. Donald Ferree, Jr., *Elites and the Idea of Equality: A Comparison of Japan, Sweden, and the United States* (Cambridge, Mass.: Harvard University Press, 1987); Kluegel and Smith, *Beliefs About Inequality*.

[34] Smith, "The Welfare State"; James A. Davis, "British and American Attitudes: Similarities and Contrast" in Jowell, Witherspoon, and Brook, eds., *The 1986 Report*, 89–114.

[35] Coughlin earlier also found this consistency in the rankings of nations, with the Anglo-American nations (U.S., Canada, United Kingdom, and Australia) at the lower end and the U.S. at the bottom. But he emphasized this less than the similarities in various attitudes in contrast to ideological differences and divergences in government policies. The countries in which public support appeared to be the highest were West Germany and France in his analysis (which also examined Sweden and Denmark) and Italy in Smith's analysis (which also included Austria, Germany, Britain, France, the Netherlands, Sweden, and Finland). Because of data limitations, it is difficult to draw clear contrasts among European nations, but more similarities in public opinion appear among them when they are compared with the United States. See Smith, "The Welfare State"; Coughlin, *Ideology*; Philip K. Armour and Richard M. Couglin, "Social Control and Social Security: Theory and Research on Capitalist and Communist Nations," *Social Science Quarterly* 66 (December 1985): 770–788.

on which Americans fare much better — and often the best — compared with other nations: educational opportunity, assistance, and spending. Overall support for education in the United States is close to that for Social Security and medical care. This is neither difficult to explain nor surprising. It stems from Americans' views and values concerning individualism and the equality of opportunity, as opposed to equality of outcomes for individuals.[36] How we judge the United States's distinctiveness depends upon whether we emphasize the direction and sources of current political trends and the evidence for convergence, or whether we stress cardinal comparisons of public preferences and policies at different points in time. The sections that follow distinguish among several different areas of social welfare policy: Social Security and old-age assistance, income assistance for the poor, employment, medical care, education, housing and urban problems, and redistribution more generally. For each we examine briefly the research and evidence concerning policy preferences on the United States and then turn to trends in other countries.

Social Security and Old-Age Assistance

The passage in the United States of the Social Security Act of 1935 marked the late and modest expansion of the American welfare state. Since then Social Security and other social welfare policies have had substantial support, and benefits from Social Security and some other programs have been perceived as rights of citizenship.[37]

It is particularly striking that during the fifty years following the passage of the Social Security Act, public polls in the United States failed to track fully trends in opinion toward old-age assistance. From 1950 to the mid-1970s we found an average of only one survey question per year — and all of those questions were worded differently. There was a fair number of questions asked in the 1930s and 1940s, showing high levels of support; and there were flurries of interest in the late 1970s and the 1980s as the federal government's financial problems as well as those of the Social Security system increased and as senior citizens and their representatives and organizations gained attention. But generally Social Security has been a less salient issue than other domestic and foreign policy matters because of the early consensus that emerged.[38]

[36] See King, "Ideas, Institutions and Policies of Government"; Wilensky, *The Welfare State and Equality*; Coughlin, *Ideology*; Smith, "The Welfare State."

[37] T. H. Marshall, *Class, Citizenship, and Social Development* (Garden City, N.Y.: Doubleday Anchor Books, 1965); Mayer N. Zald, "Political Change, Citizenship Rights, and the Welfare State" in Yeheskal Hasenfeld and Mayer N. Zald, eds., *The Welfare State in America: Trends and Prospects, The Annals of the American Academy of Political and Social Science* 479 (1985): 48–66; Erskine, "The Role of Government in Welfare," and "The Polls: Health Insurance," *Public Opinion Quarterly* 39 (Spring 1975): 128–141; Cook, *Who Should be Helped?*

[38] See Shapiro and Smith, "Social Security"; Schiltz, *Social Security*; Irving Crespi, "Social Security and the Polls: No Ado About Something," *Public Opinion* 5 (October/November 1982): 19.

The expansion of the Social Security system has been attributed to President Franklin Roosevelt's insight and ability to lead — or manipulate — public opinion. Social welfare programs are complicated policies when their costs, benefits, and administrative rules and procedures are considered. But Social Security's emphasis on workers' required contributions to a governmental social insurance system — engineered by Roosevelt and his advisers — gave people an easy way to comprehend the program, because it fit in well with the work ethic and other values concerning capitalism and democracy.[39] Although it was not originally made clear, Americans have come to realize that Social Security involves transfer payments from the young to the old and that it is not a social insurance program in which an employer and employee pay for the employee's own retirement.[40] It is still in doubt, however, whether the public understands fully the regressiveness of the payroll tax financing Social Security.

That public preferences toward redistributive policies such as Social Security may be especially susceptible to the influence of incomplete or inaccurate information has serious implications for democratic policy making.[41] Interpreting opinion concerning these policies requires great care, since pollsters have often added to the confusion by providing poor descriptions of policies in their questions. Much of the pessimism expressed about the future of Social Security can be attributed to the lack of a fully informed public discussion.[42]

The patchwork of trends in opinion toward Social Security, which has been pieced together from questions with very different wordings, shows support for Social Security since 1965 to be similar to what was found earlier. The great expansion of Social Security and other social welfare programs that occurred from the 1960s to the early 1970s no doubt required public approval. During this decade the proportion of elderly increased and, more importantly, the percentage who became eligible for retirement benefits rose dramatically. There is still support for continuing worker contributions to the retirement program.[43]

The public has persistently approved of existing or higher levels of government spending or other activity concerning Social Security. Support seems to increase

[39] McClosky and Zaller, The American Ethos; Shapiro and Smith, "Social Security."

[40] See Yankelovich, Skelly and White, Inc., A Fifty-year Report Card on the Social Secuity System: The Attitudes of the American Public. A National Survey, August 1985.

[41] See Benjamin I. Page, Who Gets What from Government? (Berkeley: University of California Press, 1983); Benjamin I. Page and Robert Y. Shapiro, "Educating and Manipulating the Public" in Michael Margolis and Gary Mauser, eds., Manipulating Public Opinion, (Chicago: Dorsey Press, 1989, forthcoming).

[42] See Paul Light, Artful Work: The Politics of Social Security Reform (New York: Random House, 1985), 71–73; Shapiro and Smith, "Social Security"; Rudolph Penner, "Spooking the Public: The Social Security Specter," Public Opinion (October/November 1982): 16–18.

[43] See Schiltz, Social Security; Shapiro and Smith, "Social Security"; David A. Rochefort, American Social Welfare Policy: Dynamics of Formulation and Change (Boulder, Colo.: Westview Press, 1986); James T. Patterson, America's Struggle Against Poverty 1900–1980 (Cambridge, Mass.: Harvard University Press, 1981).

when survey questions suggest some threat to the system, and the public's willingness to be taxed also increases when benefits are threatened. There has been continued (but perhaps diminishing) support for expanding the system to include government and uncovered employees and overwhelming support for indexing benefits to inflation. But the public is more open to limiting the size and frequency of cost-of-living increases and taxing the benefits of higher income groups. The public has tended to oppose raising the retirement age, despite increases in life expectancy and the improved health of the population. It has also favored increasing the earnings limits of retirees.[44]

To be sure, Social Security has been deemed highly successful; it has a tremendous constituency and serves a variety of interests.[45] It benefits not only the elderly, who can be influential as a growing voting block and through their pressure groups and representatives, but also those who supply goods and services to them, as well as younger generations that may be less concerned about their own retirement than about how Social Security helps assure that aging parents, grandparents, and others will not be in great financial need.

Here, as elsewhere, we can only roughly compare support across some nations for particular policies, because identical survey questions from the same time have not been available. In Great Britain there was strong support for spending more on Old-Age Pensions (OAPs) from the late 1950s through the early 1970s. Much more recently, there has been continued strong support for improving the standard of living of pensioners. Retirement pensions have ranked first in priority for increased spending among social benefits, and only one percent of survey respondents have thought that too much was being spent on OAPs.[46]

Support for such social security schemes appears to be widespread. Like Social Security in the United States, Old-Age Security is the most popular social program in Canada. The increase in this support, which started in the 1950s and continued to 1970, has remained and is quite impressive. In 1974 over two-thirds of one survey's respondents thought that Old-Age Security benefits were too low, and young people were more supportive than those receiving the benefits.[47]

There has been strong support in Italy for increasing social security contributions as long as benefits were raised to "a decent level," although from 1978 to 1982 there was a slight drop in this support. We find similar support in Finland for increasing spending on national pensions, but some drop in enthusiasm from

[44] Shapiro and Smith, "Social Security."

[45] D. Garth Taylor, "American Politics, Public Opinion, and Social Security Financing" in Felicity Skidmore, ed., *Social Security Financing* (Cambridge, Mass.: MIT Press, 1981), 235–273; Fay Lomax Cook and Edith J. Barrett, "Public Support for Social Security," *The Journal of Aging Studies*, forthcoming.

[46] Coughlin, *Ideology*; Heald and Wybrow, *The Gallup Survey of Britain*.

[47] Christopher Leman, *The Collapse of Welfare Reform: Political Institutions, Policy, and the Poor in Canada and the United States* (Cambridge, Mass.: MIT Press, 1980); Schwartz, *Public Opinion*; Coughlin, *Ideology*.

1975 to 1980 as support for using taxes to finance such pensions remained high but dropped somewhat. In Norway a large percentage of the public has favored the status quo or an expansion of the general cradle-to-grave social security system.[48]

In the case of Denmark, there has been little support — appearing to drop even further from 1973 to 1977 — for cuts in old age pensions, nursing homes, and pensions for the disabled. Danes have tended to favor greater spending for particular social purposes, and old-age pensions were one area in which from 1979 to 1985 the public increasingly felt that expenditures were too small. Even at the height of the antitax, antispending mood in 1973, few Danish survey respondents wanted cuts in old-age pensions.[49] In Germany, however, respondents in both 1981 and 1983 favored curtailing social security expenditures rather than increasing taxes or social security contributions.[50] Thus Europeans, with this possible exception, have been highly protective of their old-age and pensions systems — apparently even more defensive than Americans are toward Social Security.

Income Assistance

In contrast to all other social welfare policies, public assistance programs for the poor are the most controversial. These policies remind many Americans of deadbeats, fraud, and entangled bureaucracies; and they appear to provide serious disincentives for employment. The American public has held mixed or ambivalent attitudes toward income assistance, even as the government has done more for the poor.[51]

As is well known, Americans are uneasy toward the terms "welfare" or "relief" (related terms are used in other countries) in contrast to "assistance for the poor" or similar phrases.[52] In principle, the public has been ready to help those in need and would like to reduce the gap between the rich and the poor. But in practice, people compare the pros and cons of welfare and the needs and other characteristics of potential recipients.[53] Moreover, since Americans stop far short of seeking active efforts toward direct redistribution, they have preferred programs such as food stamps to broader policies such as a guaranteed income.

[48] Ferrera, "Italy"; Alestalo and Uusitalo, "Finland"; Stein Kuhnle, "Norway" in Peter Flora, ed., *Growth to Limits*, vol. 1, 117–196.

[49] Hibbs and Madsen, "Public Reaction"; Andersen, "Electoral Trends in Denmark"; Borre, "Recent Trends."

[50] Alber, "The West German Welfare State."

[51] For example, see Patterson, *America's Struggle Against Poverty*; Jennifer Hochschild, *What's Fair?* (Cambridge, Mass.: Harvard University Press, 1981); McClosky and Zaller, *The American Ethos*.

[52] Smith summarizes this in "That Which We Call Welfare by Any Other Name Would Smell Sweeter: An Analysis of the Impact of Question Wording on Response Patterns," *Public Opinion Quarterly* 51 (Spring 1987): 75–83; see also Golding and Middleton, *Images of Welfare*; Taylor-Gooby, *Public Opinion, Ideology, and State Welfare*.

[53] For an analysis of the complexity of this, see Cook, *Who Should Be Helped?*

Public preferences and subgroups differences concerning many of these related welfare issues do not appear to have changed very much since the 1930s. There was a modest liberalizing shift in preferences toward welfare and assistance for blacks in the 1960s; attitudes toward some issues leveled off or reversed by approximately 1974.[54] This was followed by a conservative shift up to the beginning of the 1980s. From the third quarter of 1981 to 1987 there was a liberal rebound in which opinions seemed to return to their 1970s levels. Since the political context and the meaning of many of the survey measures of preferences are not the same as those of the 1960s and 1970s, we cannot make exact comparisons. But in our judgment the public is more liberal on these issues than it was when President Jimmy Carter left office. The public reacted against the Reagan administration's original social welfare policies and especially spending reductions, some of which began under Carter and were consistent with the conservative movement of opinion during the mid to late 1970s. (See Figure 2.)[55]

There was clear liberal rebound in opinion, but it tapered off. Moreover, a full consensus toward income assistance is still far away, and the public may not have shifted back fully in its attitudes toward redistribution. The public has become more supportive of doing *something* about income inequality than it was a few years ago, but its renewed support for maintaining or expanding social welfare activity may not indicate a commensurate increase in support for significant measures to lessen the gap between the poor and those much better off. More so than before, it appears that opinion has shifted to a middle position in which citizens want both the government and individuals to take responsibility for dealing with economic hardships.[56]

To be sure, the idea that government responsibility should not be complete need not prevent further growth of social welfare programs in the United States. The Reagan administration may have helped to show, through its reluctant acceptance of government's current functions and responsibilities, what government's role should continue to be in providing public assistance — certainly like its active role in regulation of business and industry. Just as the Eisenhower and Nixon administrations provided Republican legitimacy for the foundation and expansion of the American welfare state, the Reagan administration, ironically, appears to have evoked the acceptance — even by conservative segments of the public — of government's responsibility for economic welfare.[57]

---

[54] Although this is not fully tracked by the available data; see Schiltz, *Social Security*; Erskine, "The Role of Government in Welfare"; Shapiro and Patterson, "The Dynamics of Public Opinion"; Kluegel, "Macro-economic Problems"; Tom W. Smith, "General Liberalism and Social Change in Post World War II America," *Social Indicators Research* 10 (January 1982): 1–28.

[55] Shapiro, et al., "Public Assistance"; Shapiro and Patterson, "The Dynamics of Public Opinion"; Ladd and Lipset, "Public Opinion and Public Policy"; Natalie Jaffe, "Appendix B."

[56] Shapiro et al., "Public Assistance"; Shapiro and Patterson, "The Dynamics of Public Opinion"; Karlyn H. Keene, "Who's the Fairest of Them All?" *Public Opinion* 7 (April/May 1984): 47–51.

[57] Shapiro et al., "Public Assistance"; Ladd and Lipset, "Public Opinion and Public Policy"; Hugh Heclo, "The Political Foundations of Anti-poverty Policy," paper presented at the Institute for Re-

Outside of the United States there have been some striking similarities as well as differences; and there have been similar patterns of change during some periods. During the early to mid-1970s in Canada, there was a drop in support for a guaranteed income, although majority support remained strong, especially compared to American opinion on the issue. In Great Britain, the conservative shift in opinion toward income assistance that was followed by a reversal after 1979 falls into the general pattern described earlier. But public support for "reducing poverty" was high and stable overall from 1974 to 1984. The evidence for Sweden also depicts a backlash and rebound parallel to Britain's. From 1968 to 1979 support seemed to increase for reducing allowances and assistance, and this appeared to reverse itself from 1979 to 1982. Since the survey items which have been compared are different, the stability of opinion is perhaps more impressive than the pattern of change. During part of the same period, the data for Germany showed that the substantial opposition to reducing social transfers increased a bit further from 1975 to 1978, and that this was followed by a substantial conservative shift from 1978 to 1983.[58]

Support for other forms of income assistance and supplements that are not provided in the United States has tended to be more resistant to backlash than need-based assistance to the poor. These include such policies as child allowances and maternity benefits. In Denmark, from 1973 to 1977 there were few mentions of support for cuts in child allowances. In contrast to other policy areas, from 1975 to 1980 there was a small increase in support in Finland for the position that more taxes should be used to finance child and maternity allowances.[59]

Employment

Government assistance in providing jobs is of great interest and concern everywhere. The American government has not been very active in this area since the New Deal and, to a lesser extent, since the job-training projects of the 1960s and 1970s.[60] The broader issue of employment policy has received even less attention; in fact, the lack of attention to it by American pollsters suggests that it is rarely debated in the media and consequently not much of a public issue.[61] In contrast,

search on Poverty Conference on "Poverty and Policy: Retrospect and Prospects," Williamsburg, Virginia, 6–8 December 1984.

[58] See Leman, The Collapse of Welfare Reform; Ian McAllister and Anthony Mughan, "Class, Attitudes, and Electoral Politics in Britain, 1974–1983," Comparative Political Studies 20 (April 1987): 47–71; see also Sarlvik and Crewe, Decade of Dealignment; Olson, "Sweden"; Alber, "The West German Welfare State."

[59] Hibbs and Madsen, "Public Reaction"; Alestalo and Uusitalo, "Finland."

[60] Donald C. Baumer and Carl E. Van Horn, The Politics of Unemployment (Washington, D.C.: Congressional Quarterly Press, 1985).

[61] For example, Paul Osterman, "Labor Market Policy and Labor Markets: Lessons from Abroad," prepared for the Ford Foundation Project on the Future of the American Welfare State, 1986.

unemployment compensation is a visible benefit involving substantial expenditures, and debates about it have involved the extension of benefits. In this instance, the lack of questions asked by pollsters reflects a very favorable public consensus toward this kind of assistance.

The public, of course, has been much less concerned about the amount that government spends on unemployment transfer payments than about actions directed at unemployment itself. Not surprisingly, the degree of public concern has depended upon the magnitude and duration of unemployment (versus inflation and other economic problems) and the economic status and other characteristics of citizens whose opinions are examined.[62]

Since the New Deal, there has been a recurring policy discussion about whether welfare assistance should involve work and, if needed, jobs that the government itself would help provide. Because of the work ethic and American values, there has always been overwhelming support for work in place of welfare, but the public has also disliked the unproductive work that some public jobs entail.

The public consensus is a rather nebulous one in search of a viable policy. This has provided an opportunity for national leadership and innovation that until recently had not been taken up since the actions and rhetoric of the New Deal. (The states, Congress, and the Reagan administration have virtually come to agreement on employment as a substitute for welfare). The one difference, in contrast to today's problems of structural unemployment and the "underclass," was that Roosevelt could treat employment programs as temporary until the economy heated up, which it did largely as the result of World War II. There has been no shortage of work-related proposals for dealing with the underclass.[63] Given the level of public support for providing jobs, in the abstract, it is striking that this preference has had relatively little impact on policy since the 1960s.

There is substantial variation in survey responses depending upon how questions are worded about government's role in making sure people have jobs.[64] Employment is perceived as less an entitlement than Social Security, medical care, or education. Americans clearly have mixed feelings about public service jobs, in which the government is a very active employer of last resort. In contrast, they tend to approve of more limited proposals, such as having the government provide productive work or training and education for young adults, and proposals that only vaguely describe guarantees of employment. Opposition increases as policy proposals deemphasize individual initiative or promise to guarantee an adequate

[62] Schiltz, *Social Security*; Erskine, "The Role of Government in Welfare"; Feagan, *Subordinating the Poor: Welfare and American Beliefs*; De Boer, "Attitudes Toward Unemployment"; Douglas A. Hibbs, "The Mass Public and Macroeconomic Performance: The Dynamics of Public Opinion Toward Unemployment and Inflation," *AJPS* 23 (November 1979): 705–731.

[63] For example, see Mickey Kaus, "The Work Ethic State," *The New Republic*, 7 July 1986, 22–33, and his critics.

[64] Shapiro et al., "Employment and Social Welfare"; Shapiro and Patterson, "The Dynamics of Public Opinion."

standard of living; opposition decreases when the main alternatives to government employment assistance are welfare payments. For this reason, "workfare" proposals are popular among conservative segments of the public. Many liberals also support these proposals, but they may presume that not only will jobs and job training be provided, but also support services such as child care and medical care. In contrast, conservatives interpret workfare as forced self-help in which individuals and the private sector take the main responsibility for jobs and necessary services.

Americans' support for the expansion of child care facilities has increased because of the increasing numbers of women in the labor force and the need for two-wage earners to afford a middle-class standard of living. But the public has been hesitant in seeking government-provided child care services. Americans appear to be receptive to innovations such as unpaid "parental leaves," but thus far not toward paid leaves or job-sharing.[65]

Other nations provide a significant contrast with the United States. Unemployment benefits are not in dispute anywhere, although opinions toward increases in benefits at particular times may vary.[66] Clearly, in other welfare states (and communist and socialist nations) employment itself is viewed as much more of a right. Americans' attitudes and opinions differ in fundamental ways that presumably reflect ideological differences that have been long debated and discussed. These differences become apparent when employment is considered, although not nearly as much so as in the case of policies designed to redistribute income or wealth. There have been similarities in opinion shifts across nations on the urgency of employment and other economic issues, but there are some differences in how the public has viewed government actions.

From 1976 to 1984 in Great Britain there was a more than 35 percentage point shift in the percentage of the public preferring that the government devote attention to unemployment rather than inflation. This no doubt has been the common pattern as unemployment levels have increased relative to prices in particular countries, although Americans seem to be more adverse to high inflation than citizens elsewhere. But what is striking in the case of Britain under Thatcher is that by 1984 support for the government guaranteeing jobs and a decent standard of living was 10 percentage points higher than it was in 1947 during a socialist administration.[67] In contrast, when it has come to proposals that government finance projects to create new jobs, even when American support has remained high, it has been surpassed by support in other countries.[68] There is evidence for substantial sup-

[65] Shapiro et al., "Employment and Social Welfare."
[66] See Andersen, "Electoral Trends in Denmark"; and Alestalo and Uusitalo, "Finland," who describe support for increases in expenditures on employment benefits in Denmark from 1979 to 1985, and the absence of change in opinion toward unemployment insurance in Finland from 1975 to 1980; but see Johansen, "Denmark."
[67] See King in Gergen and King, "Following the Leaders"; the data in Smith, "The Welfare State"; the data for the Netherlands in David Capitanchik and Richard Eichenberg, *Defence and Public Opinion*, Chatham House Papers 20 (London: Routledge and Kegan Paul, 1983).
[68] Coughlin, *Ideology*; Smith, "The Welfare State."

port in Canada and for large differences between the United States and Italy and Great Britain. But only slight, insignificant differences exist between the United States and West Germany and Austria.[69] Americans are also less supportive of other ways of reducing unemployment. But Americans are most distinctive concerning government's responsibility to "provide a job for everyone who wants one" or making sure "that everyone who wants a job can have one": the differences in agreement to these statements between Americans and the citizens of several European countries have been 20 percentage points or more.[70]

The available evidence on foreign support for child care programs and expenditures is limited, but it is consistent with the acceptance and continued support for these policies. There was a slight increase in public support in Denmark for expenditures on day care institutions from 1979 to 1985. Similarly, data for Yugoslavia show a comparable liberal trend during a longer period of retrenchment from 1968 to 1983.[71]

Medical Care

There are major differences in how medical care is provided and paid for in the United States and other affluent western democracies. American policies have changed slowly but substantially in recent years. Rising medical costs have been the catalyst for change, and the Reagan administration and budget cuts have altered the course of health policy. The problems of equity and access to medical care have continued for the poor and the uninsured, and there have been recurring debates about forms of national health insurance.[72] Other influences on the cost of medical care have also started to gain prominence: an aging and older population, long-term care, catastrophic care, prevention, the development and use of new technology, malpractice, and the accountability of the medical profession. The public has only begun to get acquainted with the new ways in which patient care is provided, insured, and paid for—larger insurance premiums, deductibles, out-of-pocket expenses; the uses of preferred provider organizations, health maintenance organizations, and prospective payment cost controls.

Americans' support for medical care is virtually on par with Social Security as an entitlement.[73] This support appears to have been strikingly stable for de-

[69] Schwartz, *Public Opinion*; Clarke and Zuk, "The Politics of Party Popularity"; Smith, "The Welfare State"; Roger Jowell and Sharon Witherspoon provide further evidence for very high and stable preferences in Britain during the 1980s in *British Social Attitudes: The 1985 Report* (Brookfield, Vt.: Gower Publishing Company, 1985).

[70] Smith, "The Welfare State."

[71] Andersen, Electoral Trends"; Jambrek, "Socialism Without Welfare?"; see also Johansen, "Denmark."

[72] Erskine, "Health Insurance"; John W. Kingdon, *Agendas, Alternatives, and Public Policies* (Boston: Little, Brown and Company, 1984); Theodore R. Marmor, *The Politics of Medicare* (London: Routledge and Kegan Paul, 1970).

[73] Shapiro and Young, "Medical Care"; Cook and Barrett, "Public Support for Social Security."

cades and shows some striking similarity with other affluent western countries.[74] Support for additional government medical spending and action has been consistently high in general (see Figure 1), especially because these policies benefit the elderly and the poor who are perceived to be truly needy. The public appears to be motivated by compassion and altruism, although some personal interests cannot be ruled out.[75]

Overall, the survey data suggest that changes in American health care thus far have not had substantial effect on the public's general satisfaction with medical care and insurance. In addition to challenging high costs, however, Americans appear to be more critical, litigious, and scrutinizing of doctors and hospitals than in the past. Systematic evidence concerning the consequences of various reforms and policy changes has not yet been examined fully, but given the medical services it has come to expect, the public will tend to oppose drastic changes in access or quality such as rationing of health care and abuses or widespread errors in judgment that occur in the name of "cost effectiveness."[76]

On the other hand, there appears to be an underlying ambivalence making the public receptive to incremental changes of the sort that have occurred in the past with Medicare, Medicaid, federal encouragement for health maintenance organizations and certain types of specialized treatments, and, currently, prospective payment controls and changes in employer-provided health plans. Such policies— along with persuasive efforts at opinion leadership—could move the country closer to some form of national health insurance. "National health insurance" in the abstract has generally had substantial support. But as was observed more than forty years ago, this has not necessarily been support for insurance or health services provided by the government, but rather the wish that the federal government guide private and public efforts to provide and pay for medical care.[77] Americans have always been willing and eager to look to market competition for solutions— especially a market tending toward a surplus of medical providers—but typically with desirable government regulation in the wings, should anything go wrong.[78]

The United States is quite similar to other countries in that its public views medical

[74] See Coughlin, *Ideology*; Bernice A. Pescosolido, Carol A. Boyer, and Wai Ying Tsui, "Medical Care in the Welfare State: A Crossnational Study of Public Evaluations," *Journal of Health and Social Behavior* 26 (December 1985): 276–297.

[75] Cook, *Who Should be Helped?*; Steven R. Steiber and Leonard A. Ferber, "Support for National Health Insurance: Intercohort Differentials," *Public Opinion Quarterly* 45 (Summer 1981): 179–198.

[76] Shapiro and Young, "Medical Care"; Kenneth E. John, "Americans' Satisfaction with Health Care is on the Decline," *The Washington Post National Weekly Edition*, 10 June 1985, 38.

[77] See Humphrey Taylor, "Healing the Health Care System," *Public Opinion* (August/September 1985): 16–20, 60; Stanley L. Payne, "Some Opinion Research Principles Developed Through Studies of Social Medicine," *Public Opinion Quarterly* 10 (Spring 1946): 93–98.

[78] Robert Y. Shapiro and John M. Gillroy, "The Polls: Regulation," Part I and Part II, *Public Opinion Quarterly* 48 (Summer and Fall 1984): 531–542, 666–677; Ladd and Lipset, "Public Opinion and Public Policy"; see also David A. Rochefort and Carol A. Boyer, "Use of Public Opinion Data in Public Administration: Health Care Polls," *Public Administration Review* 48 (March/April 1988): 649–660.

care as an entitlement and desires to prevent cuts in government spending and services when they are threatened. But as in the case of other entitlements, there are some differences in attitudes as well. Again, even though very large majorities view medical care as government's responsibility, public opinion is more nearly unanimous in European countries; and there has often been more support in Europe for increasing expenditures.[79]

For Great Britain, in particular, support for greater spending on the National Health Service remained steady at better than the 85 percent level from 1974 to 1983. In contrast, some authors have emphasized the increase in support that occurred for the private provision of medical care. Whether some provision of private care conflicts with the objectives of a welfare state is a complex question for the future. In Denmark, the percentage of the public responding that expenditures on health services were "too small" increased by nearly 30 percentage points from 1979 to 1985. In contrast, in Yugoslavia there was a 20 percent drop from 1968 to 1983 in support for increasing public funds on health care. In Finland, the percentage wanting more taxes spent on sickness insurance decreased from 1975 to 1980.[80]

Education

In contrast to other social welfare issues, education is the one policy area in which U.S. public opinion often stands out as more supportive than public opinion in other welfare states. Aside from the specific issues of aid to parochial schools and matters related to school desegregation, which bogged down U.S. federal action in the 1950s and early 1960s, there has been strong and steady support for aid to education (see Figure 1) and the desire for improvements in education at all levels. Several influences on opinion are unequivocally at work here: children and young adults are the well-regarded beneficiaries of this form of assistance; education provides a means to employment and upward mobility; education is not only a private good but also a public good affecting the nation's technological sophistication, productivity, and overall effectiveness (and, of course, it can also be a means of social control).[81] Unlike other social welfare issues in the United States, there

[79] Smith, "The Welfare State."

[80] Taylor-Gooby, *Public Opinion, Ideology, and State Welfare*; McAllister and Mughan "Class, Attitudes, and Electoral Politics"; Sarlvik and Crewe, *Decade of Dealignment*; Harris and Seldon, *Over-Ruled on Welfare*; Taylor-Gooby, *Public Opinion, Ideology, and State Welfare*; Andersen, "Electoral Trends"; Jambrek, "Socialism Without Welfare?"; Alestalo and Uusitalo, "Finland."

[81] See James L. Sundquist, *Politics and Policy: The Eisenhower, Kennedy, and Johnson Years* (Washington, D.C.: Brookings Institution, 1968); Susan Esser, "Public Opinion and Policy Change: A Case Study of Federal Aid for Elementary and Secondary School Construction, 1954–1965," unpublished paper, University of Chicago, 1980; Tom W. Smith, "Public Support for Education Spending: Trends, Rankings, and Models, 1971–1978" in Kevin J. Gilmartin and Robert S. Rossi, eds., *Monitoring Education Outcomes and Public Attitudes* (New York: Human Sciences Press, 1982); Fay Lomax Cook and Penny A. Sebring, "An Analysis of Public Support for Public Education," unpublished, North-

was little, if any, opinion change in a conservative direction beginning in the mid-1970s. But there has clearly been a liberal trend in support for increased government action in the 1980s, if not earlier.[82]

Comparisons with other nations on this issue are striking, since this is the one policy area for which there is greater public support and in many ways greater policy effort (for example, in the area of higher education) in the United States than in other countries. Although the publics of some other countries are more likely to consider education as an essential government responsibility, Americans are substantially more concerned about providing college opportunities for young people and spending much more on education. In contrast, however, Americans, not surprisingly, tend to prefer loans to grants for poor students and good students alike.[83]

European countries have not consistently shown the recent increase in public support for spending on education that has occurred in the United States. On the one hand, from 1973 to 1977 in Denmark there was a decline in the already low level of support for cuts in student grants; from 1979 to 1985 there was a significant increase in the percentage of the public responding that educational expenditures were too small. In contrast, the spirit of retrenchment elsewhere carried over to education. From 1968 to 1983 there was nearly a 20 percentage point drop in providing more public funds for education in Yugoslavia; and in West Germany support for reductions rose a bit from 1978 to 1983 after dropping three years earlier. In Britain, there was a dramatic decline of nearly 30 percentage points in support for "Establishing Comprehensive Schools" from 1974 to 1983, which is not easy to explain in light of other liberal trends on social welfare issues. In contrast, the increase from 1963 to 1978 in support for "contracting out to pay for private education" was consistent with other conservative shifts in preferences.[84]

Other Issues: Housing and Urban Problems

The above policy areas are not the only types of social welfare policies, and particular categories of programs and policies are not the same across nations. For some issues, there have not been studies of public preferences simply because there is

---

western University, 1982; "Opinion Roundup: Looking at Education in America," *Public Opinion* (Summer 1986): 33–39; S. M. Elam, ed., *A Decade of Gallup Polls of Attitudes Toward Education 1969–1978*," (Bloomington, Ind.: Phi Delta Kappa, 1978).

[82] "Opinion Roundup Looking at Education"; Shapiro and Patterson, "The Dynamics of Public Opinion."

[83] See Smith, "The Welfare State."

[84] See Hibbs and Madsen, "Public Reaction"; Andersen, "Electoral Trends"; Jambrek, "Socialism Without Welfare?"; Alber, "The West German Welfare State"; McAllister and Mughan "Class, Attitudes, and Electoral Politics"; Harvey Goldstein, "Educational Issues and Priorities" in Roger Jowell and Colin Airey, eds., *British Social Attitudes: the 1984 Report*, (Brookfield, Vt.: Gower Publishing Company, 1984), 105–119; Harris and Seldon, *Over-Ruled on Welfare*.

little survey data available. This is the case for housing, which has not been a major area of social welfare activity in the United States, particularly when compared to other countries. Survey data for the United States have dealt primarily with property taxes, home mortgages, tax deductions, and housing assistance for the poor, although only the latter is perceived as a social welfare benefit.

Housing is considered more of a government responsibility or entitlement in Europe than in the United States. It is a policy area, however, that has evoked positive, not negative, reactions on the part of Americans as revealed in surveys and by reactions in the media to the problem of homelessness and difficulties encountered by the poor and part of the middle class in finding suitable and affordable homes.[85]

Housing as a state responsibility is a much broader undertaking in Europe, where rent and housing allowances and public housing are more widespread than in the United States. In Britain the privatization of council houses became a controversial social welfare reform, sharply dividing the political parties, but apparently accepted as a legacy of the Thatcher years. Such privatization may not undermine the welfare state, and housing has been a less urgent issue in Britain than in the past. Housing was a serious problem in Europe after World War II. Housing shortages have been considered great national problems at various times, for example, in the Netherlands from 1977 to 1980.[86]

Public opinion toward housing assistance did not consistently demonstrate the backlash that appeared for other welfare state issues. In Denmark there was no change in support for cuts in rent allowances from 1973 to 1977; and in Yugoslavia there was an increase in support for the use of more public funds on housing from 1968 to 1978, although this reversed fully by 1983. From 1975 to 1980, in Finland there was a decline in support for financing housing allowances at a higher level.[87]

Urban problems in the United States and the related issue of assistance to blacks and minorities are social welfare matters that should be examined separately because of the connections that citizens, elites, and the media have drawn between them and other social welfare problems.[88] The policies and politics of American cities since the 1960s have involved economic problems and racial issues related to poverty and urban blight. Although Americans have not necessarily seen these issues as a piece, opinion trends for them have followed the same pattern as prefer-

[85] A sizeable majority agree that it is an important or essential government responsibility; Smith, "The Welfare State."

[86] See Elizabeth A. Roistacher, "Housing and the Welfare State in the United States and Western Europe," paper prepared for the Ford Foundation Project on the Future of the American Welfare State, 1986; Nick Bosanquet, "Interim Report: Housing" in Jowell, Witherspoon, and Brook, eds., *The 1986 Report*; Capitanchik and Eichenberg, *Defence and Public Opinion*.

[87] Hibbs and Madsen, "Public Reaction"; Jambrek, "Socialism Without Welfare?"; Alestalo and Uusitalo, "Finland."

[88] Gerald Wright Jr., "Race and Welfare Policy in America," *Social Science Quarterly* 57 (March 1977): 718–730.

ences toward welfare assistance for the poor: there have been some mixed or otherwise ambivalent feelings, although the public has always been much more supportive of aid to minorities and cities than it has been to spending on "welfare." There was the same modest liberal trend during the 1960s, leveling off by the early 1970s, followed by a conservative shift into the early 1980s and a liberal rebound into the mid-1980s.[89]

More recently the American public may have developed a different view of cities, one that is quite favorable toward state and local governments and one in which the preferred level of direct federal involvement is less than during the past twenty years. The public has supported the position that state and local governments, as the Reagan administration intended, should take on greater policy responsibilities. But the relative increase in public support for federal assistance does not seem to be commensurate with the outside help these governments would need, unless they substantially increase their revenues. This may be an important change in how the public sees cities and state governments in the American welfare state.[90]

Redistribution and Ideology

More so recently than in 1980, the American public supports doing *something* in principle about income inequality, but the renewed support for maintaining or expanding social welfare activity does not involve great fervor for directly narrowing the gap between the rich and the poor. The public appears to be content with policies that make everyone better off, involving both government action and the initiative of individuals. The public has always been ready to have the private sector do what it can, for bringing about greater equality at the expense of individuals was never the purpose of the American welfare state. The public agrees that redistribution is desirable, but it is not essential that government work actively toward it.[91]

Moreover, the public has become even more critical of the seemingly progressive income tax than of other taxes. It continues to complain least about regressive Social Security taxes.[92] Liberal and progressive leaders in the United States have apparently failed to educate citizens about the effects of taxes and spending on redistribution; or the public may be relatively easy to manipulate or deceive in such fundamental but complex economic matters.[93] This may be why the public has generally opposed measures that would explicitly and substantially redistribute wealth. To the extent efforts to equalize wealth are considered important activities

---

[89] Shapiro and Patterson, "The Dynamics of Public Opinion."

[90] Ibid.

[91] Ibid.

[92] Shapiro and Smith, "Social Security."

[93] Ralph Miliband, *The State in Capitalist Society*, (London: Quartet Books, 1969); David Stockman, *The Triumph of Politics* (New York: Harper and Row, 1986); Page, *Who Gets What from Government?*

of welfare states, redistributive policies in the United States — which have never been extensive or effective to begin with[94] — may have received an enduring setback in the public mind during the Reagan years. The one exception is the public's support for closing tax loopholes that benefit mainly the wealthy.

Americans would like everyone to have a job but prefer that government provide these jobs only when the alternative solutions are worse from the standpoint of individualism, the work ethic, and related values. This reasoning applies to an even greater extent to public preferences toward redistributive policies. These opinions reflect an ideology that is not yet reconciled with the principles underlying other more extensive welfare states. The differences among welfare states may have resulted largely from these ideological differences. Although the processes by which ideologies or ideas have particular consequences have not been fully described, the public opinion evidence is consistent with this argument.[95] American elites as well as the mass public have consistently shown the least support among welfare states for reducing differences in economic status.[96] Past and especially present data have shown that Americans are about half as likely as Europeans to respond that the government is responsible for reducing income differences between the rich and poor. Americans apparently prefer to rely on their open society and the upward mobility of new generations — or they have come to accept or support inequality.[97]

Overall, American opinion toward redistribution has been quite stable. The data show a conservative movement that had reversed, but not fully, and in such a way that the public in the mid-1980s tended toward a middle position. There is some evidence that public opinion became slightly less supportive of efforts to reduce inequality at times during the late 1970s and early 1980s in West Germany, France, the Netherlands, Italy, Great Britain, Northern Ireland, and Denmark.[98] But we can track later reversals in Great Britain and Northern Ireland and in Denmark,

[94] For example, Wilensky, *The Welfare State and Equality*; and Page, *Who Gets What from Government?*

[95] Coughlin, *Ideology*; King, "Ideas, Institutions, and the Policies of Governments"; Wilensky, *The Welfare State and Equality*; Heclo, "The Political Foundations of Anti-poverty Policy"; Judith Russell, "Ideas, Elites, and Antipoverty Policy," paper presented at the annual meeting of the American Political Science Association, Chicago, 1987.

[96] For example, Verba and Orren, *Equality in America*; see also Verba et al., *Elites*.

[97] Coughlin, *Ideology, Public Opinion, and Welfare Policy*; Smith, "The Welfare State"; Robert E. Lane, *Political Ideology*, (New York: The Free Press, 1962); Hochschild, *What's Fair?*; McClosky and Zaller, *The American Ethos*; Stanley Feldman, "Structure and Consistency in Public Opinion: The Role of Core Beliefs and Values," *AJPS* 32 (May 1988): 416–440.

[98] Eichenberg, *Society and Security in Western Europe*; McAllister and Mughan, "Class, Attitudes, and Electoral Politics"; Sarlvik and Crewe, *Decade of Dealignment*; Laura Crockett and Christopher Wlezien, "Corporatism, Pluralism, and Representation: Public Opinion and Social Welfare Policy in the European Economic Community," paper presented at the annual meeting of the Midwest Political Science Association, Chicago. 1987; Capitanchik and Eichenberg, *Defence and Public Opinion*, 28; Olaf Petersson and Henry Valen, "Political Cleavages in Sweden and Norway," *Scandinavian Political Studies* 2 (1979): 313–331.

where the rebound may have been especially great.[99] Since these findings are based on comparisons of survey question that have different wordings, and because changes in opinion were small, our conclusion is that opinion in the above countries was quite stable (and in Belgium and Ireland public support may have increased slightly), showing persistent and large majority support for reducing inequality.

EFFECT OF PUBLIC OPINION ON POLICY

Given the interesting but sparse comparative research on the nature and dynamics of public preferences, it was not surprising to find little systematic research on the effects of public preferences on policies. Some relevant discussion occurred in the studies we have already reviewed, especially those addressing the effect of public opinion and ideology on the development of welfare states. But little of the research examined the degree or frequency of the influence of public preferences on policies, a matter central to theories about democracy. Such theories ought to be pertinent not only to the United States but to other ostensibly democratic nations as well.[100]

One might have expected concern for the future of the welfare state in the West to have produced more research beyond important early discussions, which considered the role that public opinion might play in policy making.[101] Even if public preferences did not generally affect policies, they might be more likely to do so under certain forms of representation of interests. The only genuinely comparative study that examined this matter directly found that greater representation on issues of redistribution and welfare occurred under corporatist forms of interest organization.[102]

While the overall findings are mixed and some authors have argued that public opinion has little to do with social welfare policy making beyond providing a broad

[99] Crockett and Wlezien, "Corporatism, Pluralism, and Representation"; Andersen, "Electoral Trends"; but see the data in Johansen, "Denmark."

[100] See Robert A. Dahl, *A Preface to Democratic Theory* (Chicago: University of Chicago Press, 1956); Donald J. Devine, *The Attentive Public: Polyarchial Democracy* (Chicago: Rand McNally, 1970); Anthony Downs, *An Economic Theory of Democracy* (New York: Harper, 1957); Robert Weissberg, *Public Opinion and Popular Government* (Englewood Cliffs, N.J.: Prentice-Hall, 1976).

[101] Schiltz, *Social Security*; Coughlin, *Ideology*; Wilensky, *The Welfare State and Equality*; Wilensky, "Democratic Corporatism, Consensus, and Social Policy"; and Wilensky, "Political Legitimacy and Consensus: Missing Variables in the Assessment of Social Policy" in S. E. Spiro and E. Yuchtman, ed., *Evaluating the Welfare State: Social Political Perspectives* (New York: Academic Press, 1983), 51–74; see also Flora, ed., *Growth to Limits*, vol. 1 and vol. 2. Although there has been much analysis of welfare spending and policies in advanced industrial democracies, the impact of public preferences has received little consideration. For a good example and review of this literature, see Fred C. Pampel and John B. Williamson, "Welfare Spending in Advanced Industrial Democracies, 1950–1980," *American Journal of Sociology* 93 (May 1988): 1424–1456.

[102] Crockett and Wlezien, "Corporatism, Pluralism, and Representation."

constraint, there is considerable evidence that changes in American government policies have corresponded in a number of ways with public preferences.[103] Less — and less direct — evidence has been presented for this in Great Britain than the United States, and this has been even more so for other countries. Moreover, competing views have been offered by British scholars in evaluating elitist versus pluralistic or more populistic theories about political power and democracy.[104]

Studies of representation in Congress, which do not deal directly with enacted policies, have found stronger relationships between constituency preferences and members' roll call voting on social welfare issues than was initially reported in Warren Miller and Donald Stokes' classic study.[105] Greater correspondence can also be found when the analysis shifts from pairings of district-member dyads to collective representation.[106] Neither the representation studies nor the studies

[103] Heclo, "The Political Foundations of Anti-poverty Policy"; Kluegel, "Macro-economic Problems"; Devine, The Attentive Public; Alan D. Monroe, "Consistency Between Public Preferences and National Policy Decisions, American Politics Quarterly 7 (January 1979): 3–19; and Monroe, "American Party Platforms and Public Opinion," AJPS 27 (February 1983): 27–42; Page and Shapiro, "Effects of Public Opinion on Policy; "Robert Y. Shapiro, The Dynamics of Public Opinion and Public Policy, diss., University of Chicago, 1982; Rochefort, American Social Welfare Policy; Jack Knight, "Welfare Spending 1972–1978: A Case Study in Democratic Responsiveness," M. A. paper, University of Chicago, 1980; Lawrence R. Jacobs, A Social Interpretation of Institutional Change, diss., Columbia University, 1989; Robert Y. Shapiro and Lawrence R. Jacobs, "The Relationship Between Public Opinion and Public Policy" in Samuel Long, ed., Political Behavior Annual (Boulder, Colo.: Westview Press, 1989); Ernest H. Wohlenberg, "A Regional Approach to Public Attitudes and Public Assistance," Social Service Review 50 (September 1976); Gerald C. Wright, Robert S. Erikson, and John P. McIver, "Public Opinion and Policy Liberalism in the American States," AJPS 31 (November 1987): 980–1001; David Lowery, Virginia Gray, and Gregory Hager, "Public Opinion and Policy Change in the American States," American Politics Quarterly, forthcoming.

[104] See Paul Whitely, "Public Opinion and the Demand for Social Welfare in Britain," Journal of Social Policy 10 (1981): 453–475; Christopher Hewitt, "Policy-making in Postwar Britain: A National-level Test of Elitist and Pluralist Hypotheses," British Journal of Political Science 4 (April 1974): 187–216; and Hewitt, "Elites and the Distribution of Power" in Philip Stanforth and Anthony Giddens, eds., Elites and Power in British Society (Cambridge, England: Cambridge University Press, 1974); Rudolf Klein, "The Case for Elitism: Public Opinion and Public Policy," The Political Quarterly 45 (October-December 1974): 406–417; Joel E. Brooks, "Democratic Frustration in the Anglo-American Polities: A Quantification of Inconsistency Between Mass Public Opinion and Public Policy," The Western Political Science Quarterly 30 (June 1985): 250–261; Jacobs, A Social Interpretation of Institutional Change.

[105] Robert S. Erikson, "Constituency Opinion and Congressional Behavior: A Reexamination of the Miller-Stokes Data, AJPS 22 (August 1978): 511–535; Benjamin I. Page, Robert Y. Shapiro, Paul W. Gronke, and Robert M. Rosenberg, "Constituency, Party, and Representation in Congress," Public Opinion Quarterly 48 (Winter 1984): 741–756; Walter J. Stone, "Electoral Change and Policy Representation in Congress: Domestic Welfare Issues from 1956–1972," British Journal of Political Science 12 (January 1982): 95–115; Donald J. McCrone and Walter J. Stone, "The Structure of Constituency Representation: On Theory and Method," Journal of Politics 48 (November 1986): 956–975; Warren E. Miller and Donald E. Stokes, "Constituency Influence in Congress," APSR 57 (March 1963): 45–56.

[106] Robert Weissberg, "Collective vs. Dyadic Representation in Congress," APSR 72 (June 1978): 535–547; Patricia A. Hurley, "Collective Representation Reappraised," Legislative Studies Quarterly 7 (February 1982): 119–136.

of different types of opinion-policy congruence, however, have been able to distinguish among different types of social welfare policies.

Outside the United States the overall evidence is less clear. It may be the case that the relationship between opinion and policy is weaker than in the United States. Some interesting evidence suggests that even when preferences and policies do show some congruence, this occurs less frequently for redistributive policies than for other domestic issues. This is consistent with theories about the politics of distribution, regulation, and redistribution.[107]

Constituency representation in European legislatures on economic welfare issues has been difficult to disentangle in studies of Italy, France, and elsewhere. Greater constituency-legislator agreement has been found when the representives' constituents within their party are distinguished from other constituents.[108] Also, one study comparing mass and elite preferences across several European nations found a substantial and more general mass-elite link on redistributive issues.[109] A moderately large correlation has been found between West German constituencies' and representatives' opinions, but the relationship was weaker than on non-welfare issues.[110] Moreover, a recent study directly examining majority opinion and policy found that overall there was little opinion-policy congruence in France, Britain, and Canada, and that public opinion was less influential on redistributive issues than on non-redistributive ones. This weaker relationship for redistributive policies has also been found for the United States.[111]

CONCLUSION

The observation in this article that there is a dearth of comparative research is certainly not new. In 1973 Anthony King noted that it was a reflection on the interests of political scientists at that time that no one since the publication of Hadley Cantril and Mildred Strunk's *Public Opinion, 1935-1946* had been interested in compiling across nations — to say nothing of analyzing — data on public opinion

[107] Theodore J. Lowi, "American Business, Public Policy Case Studies, and Political Theory," *World Politics* 16 (July 1964): 677-715.

[108] Samuel Barnes, *Representation in Italy* (Chicago: University of Chicago Press, 1977); Philip E. Converse and Roy Pierce, *Political Representation in France* (Cambridge, Mass.: Harvard University Press, 1986).

[109] Russel J. Dalton, "Political Parties and Political Representation: Party Supporters and Party Elites in Nine Nations," *Comparative Political Studies* 18 (October 1985): 267-299; Verba and Orren, *Equality in America*; Verba et al., *Equality*.

[110] Barbara G. Farah, *Political Representation in West Germany*, diss., University of Michigan, 1980; and Farah, "The Institution and Maintenance of Representation in West Germany" in W. Phillips Shively, ed., *The Research Process in Political Science* (Itasca, Ill.: Peacock Publishers, 1984).

[111] See Joel E. Brooks, "Democratic Frustration in the Anglo-American Polities"; and "The Opinion-policy Nexus in France: Do Institutions and Ideology Make a Difference?" *The Journal of Politics* 49 (May 1987): 465-480; Monroe, "Consistency Between Public Preferences and National Policy Decisions"; Page and Shapiro, "Effects of Public Opinion on Policy"; Shapiro, *The Dynamics of Public Opinion and Public Policy*."

toward social welfare policy or other domestic issues.[112] In the last fifteen years there has not been very much progress, despite the growth of survey research and the greater availability of public opinion and other data.[113]

Even in the case of the United States there is much to be learned, as Fay Lomax Cook most notably has pointed out. We can only expand upon her appraisal and emphasize that we should not be concerned only with public opinion and policy making in the United States, but in other countries as well. It is necessary to understand further the multidimensional nature of policies and preferences toward social welfare issues: different kinds of programs, the needs of different beneficiaries, and the different origins of preferences found in ideology, values, and beliefs.[114]

We must also ask systematically and comparatively: What are the psychological referents of "welfare" (and terms with analogous connotations in different countries) and the "welfare state?" How are mass (aggregate and subgroups') and elite beliefs structured and organized? How homogeneous or heterogeneous is the public in its patterns of policy preferences, and why? To what extent are preferences motivated by personal interests versus concerns for the well-being of others or the nation? In what ways are constraints taken into account in opinion formation and change, as in the taxing/spending tradeoff?[115] To what extent are the public and policy makers aware of and influenced by opportunities for change? In what ways are possible negative side effects of policies and reforms taken into account? How do citizens think about the appropriate role for government, the private sector, and individuals and their families in a welfare state? What are the decision makers' sources of information about public opinion? To what extent have governments been responsive to public preferences toward different policies? In what countries and types of political systems? Under what sorts of government structures, party

---

[112] King, "Ideas, Institutions, and the Policies of Governments Part II," 412–413 and n. 8; Hadley Cantril with Mildred Strunk, *Public Opinion, 1935–1946* (Princeton, N.J.: Princeton University Press, 1951).

[113] There are survey organizations in at least fifty countries, and election studies somewhat analogous to the American National Election Studies have been done in twenty or more. There have also been an increasing number of published and unpublished reports of survey results and trends. See Elizabeth Hann Hastings and Philip K. Hastings, eds., *Index to International Public Opinion, 1977–1984*, several volumes, (Westport, Conn.: Greenwood Press, 1978–1985); Paul de Guchteneire, Lawrence Leduc, and Richard G. Niemi, "A Compendium of Academic Survey Studies of Elections Around the World," *Electoral Studies* 4 (August 1985): 159–174; Robert Y. Shapiro and John T. Young, "Public Opinion and Policy Change: Comparisons Across Nations," Columbia University, 1987.

[114] See Fay Lomax Cook, "Public Opinion and Social Welfare Policy," from which some of the remainder of this article is drawn; Heclo, "The Political Foundations of Anti-poverty Policy"; Cook, *Who Should Be Helped?*; Coughlin, *Ideology*; Hochschild, *What's Fair?*; McClosky and Zaller, *The American Ethos*; Feldman, "Structure and Consistency in Public Opinion."

[115] Susan Welch, "The 'More for Less' Paradox: Public Attitudes on Taxing and Spending," *Public Opinion Quarterly* 49 (Fall 1985): 310–316; Terry Nichols Clark, ed., *Citizen Preferences and Urban Public Policies: Models, Measures, and Uses* (Beverly Hills, Calif.: Sage Publications, 1976).

systems, and ways in which interests are organized?[116] What types of influences do the mass media have? Do policy makers currently have such great interest in what the press report that it is important to know how social welfare issues are portrayed?[117] How have welfare issues been reported and how has this changed our time?

We think that these are the kinds of important and specific questions that ought to be examined. Further research should follow up more actively than has been done thus far on King's rather penetrating observation about the interests of political scientists — and political science.

[116] Dalton, "Political Parties and Political Representation"; Wilensky, *The Welfare State and Equality*, "Democratic Corporatism, Consensus, and Social Policy," and "Political Legitimacy and Consensus"; Coughlin, *Ideology*; Crockett and Wlezien, "Corporatism, Pluralism, and Representation."

[117] For example, see Goldberg and Middleton, *Images of Welfare*; Shanto Iyengar and Donald R. Kinder, *News that Matters* (Chicago: Chicago University Press, 1987).

* Fay Lomax Cook, Lewis Edinger, Richard Eichenberg, Lawrence Jacobs, Mark Kesselman, Philip Oldenburg, Judith Russell, Tom W. Smith, Hilary Silver, Barbara Farah, Ester Fuchs, Terry Nichols Clark, Steven Farkas, Charles V. Hamilton, Kelly Patterson, Harpreet Mahajan, Benjamin Page, Douglas Chalmers, Demetrios Caraley, and Kurt von Mettenheim provided useful discussions concerning this article. This is part of a larger project on public opinion, policy making, and the media at Columbia University's Center for the Social Sciences. Support has been provided by the Spencer Foundation, the Ford Foundation Project on Social Welfare and the American Future, and Columbia University. The responsibility for analysis and interpretation is our own.

What Is a Nation?

ROBERT B. REICH

History is replete with examples of people wishing to secede from alliances with certain other people. In the nineteenth century, the American southern states tried to secede from the Union. Centuries before, Martin Luther led a secession from the Holy See. In 1991, Lithuanians, Latvians, and many others are attempting much the same from the Soviet empire. Staten Island would like to secede from New York City. Secession is also common to high-tech engineers, investment bankers, and lawyers, who often defect from their business associates to form their own firms. Many working women these days are able to secede from unhappy or unrewarding marriages. While the reasons for such withdrawals vary, where an economic motive exists it is usually because the defectors conclude that they will do better on their own. The union is unnecessarily costly or constraining, and the defectors no longer wish to subsidize partners who fail to pull their own weight. Secession need not be explicit. It does not require a declaration of war nor even a formal revocation of contract. It can happen quietly, almost imperceptibly, as in a marriage whose partners slowly drift apart. One day the players awaken to a new reality. They discover they are no longer part of the same team.

Something of this sort has been occurring in the United States. America's highest income earners (whom I have labeled "symbolic analysts" in light of the problem-solving functions they perform in the emerging global economy, usually by manipulating numerical or verbal symbols) have been seceding from the rest of the nation. The secession has taken many forms, but it is grounded in the same emerging economic reality. This group of Americans no longer depends, as it

ROBERT B. REICH, a former official in both the Ford and Carter administrations, teaches political economy and management at Harvard's John F. Kennedy School of Government. This article is drawn from his most recent book, *The Work of Nations: Preparing Ourselves for 21st Century Capitalism*, published by Alfred A. Knopf.

once did, on the economic performance of other Americans. Symbolic analysts are linked instead to global webs of enterprise to which they add value directly as engineers, lawyers, management consultants, investment bankers, research scientists, corporate executives, and other deployers of abstract analysis.

The secession is occurring gradually, without fanfare. For many symbolic analysts (including me and, perhaps, you), it has been taking place without explicit knowledge or intent. While symbolic analysts pledge national allegiance with as much sincerity and resolve as ever, the new global sources of their economic well-being have subtly altered how they understand their economic roles and responsibilities in society.

One form of secession takes the form of a decreasing tax burden on symbolic analysts and an increasing tax burden (including Social Security payroll taxes, sales taxes, user fees, property taxes, and lottery fees) on lower-income Americans. Corresponding with this shift in the tax burden has been a withdrawal of government funding from programs that would make the less fortunate four-fifths of the population more productive by improving their skills and helping them transport themselves and their products to market.

The two phenomena—the shift of the tax burden from wealthier to poorer Americans and the withdrawal of public funding—are of course related, since poorer Americans cannot afford to pay more taxes to support public programs even if the programs would improve their earnings over the long term. Tax revolts by middle and lower-income Americans whose real earnings have slowly declined are only to be expected when tax burdens shift further in their direction.

In the early postwar years, government expenditures on education, training, highways, and other "public improvements" were justified to the more fortunate by pointing to their salutary effects on the the nation as a whole. Alexis de Tocqueville's logic of "self-interest properly understood" lay behind many of the initiatives of the era. But in more recent years, as symbolic analysts have come to depend less on other Americans, the traditional justification has apparently lost some of its potency.

Consider infrastructure. Many of America's symbolic analysts transmit their concepts through the air via private telecommunications systems and transport their bodies through the air via private airlines. Most other workers rely primarily on public highways, bridges, ports, trains, buses, and subways in order to add much economic value. Yet in the United States, spending to maintain and upgrade these latter sorts of facilities has declined steadily. In the 1950s, the nation committed itself to building a modern transportation system. Infrastructure then absorbed around 6 percent of the nation's nonmilitary federal budget each year, or just under 4 percent of gross national product (GNP), where it remained through most of the 1960s. Public spending on the nation's transportation system declined in the 1970s and declined even more sharply in the 1980s to the point where the nation was spending only 1.2 percent of its nonmilitary budget (about 3 percent of GNP) on building and maintaining infrastructure. Hence the specter of collapsing bridges and crumbling highways. In 1989, the U.S. Department of

Transportation estimated that simply to repair the nation's 240,000 bridges would require an expenditure of $50 billion; to repair the nation's highways, $315 billion. Spending on *new* infrastructure has fallen even more dramatically, from 2.3 percent of GNP in 1963 to only 1 percent in 1989.[1]

The federal government's withdrawal has been especially precipitous. By the end of the 1980s, Washington was annually investing about the same amount of money in infrastructure (in constant dollars) as it invested thirty years before, although the gross national product had grown 144 percent in the interim. Physical capital investment dropped from over 24 percent of total federal outlays in 1960 to less than 11 percent in 1991.[2] And much of what the federal government has underwritten in recent years has been dedicated to downtown convention centers, office parks, research parks, and other amenities utilized mostly by symbolic analysts.

Expenditure on public elementary and secondary education has shown a similar pattern. Many politicians, business leaders, and many average citizens are quick to claim that the crisis in public education is unrelated to a lack of public funding. A premise of their argument — that there are many means of improving American schools that do not require large public outlays — is surely correct. Pushing responsibility for what is taught and how it is taught down to teachers and parents, and away from educational bureaucracies, is one such step (analogous to the shift in responsibility within the corporation from high-volume hierarchies to high-value webs). Giving parents some choice over which school their child attends is another, so long as the poorest children, whose parents are least likely to be able or willing to shop, do not get left behind in the worst schools. But to claim that these types of reforms will be sufficient is being less than ingenuous. In order to have smaller classes and attract better qualified teachers, more money is also necessary.[3]

Controlled for inflation, public spending on primary and secondary education per student has increased since the mid-1970s, but not appreciably faster than it did during the fifteen years before. Between 1959 and the early 1970s, annual spending per student grew at a brisk 4.7 percent in real terms — more than a full percentage point above the increase in the gross national product per person.

[1] See calculations by Brian Cromwell, "Corporate Subsidies and the Infrastructure Crisis," *Economic Review*, Federal Reserve Bank of Cleveland, March 1989.

[2] Figures from David Aschauer, "Is Public Expenditure Productive?" *Journal of Monetary Economics* 17 (March 1989): 177–200; and from Alicia Munnell, "Productivity and Public Investment," *New England Economic Review* 17 (January–February 1990): 3–22.

[3] That smaller classes and better qualified teachers result in a better education is one of the few propositions on which most educational researchers agree. See, for example, David Cord and Alan Krueger, "Does School Quality Matter? Returns to Education and the Characteristics of Public Schools in the U.S." (Cambridge, MA: National Bureau of Economic Research, Working Paper No. 3358, May 1990). See also R. Eberts, E. Schwartz, and J. Stone, "School Reform, School Size, and Student Achievement," *Economic Review*, Federal Reserve Bank of Cleveland, vol. 26, June 1990.

Since 1975, annual spending per pupil has continued to rise about 1 percent faster than the rate of growth of GNP per person. But there are several reasons for believing that the more recent increases have been inadequate. First is the comparative measure of what other nations are spending. By the late 1980s, America's per-pupil expenditures (converted to dollars using 1988 exchange rates) were below per-pupil expenditures in eight other nations – Sweden, Norway, Japan, Denmark, Austria, West Germany, Canada, and Switzerland.[4]

Comparisons aside, the demands on public education in the United States have significantly increased during the past fifteen years due to growing numbers of broken homes, single parents, immigrants (both legal and illegal), and poor children. There is also the undeniable fact that talented individuals are no longer drawn to teaching as readily as they were two decades ago. Previous generations of American school children benefited from limited career options available to talented women, other than teaching. By the late 1980s, that free ride was over. Talented women (and men) were in demand in a wide range of occupations. The law of supply and demand is not repealed at the schoolhouse door: if talented people are to be attracted to teaching, teachers must be paid enough to attract such individuals. Yet average teacher salaries in 1990 (adjusted for inflation) were only 4 percent higher than in 1970, when career choices were far more limited.

Finally the average figures on per-pupil expenditure in the United States disguise growing disparities among states and among school districts. During the 1980s, federal support for elementary and secondary education dropped by a third. States and localities picked up the bill, but for some of them the burden has been especially heavy. Although per-pupil expenditures increased in wealthier states and school districts, many poorer states and districts – already coping with the most intractable social problems – have barely been able to fund even a minimum quality public education.

Meanwhile, even as tax-free day care for children of symbolic analysts has become a de rigueur provision of law firms, management consulting companies, and investment banks, public funding for preschool education for poor children has appreciably dwindled. In 1989, fewer than a fifth of poor three and four-year-olds were able to participate in Head Start – a pre-school program costing approximately $4,000 per child – whose graduates are more likely to gain a high

---

[4] International comparisons are hazardous, not only because of differences in the measurements used by different countries, but also because different societies may have different objectives for their educational systems. There is also the question of how the measurements are to be done, given different exchange rates. Using a 1985 exchange rate, when the dollar was at its height in comparison with the currencies of other industrialized nations, puts the United States in fourth place. But this comparison obviously is skewed by the abnormally high dollar at the time. For these and related calculations see *Digest of Educational Statistics* (National Center for Education Statistics, United States Department of Education, Washington, DC, 1988). See also, M. E. Rasell and L. Mishel, "Shortchanging Education: How U.S. Spending on Grades K–12 Lags Behind Other Industrialized Nations," Economic Policy Institute, Washington, DC, January 1990.

school diploma, attend college, and find employment than comparable children not enrolled in the program.[5] By contrast, nearly two out of three four-year olds whose families have incomes over $35,000-a-year attended preschool in 1989.[6] In 1991, the Bush administration proposed increased funding to permit most poor four-year-olds to participate in Head Start. This is a welcome initiative, but even with this boost the program still will serve less than a third of all eligible children.[7]

Also because of government cutbacks, many capable young people in the United States no longer receive the federal dollars that were their only hope of affording a college education. Tuitions at public and private universities rose during the 1980s by 26 percent on average (adjusted for inflation), while the incomes of families in the middle and lower ranks of American households declined. Instead of filling the growing gap, however, the government helped widen it. During the 1980s, guaranteed student loans fell by 13 percent, marking yet another previous commitment reneged upon.

In 1965, the nation decided that all students qualified to attend college should have access to higher education. The resulting Higher Education Act established a system of grants and loan guarantees for low-income students, thus increasing from 22 to 26 percent the portion of university students from families with incomes at or below the median. But by 1988, with grants and loan guarantees drying up, the proportion of low-income university students fell back below 20 percent.[8] For the first time in the nation's history, the proportion of the population attending college has begun to decline; younger men, aged 25 to 34, are now less likely to have completed four years of college than were the baby boomers just ahead of them. The high costs of education have helped push them out.[9]

Public funding to train and retrain workers, meanwhile, dropped by more than

---

[5] For an assessment of the Head Start program, see R. Darlington and T. Lazar, "The Lasting Effects After Preschool," U.S. Department of Health and Human Services (Washington, DC: United States Government Printing Office, 1979).

[6] Figures from the Children's Defense Fund, Washington, DC.

[7] See "Competitive Assessment of the President's Fiscal Year 1991 Budget," (Washington, DC: Council on Competitiveness, May 1990), 6–7. Where preschool programs for poor children have had more teachers and social workers than in the typical Head Start program, children have shown even larger gains. See Jean Layzer, "Evaluation of New York City Project Giant Step," (Cambridge, MA: Apt Associates, April 1990). See also Amy Stuart Wells, "Preschool Program in New York City is Reported to Surpass Head Start," *New York Times*, 16 May 1990.

[8] Data from the American Higher Education Research Program, American Council on Education, 1989. See also, Barbara Vobejda, "Class, Color, and College: Higher Education's Role in Reinforcing the Social Hierarchy," *Washington Post Weekly Edition*, 15–21 May 1989, 6.

[9] Until the 1990s, each generation of Americans had been better educated than the generation preceding it. In 1980, 25 percent of men age 35 to 44 had completed four years of college; by 1990, 31 percent of men within this age group had done so. But by 1990, *younger* men were less educated than the generation before them: 25 percent of them had completed four years of college, compared to 27 percent of the same age group in 1980. Younger women were becoming slightly better educated, however: in 1990, 24 percent of women age 25–34 had completed four years of college; 23 percent of women age 35–44 had done so. Ibid.

50 percent during the 1980s from $13.2 billion to $5.6 billion.[10] Private training, the costs of which corporations deduct from their taxable income, has hardly made up the difference. American corporations claim to spend some $30 billion a year training their employees, but most of these funds have been used on what is termed, euphemistically, executive training.[11] Such training is, of course, available only to the most dedicated and already valuable employees. College graduates are 50 percent more likely to be trained by their corporations than are high school graduates; employees with post-graduate degrees within high-tech industries are twice as likely as mere college graduates.[12] Training, then, is typically provided to those who need it least.

The official reason given for why America cannot invest more money in infrastructure, education, and training is that we cannot afford it. In his inaugural address, George Bush noted regretfully, "We have more will than wallet" – a frequent lamentation. But only excessive politeness should constrain one from inquiring: Whose will? Whose wallet? Even if the necessary funds cannot be reallocated from elsewhere in the federal budget – surely an heroic assumption, given the number of B-1 bombers and other military exotica being created to ward off communists, most of whom no longer exist (as such) – the claim that America cannot afford to spend more on the productivity of all its citizens remains a curious one.

In 1989, Americans had about $3,500 billion to spend after paying taxes. The lower four-fifths of the population received a little under half of this sum (about $1745 billion), which did not permit them any more consumption than a decade earlier; their belts were as tight as before.[13] The top fifth of the population, mostly comprising symbolic analysts, received the rest (about $1755 billion) – more than the other four-fifths of the population combined. Accordingly, symbolic analysts loosened their belts considerably. Their incomes have been increasing on average by 2 to 3 percent a year after inflation (and if they are in the most fortunate tenth of earners, faster than this), even as the incomes of other Americans have stagnated or declined.

[10] Figures from "Unprotected: Jobless Workers," Center on Budget and Policy Priorities, Washington, DC, 1989.

[11] While the precise content of this elusive process is difficult to determine, I have personal experience that may shed some light. On more than one occasion I have been hired to lecture to a group of executives who, after two intellectually strenuous hours with me, proceed through a similarly rigorous day-long schedule: a sumptuous lunch, followed by an afternoon of tennis and golf, culminating with top-shelf cocktails and five-course dinner.

[12] L.A. Lillard and H.W. Tan, "Private Sector Training: What Are Its Effects?" Report to the Department of Commerce, Rand Corporation, Santa Monica, CA, 1986.

[13] Contrary to popular wisdom about Americans saving too little and spending too much, actual consumption by the bottom four-fifths of the American population hardly increased at all during the 1980s. Only the fortunate fifth of households experienced growth of real consumption during these years. See Robert R. Blecker, *Are We On A Consumption Binge? The Evidence Reconsidered* (Washington, DC: Economic Policy Institute, January 1990).

While average working Americans may justly feel that they have been surrendering a larger percentage of their earnings in taxes (including Social Security payroll taxes, sales taxes, and property taxes), tax burdens on Americans *overall* have not increased since the mid-1960s. Total tax receipts amounted to 31.1 percent of gross national product in 1969, 31.1 percent in 1979, and 32 percent in 1989. It is just that the burden has been shifted from relatively wealthier Americans to relatively poorer Americans.

Were the tax code as progressive as it was even as late as 1977, symbolic analysts would have paid at least $93 billion more in taxes than they in fact paid in 1989.[14] Between 1990 and 2000, they would have contributed over a trillion dollars more. This tidy sum, when added to the money released from making relatively modest cuts in defense spending[15] would yield approximately $2 trillion — a significant down payment on the productivity of the rest of the population.[16]

I am not aware of a groundswell of support among business leaders or politicians for increasing the taxes on the top fifth of American earners. In fact, the administration currently in Washington has sought instead to reduce tax rates on appreciating capital assets. The apparent justification for lowering, rather than raising, federal taxes on wealthy individuals (who own most of these capital assets) is that such a step would motivate them to invest their savings in new enterprise. Profit-seeking, resolutely self-interested individuals, it is assumed, will spur the American economy forward. Should there come to be substantial fiscal savings due to the collapse of Soviet communism and a concomitant difficulty of finding dangerous enemies against whom we must arm, the administration (in cooperation with a coterie of economists, business lobbyists, and conservative pundits) has signaled its determination to apply such savings to further tax cuts and reductions in the federal budget deficit rather than to public investments in education, training, and infrastructure.

What is the role of a nation within the global economy? Rather than increase the profitability of corporations flying its flag or enlarge the worldwide holdings of its citizens, a nation's economic role is to enhance its citizens' standard of living by increasing the value that they add to the world economy. The concern over national competitiveness is often misplaced. It is not what we own that counts; it is what we do.

---

[14] Almost all of this sum would have been paid by the top 10 percent of income earners. Calculations from *Inequality and the Federal Budget Deficit* (Washington, DC: Citizens for Tax Justice, March 1990).

[15] Were military spending steadily reduced through the decade of the 1990s by about 50 percent, the total savings by the year 2000 would come close to $1 trillion.

[16] I have not included the costs of the current savings and loan bailout in my calculations, since the bailout is nothing more than a huge transfer of money from American taxpayers to other Americans. The bailout does not actually use up scarce resources.

Viewed in this way, America's problem is that while some Americans are adding substantial value, most are not. In consequence, the gap between those few in the first group and everyone else is widening. To improve the economic position of the bottom four-fifths will require that the fortunate fifth share its wealth and invest in the wealth-creating capacities of other Americans. Yet as the top becomes ever more tightly linked to the global economy, it has less of a stake in the performance and potential of less fortunate compatriots. Thus our emerging dilemma.

History rarely proceeds in a direct line, however. Those who project that today's steady improvement (or deterioration) over yesterday's will become even more pronounced tomorrow often end up embarrassed when the future finally arrives. In the intervening moments a new leader will come, or an earthquake, a potent idea, a revolution, a sudden loss of business confidence, a scientific discovery—reversing the most seemingly intransigent of trends and causing people to wonder how they could ever have been deluded into believing that any other outcome was ever remotely possible. The predictable failure of all prediction notwithstanding, the public continues to pay attention to stock analysts, trend-spotters, futurologists, weather forecasters, astrologers, and economists. Presumably, such respect is due less to the accuracy of their prophesies than to their bravery in making them.

The reader of these pages is duly warned. A simple extrapolation of the past into the future would show a continuing rise in the fortunes of symbolic analysts and a steady decline in the fortunes of almost everyone else. The costs of worldwide transportation and communications will continue to decline and create an ever larger market and burgeoning demand for the services of America's symbolic analysts. But this will simultaneously generate an ever larger supply of unskilled workers. In consequence, America's symbolic analysts will become even wealthier; routine producers will grow poorer and fewer in number; and with the enhanced mobility of world labor and the dexterity of labor-saving machinery, in-person servers (unskilled local service workers) will become less economically secure.

The fortunes of the most well-off and the least will thus continue to diverge. By 2020, the top fifth of American earners will account for more than 60 percent of all the income earned by Americans; the bottom fifth, for 2 percent. Symbolic analysts will withdraw into ever more isolated enclaves within which they will pool their resources rather than share them with other Americans or invest them in ways that improve other Americans' productivity. An ever smaller proportion of their incomes will be taxed and thence redistributed or invested on behalf of the rest of the public. Government spending on education, training, and infrastructure will continue to decline as a proportion of the nation's total income; any savings attributable to a smaller defense budget will result in further tax reductions and the diminution of the fiscal deficit. Poorer cities, townships, and states will be unable to make up the difference.

Distinguished from the rest of the population by their global linkages, good schools, comfortable lifestyles, excellent health care, and abundance of security guards, symbolic analysts will complete their secession from the union. The townships and urban enclaves where they reside and the symbolic analytic zones where they work will bear no resemblance to the rest of America; nor will there be any direct connections between the two. America's poorest citizens, meanwhile, will be isolated within their own enclaves of urban and rural desperation; an even larger proportion of their young men will fill the nation's prisons. The remainder of the American population, growing gradually poorer, will feel powerless to alter any of these trends.

It is not that simple, of course. Other events will likely intervene to set this trajectory off course. Not the least is the inability of symbolic analysts to protect themselves, their families, and their property from the depredations of a larger and ever more desperate population outside. The peace of mind potentially offered by platoons of security guards, state-of-the-art alarm systems, and a multitude of prisons is limited.

There is also the possibility that symbolic analysts will decide that they have a responsibility to improve the well-being of their compatriots, regardless of any personal gain. A new patriotism would thus be born, founded less upon economic self-interest than upon loyalty to nation. What do we owe one another as members of the same society who no longer inhabit the same economy? The answer will depend on how strongly we feel that we are, in fact, members of the same society.

Loyalty to place—to one's city or region or nation—used to correspond more naturally with economic self-interest. Individual citizens supported education, roads, and other civic improvements, even when the individual was unlikely to enjoy but a fraction of what was paid out in the short term, because it was assumed that such sacrifices would be amply rewarded eventually. Civic boosterism, public investment, and economic cooperation were consistent with Tocqueville's principle of "self-interest rightly understood." As one group of citizens grew wealthier and more productive, the other citizens benefited by their ability to give more in exchange for what was offered them. And as one group resisted opportunistic behavior, so did the other, with the result that all benefited. The resulting networks of economic interdependence induced the habits of citizenship.

Between 1950 and the early 1970s, the American economy as a whole began to exemplify this principle. Labor, business, and the broader public, through its elected representatives, tacitly cooperated to promote high-volume production; the resulting efficiencies of scale generated high profits; some of the profits were reinvested to create even vaster scale, and some were returned to production workers and middle-level managers in the form of higher wages and benefits. As a result, large numbers of Americans entered the middle class ready to consume the output of this burgeoning system.

But as the borders of cities, states, and even nations no longer come to signify special domains of economic interdependence, Tocqueville's principle of enlightened self-interest is less compelling. Nations are becoming regions of a global economy; their citizens are laborers in a global market. National corporations are turning into global webs whose high-volume, standardized activities are undertaken wherever labor is cheapest worldwide, and whose most profitable activities are done wherever skilled and talented people can best conceptualize new problems and solutions. Under such circumstances, economic sacrifice and restraint exercised within a nation's borders is less likely to come full circle than it was in a more closed economy.

The question is whether the habits of citizenship are sufficiently strong to withstand the centrifugal forces of the new global economy. Is there enough of simple loyalty to place—of civic obligation unadorned by enlightened self-interest—to elicit sacrifice nonetheless? We are, after all, citizens as well as economic actors; we may work in markets, but we live in societies. How tight is the social and political bond when the economic bond unravels?

The question is, of course, relevant to all nations subject to global economic forces, which are reducing the interdependence of their own citizens and simultaneously separating them into global winners and losers. In some societies, the pull of the global economy notwithstanding, national allegiances are sufficiently potent to motivate the winners to continue helping the losers. The we're-all-in-it-together nationalism that characterizes such places is founded not only on enlightened self-interest but also on a deeply ingrained sense of shared heritage and national destiny. The Japanese, Swedes, Austrians, Swiss, and Germans, for example, view themselves as cultures whose strength and survival depend to some extent on sacrifices by the more fortunate among them. It is a matter of national duty and pride. Partly as a result, the distribution of income within these nations has been among the most equal of any countries, although the global division of labor is driving a wedge between their rich and poor, and testing their commitments to equality. These nations, incidentally, experienced during the decades of the 1960s and 1970s among the most spectacular records of economic growth of all industrialized nations, benefiting all their citizens.[17]

Could such sentiments be nurtured in America? Should they be? Nationalism is a hazardous sentiment. The same we're-all-in-it-together attitude that elicits mutual sacrifice within a nation can easily degenerate into jingoistic contempt for all things foreign. Indeed, the two emotions tend to reinforce one another. It is a commonplace notion in Britain that the nation's citizens never again dis-

[17] Much has been written about the developmental state of modern Japan. South Korea and Hong Kong, once touted by orthodox free marketers as models of laissez-faire economic individualism, on closer inspection look remarkably like their more advanced neighbor to the north. See, for example, Alice Amsden, *Asia's Next Giant* (New York: Oxford University Press, 1989); and M. Castells and L.Tyson, "High Technology and the Changing International Division of Production" in R. Purcell, ed., *The Newly Industrializing Countries in the World Economy* (Boulder, CO: Lynne Rienner, 1989). Austria, Switzerland, and Sweden represent a different path, of course, but these nations also are characterized by systems of internal bargaining that soften adjustment for their least fortunate citizens and elicit sacrifices from their most fortunate. See, for example, Peter Katzenstein, *Corporatism and Change: Austria, Switzerland, and the Politics of Industry* (Ithaca, NY: Cornell University Press, 1989).

played such virtue and solidarity as when they fought Hitler. America's cold war with the Soviet Union inspired and provided justification for billions of dollars of public expenditure on highways, education, and research. The willingness of talented Japanese citizens to work long hours and receive relatively low incomes for the honor of doing their part for their country is fueled by the same set of emotions that makes it difficult for the Japanese to open their borders to foreign products and immigrants.

History offers ample warning of how zero-sum nationalism—the assumption that either we win or they win—can corrode public values to the point where citizens support policies that marginally improve their own welfare while harming everyone else on the planet, thus forcing other nations to do the same in defense. Armaments escalate; trade barriers rise; cold wars turn hot. National allegiances, once unleashed, can lead to much worse. The same social discipline and fierce loyalty that have elicited sacrifices among Germans and Japanese have also in this century generated mind-numbing atrocities.

Unbridled nationalism can cause civic values to degenerate at home. Nations grow paranoid about foreign agents in their midst; civil liberties are restricted on grounds of national security. Neighbors begin to distrust one another. Tribal allegiances can even tear nation-states apart. The violence that periodically erupts between Greek and Turkish Cypriots, Armenians and Azerbaijanis, Albanians and Serbs, Flamands and Walloons, Vietnamese and Cambodians, Israelis and Palestinians, Sikhs and other Indians, Tamils and Sinhalese, and Lebanon's Christian and Moslem sects is grim evidence of the costs of tribal loyalty.

The argument against zero-sum nationalism, and in favor of a larger and more cosmopolitan perspective, seems especially strong in light of the growing inequalities in the world. The gap between the top fifth and bottom four-fifths of incomes within the United States is negligible in comparison with the gap between the top fifth and bottom four-fifths of the world's population. North America, Western Europe, and East Asia—together comprising the top fifth—account for three-quarters of gross world product and 80 percent of the value of world trade. As these wealthy regions have become uncoupled from the rest of the world, much of what remains behind is sinking precipitously into hopeless poverty. Between 1970 and 1980, the number of undernourished people in developing nations (excluding China) increased from 650 million to 730 million. Since 1980, economic growth rates in most of these nations have slowed, and real wages have dropped further. In Africa and Latin America, per capita incomes were substantially lower in 1990 than in 1980. Commodity prices have plummeted; indebtedness to global banks has crippled many underdeveloped economies, as more than $50 billion is transferred each year to advanced nations. The ravages of deforestation, erosion, and large-scale farming have taken their toll on much of the Third World. Meanwhile, the world's poor populations are giving birth at a much higher rate than are the world's rich. Sixty percent of the 12,000 children born into the world each hour join families whose annual per person incomes are lower than $350. In 1990, just over 5 billion human beings lived on the planet;

their number is expected to reach 8 billion by 2025, and 16 billion by the end of the 21st century. The number of impoverished people has grown dramatically in Brazil, Chile, Ghana, Jamaica, Peru, and the Philippines. Life expectancy has declined in nine sub-Saharan African countries; deaths from malnutrition among infants and children have increased.[18]

A focus on national well-being is also dangerously narrow in relation to other problems on which global cooperation is essential: acid rain, the depletion of the ozone, the pollution of oceans, the use of fossil fuels and global warming, the destruction of species-rich tropical rain forests, the proliferation of nuclear weapons, the assimilation of refugee populations, the drug trade, the spread of AIDS, international terrorism. Nationalist attitudes render solutions to these and other transnational crises all the more difficult to achieve.

Zero-sum nationalism also endangers global economic prosperity. The neomercantilist premise that either they win or we win is simply incorrect. As one nation's workers become more insightful and educated, they are able to add more wealth to the world. Everyone on the planet benefits from smaller and more powerful semiconductor chips regardless of who makes them.

It is true, of course, that the nation whose workers first gain the insights are likely to benefit disproportionately. This advantage may cause other nations' citizens to feel relatively poorer, notwithstanding their absolute gain. Sociologists have long noted the phenomenon of relative deprivation, whereby people evaluate their well-being in light of others' wealth. The average citizen of Great Britain is far better off than twenty years ago, but feels poorer now that the average Italian has pulled ahead. When I ask my students whether they would prefer living in a world in which every American is 25 percent wealthier than now and every Japanese was much wealthier than the average American, or one in which Americans were only 10 percent wealthier but still ahead of the average Japanese, a large number usually vote for the second option. Thus, people may be willing to forego absolute gains to prevent their perceived rivals from enjoying even greater gains. While understandable, such zero-sum impulses are hardly to be commended as a principle of international economic behavior. Since economic advances rarely benefit the citizens of all nations in equal proportion, such an approach, if widely adapted, would legitimize the blocking of most efforts to increase global wealth.

Economic interdependence runs so deep, in fact, that any zero-sum strategy is likely to boomerang, as the members of the Organization of Petroleum Exporting Countries discovered in the 1970s when their sky-high oil prices plunged the world into recession and reduced the demand for oil. Today no nation's central banker can control its money supply or the value of its currency without the help of other nations' central bankers; nor can a nation unilaterally raise its interest rates or run large budget surpluses or deficits without others' cooperation or acquiescence. These days, every advanced nation depends on others as a market for and

---

[18] See *Global Outlook 2000* (New York: United Nations Publications, 1990).

source of its goods. The Japanese need a strong and prosperous America as a market for their goods and a place to invest their money. If any step they might take were to precipitate a steep economic decline in the United States, the results would be disastrous for the Japanese as well.

But what if foreigners dominate a major technology, as it seems likely the Japanese soon will with advanced semiconductors, high definition television, and dozens of other gadgets? Again, we should beware zero-sum assumptions. The Japanese mastery of particular technologies will not foreclose technological progress in the United States or elsewhere. Technologies are not commodities for which world demand is finite, nor do they come in fixed quantities that either they get or we get. Technologies are domains of knowledge. They are like the outer branches of a giant bush on which countless other branches are growing all the time. While Americans need direct experience in researching, designing, and fabricating technologies on outer branches if they are to share in future growth, these need not be exactly the same branches as occupied by another nation's work force.

The cosmopolitan man or woman with a sense of global citizenship is thus able to maintain appropriate perspective on the world's problems and possibilities. Devoid of strong patriotic impulse, the global symbolic analyst is likely to resist zero-sum solutions and thus behave more responsibly (in this sense) than citizens whose frame of reference is narrower.

But will the cosmopolitan with a global perspective choose to act fairly and compassionately? Will our current and future symbolic analysts—lacking any special sense of responsibility toward a particular nation and its citizens—share their wealth with the less fortunate of the world and devote their resources and energies to improving the chances that others may contribute to the world's wealth? Here we find the darker side of cosmopolitanism. For without strong attachments and loyalties extending beyond family and friends, symbolic analysts may never develop the habits and attitudes of social responsibility. They will be world citizens, but without accepting or even acknowledging any of the obligations that citizenship in a polity normally implies. They will resist zero-sum solutions, but they may also resist all other solutions that require sacrifice and commitment. Without a real political community in which to learn, refine, and practice the ideals of justice and fairness, they may find these ideals to be meaningless abstractions.

Senses of justice and generosity are learned. The learning has many roots, but significant among them is membership in a political community. We learn to feel responsible for others because we share with them a common history; we participate with them in a common culture; we face with them a common fate. "We think of ourselves not as human beings first, but as sons, and daughters ... tribesmen, and neighbors. It is in this dense web of relations and the meanings which they give to life which satisfies the needs which really matter to us."[19]

[19] Michael Ignatieff, *The Needs of Strangers* (New York: Viking Penguin, 1985), 29.

That we share with others nothing more than our humanity may be insufficient to elicit much sacrifice. The management consultant living in Westchester County, New York, commuting to a steel and glass tower on Park Avenue, and dealing with clients all over the world, may feel slightly more responsibility toward a poor family living 3,000 miles away in East Los Angeles than to a poor family of Mexicans living 3,200 miles away in Tijuana. But the extra measure of affinity is not enough to command his or her energies or resources. A citizen of the world, the management consultant feels no particular bond with any society.

Cosmopolitanism can also engender resignation. Even if the symbolic analyst is sensitive to the problems that plague the world, these dilemmas may seem so intractable and overpowering in their global dimension that any attempt to remedy them appears futile. The greatest enemy of progress is a sense of hopelessness; yet from a vantage point that takes in the full enormity of the world's ills, real progress may seem beyond reach. Within smaller political units like towns, cities, states, and even nations, problems may seem soluble; even tiny improvements can seem large on this smaller scale. As a result, where the nationalist or localist is apt to feel that a sacrifice is both valorous and potentially effective, the cosmopolitan may be overcome by its apparent uselessness.[20]

The reader has only to reflect upon personal experience. Nothing more surely stills reformist zeal than a faithful reading of *The New York Times* or other great newspapers of the world, in which the global dimensions of hunger, disease, racism, environmental depredation, and political injustice are detailed daily. It should not come as a surprise, then, that all great social movements have begun locally. Those who aim to reform the world in one great swoop often have difficulty signing up credulous recruits.

In short, while a cosmopolitan view provides a useful and appropriate perspective on many of the world's problems and avoids the pitfalls of zero-sum thinking, it may discourage the very steps necessary to remedy the problems it illuminates. It is not clear that humanity is significantly better off with an abundance of wise cosmopolitans feeling indifferent or ineffective in the face of the world's ills than it is with a bunch of foolish nationalists intent on making their society Number One.

But must we choose between zero-sum nationalism and impassive cosmopolitanism? Do these two positions describe the only alternative modes of future citizenship? Unfortunately, much of the debate we hear about America's national interest in the global economy is framed in just these dichotomous terms. On one side are zero-sum nationalists, typically representing the views of routine producers and in-person servers, urging that government advance America's economic interests, even at the expense of others around the globe. In their view, unless Americans become more assertive, foreigners will continue to increase their market shares at America's expense in industry after industry — exploiting

[20] Jonathan Glover, "It Makes No Difference Whether or Not I Do It," *Supplemental Proceedings of the Aristotelian Society*, 1975.

American openness, gaining competitive advantage, ultimately robbing Americans of control over their destinies. On the other side are laissez-faire cosmopolitans, usually representing the views of symbolic analysts, arguing that government should simply stay out. In their view, profit-seeking individuals and firms are far better able to decide what gets produced where; governments only mess things up. Free movement of all factors of production across national boundaries ultimately will improve everyone's lot.

What is being lost in this debate is a third, superior position: a positive economic nationalism, in which each nation's citizens take primary responsibility for enhancing the capacities of their countrymen for full and productive lives, but who also work with other nations to ensure that these improvements not come at others' expense. This position is not that of the laissez-faire cosmopolitan, because it rests on a sense of national purpose—of principled historic and cultural connection to a common political endeavor. It seeks to encourage new learning within the nation, to smooth the transition of the labor force from older industries, to educate and train the nation's workers, to improve the nation's infrastructure, and to create international rules of fair play for accomplishing all these things. The sources and objectives of such investments are unambiguously public.

Neither is this the position of a zero-sum nationalist: here the overarching goal is to enhance global welfare rather than to advance one nation's well-being by reducing another's. There is not a fixed amount of world profit to be divided or a limited market to be shared. It is not their corporations against ours in a fight for dominance of world commerce. We meet instead on an infinitely expanding terrain of human skills and knowledge. Human capital, unlike physical or financial capital, has no inherent bounds.

Indeed, these nationalist sentiments are likely to result in greater global wealth than will cosmopolitan sentiments founded upon loyalty to no nation. For like villagers whose diligence in tending to their own gardens results in a bounteous harvest for all, citizens who feel a special obligation to cultivate the talents and abilities of their compatriots end up contributing to the well-being of compatriots and noncompatriots alike. One nation's well-being is enhanced whenever other nations improve the capacities of their own citizens. To extend the metaphor, while each garden tender may feel competitive with every other, each also understands that the success of the total harvest requires cooperation. While each has a primary responsibility to tend his own garden, each has a secondary responsibility to ensure—and a genuine interest in seeing—that all gardens flourish.

Thus positive economic nationalism would eschew trade barriers against any workforce's labors, as well as obstacles to the movement of money and ideas across borders. Even were such obstacles enforceable, they would only serve to reduce the capacity of each nation's work force to enjoy the fruits of investments made in them and in others. But not all government intervention would be avoided. Instead, this approach would encourage public spending within each nation in any manner that enhanced the capacities of its citizens to lead full and productive lives—including pre- and postnatal care, preschool preparation, excellent primary and secondary education, access to college regardless of financial condition, training and retraining, and good infrastructure. Such investments would form the core of national economic policy.

Positive nationalism also would tolerate—even invite—public subsidies to firms that undertook within the nation's borders high value-added production (complex design, engineering, fabrication, systems integration, and so forth), so that the subsidy-granting nation's work force could gain sophisticated on-the-job skills. But it would draw no distinctions based on the nationalities of the firm's shareholders or top executives. To ensure against zero-sum ploys in which nations bid against one another to attract the same set of global firms and related technologies, nations would negotiate appropriate levels and targets of such subsidies. The result would be a kind of GATT for direct investment—a logical extension of the General Agreement on Tariffs and Trade that the United States sponsored after World War II—setting out the rules by which nations could bid for high value-added investments by global corporations. Barred would be threats to close the domestic market unless certain investments were undertaken within it, for such threats would likely unravel into zero-sum contests. Instead, the rules would seek to define fair tactics, depending upon the characteristics of the national economy and the type of investment being sought. For example, the amount of permissible subsidy might be directly proportional to the size of the nation's work force but inversely proportional to its average skills. Thus nations with large and relatively unskilled work forces would be allowed greater leeway in bidding for global investment than nations with fewer and more highly-skilled workers.

Other kinds of subsidies would be pooled and parceled out to where they could do the most good, as the European Community has begun to do regionally. For example, nations would jointly fund basic research whose fruits were likely to travel almost immediately across international borders—projects such as the high-energy particle accelerator, the human genome, and the exploration of space. (Single governments are unlikely to support many of such projects on their own, given that the entire world so easily benefits from them.) How such funds were apportioned and toward what ends would of course be subject to negotiation.

Positive economic nationalism also would ease the transition of a work force out of older industries and technologies in which there was worldwide overcapacity. This might take the form of severance payments, relocation assistance, extra training grants, extra unemployment insurance, regional economic aid, and funds for retooling or upgrading machinery toward high value-added production. Since every nation benefits when overcapacity anywhere is reduced, these subsidies might come from a common fund established jointly by all nations. Payments into the fund could be apportioned according to how much of that particular industry's capacity lay within each nation's borders at the start.

Finally, positive economic nationalism would seek to develop the capacities of the work forces of the Third World—not as a means of forestalling world communism or stabilizing Third World regimes so that global companies can safely extract raw materials and sell products within them — but as a means of promoting indigenous development and thereby enhancing global wealth. To this end, the shift of high-volume, standardized production to Third World nations would be welcomed; and markets in advanced economies would be open to them. Advanced nations would reduce the Third World's debt burden and make new lending available.

The pressures of global change have fragmented the American electorate. Blue collar and local service workers — tending toward zero-sum nationalism — fear that foreigners, the Japanese in particular, are taking over the nation's assets and secretly influencing American politics. They resent low-wage workers in Southeast Asia and Latin America who are inheriting many of America's routine production jobs and seem to be swarming into American cities. Many symbolic analysts — tending toward laissez-faire cosmopolitanism — feel no particular urgency about the economic plight of other Americans, and feel ineffectual and overwhelmed with regard to many of the larger problems facing the rest of the world.

Neither constituency, in other words, is naturally disposed to positive nationalism. Those who are threatened by global competition feel that they have much to lose and little to gain from an approach that seeks to enhance world wealth, while those who are benefiting the most from the blurring of national borders sense that they have much to lose and little to gain from government intervention intended to spread such benefits.

The direction we are heading is reasonably clear. If the future could be predicted on the basis of trends already underway, laissez-faire cosmopolitanism would become America's dominant economic and social philosophy. Left to unfold on its own, the worldwide division of labor will not only create vast disparities of wealth within nations, but may also reduce the willingness of global winners to do anything to reverse this trend toward inequality — either within the nation or without. Symbolic analysts, who hold most of the cards in this game, could be confident of "victory." But what of the losers?

The forces of history have presented us with a rare moment in which the threat of worldwide conflict seems remote and the transformations of economics and technology are blurring the lines between nations. The 1991 Persian Gulf war is notable for not aggravating global tensions or extending beyond Iraq and Kuwait. The modern nation-state, some 200 years old, is no longer what it once was: vanishing is a nationalism founded upon the practical necessities of economic interdependence within borders and security against foreigners outside. There is thus an opportunity to redefine who we are, why we have joined together, and what we owe each other and the other inhabitants of the world. The choice is ours to make. We are no more slaves to present trends than to vestiges of the past. We can, if we choose, assert that our mutual obligations as citizens extend beyond our economic usefulness to one another and act accordingly.